OBSERVING THE ECONOMY

ASSOCIATION OF SOCIAL ANTHROPOLOGISTS

ASA Research Methods in Social Anthropology

Panel of Honorary Editors:-
A.L. Epstein   James J. Fox   Clifford Geertz
Adam Kuper   Marilyn Strathern

Series Editor:
Anthony Good,
University of Edinburgh

RESEARCH PRACTICES IN THE STUDY OF KINSHIP,
Alan Barnard and Anthony Good (Academic Press) 1984

ETHNOGRAPHIC RESEARCH:
A GUIDE TO GENERAL CONDUCT,
R.F.Ellen (ed.) (Academic Press) 1984

OBSERVING THE ECONOMY,
C.A. Gregory and J.C. Altman (Routledge) 1989

OBSERVING THE ECONOMY

C.A. GREGORY
and
J.C. ALTMAN

ROUTLEDGE
London and New York

First published in 1989 by Routledge
11 New Fetter Lane, London EC4P 4EE

Simultaneously published in the USA and Canada
by Routledge
a division of Routledge, Chapman and Hall, Inc.
29 West 35th Street, New York, NY 10001

Typeset by LaserScript Limited, Mitcham, Surrey
Printed and bound in Great Britain by Mackays of Chatham PLC, Kent

British Library Cataloguing in Publication Data
Gregory, C.A. (Christopher A.)
Observing the economy. – (ASA research methods series)
1. Economics. Methodology
I. Title II. Altman, J.C. III. Series
330'.01'8

Library of Congress Cataloging in Publication Data
Gregory, C. A. (Chris A.)
Observing the economy / C.A. Gregory and J.C. Altman.
p. cm. — (ASA research methods in social anthropology: 3)
Bibliography: p.; includes index.
1. Economic anthropology—Methodology. I. Altman,
Jon C., 1954–
II. Title. III. Series.
GN448.2.G74 1989 306'.3—dc19
89–5963 CIP

ISBN 0-415-01754-8 (Hbk)
ISBN 0-415-01755-6 (Pbk)

CONTENTS

TABLES

SERIES EDITOR'S FOREWORD

The *Research Methods* series was initiated by the Association of Social Anthropologists, originally under the editorship of Roy Ellen. By a happy coincidence the series will henceforth be published by Routledge, who for many years produced successive editions of its celebrated predecessor, *Notes and Queries on Anthropology*.

In his foreword to the two previous volumes in the present series, Sir Raymond Firth set their agenda: not to enjoin blind adherence to prescribed mechanical techniques, but to complement the personal ingenuity and skill of the field researcher. As the second Series Editor, my aim is to pursue that agenda in two ways.

Future volumes already commissioned will of course take account of the new methods and interests which have arisen during the almost forty years since *Notes and Queries* was last revised. But if it is to be of maximum benefit to the next generation of fieldworkers, and to provide a comprehensive account of current theoretical approaches in anthropology for undergraduates and non-specialists, then the series must also reflect continuing developments in areas of more traditional concern.

The present volume falls squarely under this second rubric, for economic anthropology has been central to the discipline since the very beginning of modern-style field research, largely of course thanks to the pioneering work of Firth himself. The present authors, both of whom are trained economists as well as experienced anthropological fieldworkers, have set out to demystify economic theory for the general reader, as well as to deal with the systematic procedures of data collection and analysis which their subject obviously requires. In my view they have succeeded splendidly in both aims.

Anthony Good

PREFACE

Work on this book began just after the Wall Street stock-market crash of October 1987. This event, which spread to stock-markets around the world at a speed constrained only by the rotation of the earth, serves to remind us of the highly interdependent nature of the contemporary world economy. Furthermore, comparisons with the events of October 1929 recall the dramatic economic changes that have occurred since that time and the widespread anxieties about a future which seems to contain more uncertainties than usual. What are the implications of these global events for anthropology? In particular, what is the contemporary relevance of ethnographic approaches to the economy?

Anthropology can be defined by its traditional exotic subject, the pristine tribal society, or by its direct observation method of ethnographic analysis. In the former sense anthropology is a subject with a great past; in the latter sense it is a subject with a great future, a thesis we hope to demonstrate in this book. The response of individuals to global changes is everywhere different. If the nature and causes of wealth and poverty in the world are to be understood, then microeconomic studies of an ethnographic kind, whether they be in the factories and households of England or in the islands of Melanesia, are urgently needed and always will be.

We are of the 'sink or swim' school of fieldwork methods; but, as the fathers of young children, we are well aware of the advantages of 'floaties' for teaching beginners how to swim. *Observing the Economy*, then, can be considered as an aid of this type. It owes much to our own experiences in Australia, Papua New Guinea, and India. We are conscious of the fact that many of the examples used are drawn from these countries, but this material is intended to illustrate general points, rather than country-specific techniques. The general framework we use is, of course, subject to criticism and the student who uses our book should keep this in mind. Ethnographic analysis is a creative analytical process and if we stimulate people to think about fieldwork in this way then we will have achieved one of our principal aims.

We begin our acknowledgements with thanks to Anthony Forge and Jamie Mackie, the heads of our respective departments. Both have supported the project whole-heartedly, and have encouraged our collaboration across teaching and research 'enclaves' of the Australian National University. Jamie Mackie also provided essential logistical support at a time when university resources are diminishing: without adjacent offices and uninterrupted access to two microcomputers we would never have met our deadline. At the Department of Political and Social Change, Linda Allen provided invaluable research assistance in preparing bibliographical material and in reading and commenting on a number of draft chapters; Claire Smith also assisted by keying in our bibliography. Terry Hull, Bryant Allen, Michael Bourke, Robert Attenborough, Roy Green and Stephen Beare assisted greatly by pointing out relevant literature in unfamiliar areas. Don Gardner, Stephen Henningham, Francoise Dussart, Jim Fox, Ranajit Guha, Bob Layton, Doug Miles, and Michael Young all made helpful comments on various draft chapters. Our series editor, Anthony Good, read all our draft chapters meticulously; he made many extremely useful general comments and specific points.

We both realize that we have been a little obsessive and tedious at times while writing and we thank our families, Judith Robinson, Polly and Melanie (in CAG's case) and Francesca Baas Becking and Tessa (in JCA's) for their encouragement and support.

Our greatest gratitude is reserved for Raymond Firth and Polly Hill, who between them have done so much to establish an ethnographic approach to economic analysis. We sent them our draft chapters as they were written and received long, detailed, incisive comments, some of which were devastating, but all of which were thought-provoking. With their cumulative field experience that totals many years and includes many geographic areas, we have been extremely fortunate to have two of the most sophisticated and critical readers possible. We dedicate this book to them.

Despite the assistance of all these people, we would like to stress that the ideas and opinions expressed, and any errors, are our own.

Chris Gregory
Jon Altman

Canberra, September 1988

Chapter One

INTRODUCTION

SCOPE AND LIMITS

This book outlines some general techniques for the collection and analysis of primary data on the economy. It argues that fieldwork is not a passive registering of facts, but an analytical process involving direct observation and, where possible, participation in the daily lives of the people whose economy is the object of investigation (Malinowski 1935: 317). The book also argues for the use of historically, politically, and theoretically informed comparative methods.

The scope and limits of the book are defined by the terms 'economy' and 'ethnographic analysis'.

By 'economy' we mean the social relations people establish to control the production, consumption, and circulation of food, clothing, and shelter. The categories 'production', 'consumption' and 'circulation' are common to all societies. Logically, production is opposed to consumption and the two are mediated by circulation; they are all phases in a cyclical process of reproduction. Thus, while consumption can be seen as the end of one production process, it is simultaneously the beginning of another. Circulation includes the distribution of raw material and labour inputs, and the exchange and redistribution of outputs. These logical and universal economic relations are not to be confused with the empirical and contingent relations that hold between them in particular situations. Concrete economic situations reveal a bewildering diversity of form and character, and are always the expression of relations between people. Wages in England and harvest gifts in the Trobriand Islands are similar as

1

both are divisions of total output; but they are different in that wages are an expression of a relation between employer and employee, while harvest gifts are an expression of relations between the wife's brother and the sister's husband (Malinowski 1935: 189). Relations between parents and children, between males and females, and among groups of people are formed everywhere for the purpose of dividing labour and output; but the content of these relations, and their relative sociological significance, can only be determined empirically.

By 'ethnographic analysis' we mean the direct observation of living people and the collection of data on their immediate history. It is concerned first and foremost with primary data collection and analysis. The object of study for an ethnographer is a select group of people located in time and place. Subjects such as rural Kano in 1900 and 1970 (Hill 1977), Roti island ecology and economy 1600 to 1970 (Fox 1977), economy, society, and religion in a Siberian collective farm 1900 to 1975 (Humphrey 1983), the ideology of working class youths in an English industrial city, 1972-5 (Willis 1977), and Vunamami village economy 1880 to 1970 (Salisbury 1970) exemplify the concerns of the ethnographer. The Tolai of Papua New Guinea use 'shell money' to transmit clan land; they produce cash crops such as cocoa and copra for the world market, work as wage labourers, and run business enterprises. Ethnographers like Salisbury are concerned to analyse concrete economies like this in all their complexity rather than to examine an attribute such as wage labour in the abstract. Thus the ethnographer's subject is 'micro' rather than 'macro'; but, like the historian's subject, the concern is with the microcosmic rather than the microscopic (Postan 1970: 20). In other words, what the ethnographer studies is not an invisible isolate, but a very small part of the global population. The aim is to search for the general in the particular by use of comparative analysis; the method 'implies a recognition of the need for making investigations relevant to the wider issues of social science and yet further recognition of the special difficulties and peculiar shortcomings of social investigation' (Postan 1970: 21).

The micro methods of the ethnographer are to be distinguished from the macro methods employed by some anthropologists such as Hart (1982) in his study of the political economy of west African agriculture from 1800 to 1980, and

Geertz (1963) in his analysis of the processes of agricultural and ecological change in Indonesia from 1600 to 1960. These are examples of secondary data analysis based on the primary data collected by a large number of researchers, including the authors themselves. They achieve greater coverage in population and geographic terms but only by making simplifications. Ethnographic analysis, by way of contrast, achieves a greater understanding of the complexity of economic relationships, but at the expense of narrowness in coverage. These two modes of analysis are complementary rather than contradictory. However, in order to limit the scope of this book, we shall be concerned only with methods of primary data collection and analysis.

While we have made no assumptions about the reader's knowledge of economic theory, this book is in no sense an elementary economics textbook. Our aim is to demystify economic theory rather than to simplify it. It is our contention that the contemporary world economy is changing so rapidly that many people, including a large number of economists, do not understand what is happening; but we believe that anyone who is prepared to do the necessary hard work can make some contribution to economic knowledge. An understanding of abstract economic theory (or 'tertiary data analysis' as we call it) can be of assistance in this task, but it is important to realize also that ethnographic studies can contribute to the development of economic thought.

Economics is not economy. Economics is what economists do; it is a mode of analysis concerned with ideas about the economy. These ideas have a long and complicated history. Economy, on the other hand, is a mode of living; it describes how people organize production, consumption and circulation of wealth in order to reproduce themselves. The history of the economy is related to, but different from, the history of economic thought. The study of the economy, then, must be distinguished from the study of economics.

Economists do not have a monopoly over the study of the economy; there is no reason why anthropologists, historians, sociologists, political scientists, or indeed anyone for that matter cannot study the economy. Conversely, there is no reason why all economists should be concerned with the direct observation of the economy. Many economists are interested only in logical relations

INTRODUCTION

between economic concepts such as wages and prices; this is a perfectly legitimate preoccupation when seen in the context of the intellectual division of labour. The existence of primary data on the economy is the basis for higher-level abstraction, but the relationship between primary data analysis and tertiary data analysis is by no means simple and has been the subject of much philosophical debate (Kaplan 1964).

While the book is addressed primarily to anthropologists, it is hoped that it will be of use to economists and others who wish to study the economy by using direct observation methods. Economists are mainly concerned with the analysis of secondary, rather than primary, data; very few go to the factories or the fields to collect their own data and the numbers who stay for more than a few weeks are very rare indeed. This fact is the basis of our belief that ethnographic studies of the economy can contribute to the development of economic thought.

ECONOMY AND ANTHROPOLOGY

The needs for food, clothing and shelter are such basic facts of life everywhere that it is only with the greatest difficulty that an ethnographer can avoid discussing them. The 'real' history of economic anthropology is, therefore, as old as the discipline of anthropology itself. Consider the case of Lewis Henry Morgan, one of the founding fathers of anthropology. For him the analysis of the economy was of central concern: his *Ancient Society* (1877) is an analysis of property and politics, while his *Houses and House Life of the American Aborigines* (1881) presents some original data on a topic that has received little attention since his time (Humphrey 1988). Malinowski's classic study, *Argonauts of the Western Pacific* (1922), gave the subject a whole new direction. However, what distinguished Malinowski's approach to the study of agrarian economies was his method (ibid: 60). At the same time that Malinowski was developing his research techniques in the Trobriands, Russian officials, under the guidance of economists such as Chayanov (1925), were spending up to two days in Russian villages administering, with the aid of a translator, complicated questionnaires consisting of up to 677 questions (Kerblay 1966). Malinowski's method of spending up to two years in a single district conversing with the people in vernacular contrasted

4

sharply with the sample survey questionnaire method; his work, along with that of later scholars such as Raymond Firth, Audrey Richards, Polly Hill, and many others, has revolutionized our understanding of agrarian economies.

This 'real' history of economic anthropology can be contrasted with a 'mythical' history which describes the emergence of the sub-discipline of economic anthropology in terms of the formalist-substantivist-neomarxist debate (Ortiz 1983). This debate, is, at best, of secondary importance to the fieldworker concerned with the economy; at worst, it is an irrelevance (see pp. 27-34). At the centre of this debate is a distinction between 'theory' and 'empirical evidence'; different protagonists argue the case for their particular theory on the grounds of applicability and explanatory power. But the distinctions that need to be drawn, we argue, are those between primary, secondary and tertiary methods of analysis, not those between 'formalist', 'substantivist', and 'neomarxist' theory.

The distinction between the different methods of analysis is, of course, a matter of degree. All ethnographers who study the economy must engage in secondary data analysis of some type, as the works of Salisbury (1970), Fox (1977), Hill (1977), Humphrey (1983), and others illustrate. In all these cases, however, the prime concern is with the collection and analysis of original material. The books by Geertz (1963) and Hart (1982), by way of contrast, are quite different. While the work of these authors is informed by their own fieldwork experiences, the main aim of these studies was to analyse data collected by other researchers on the Indonesian and west African economies respectively. Mauss's *The Gift* (1925) and Polanyi's *The Great Transformation* (1944) are of a different order again. The broad spatio-temporal scope of these books places them in the secondary/tertiary range of analysis; neither Mauss nor Polanyi engaged in primary data analysis.

These books illustrate the fact that the relationship between different levels of economic analysis tends to be asymmetrical: all primary data analysts tend to be involved in some secondary and tertiary analysis, but the converse is not necessarily the case. Some secondary data analysts and many tertiary data analysts do not collect and analyse any primary data.

ECONOMY AND ECONOMICS

What distinguishes the discipline of economics from that of anthropology is method. Whereas anthropologists tend to specialize in primary and secondary data analysis, economists tend to specialize in secondary and tertiary data analysis. The number of economists who have engaged in primary data analysis is very small indeed (e.g. Bliss and Stern 1982; Hayami *et al.* 1978). Economists rely mainly on official statistics for their data needs; large-scale sample surveys are sometimes used to collect other statistics. Historical documents are also used at times for data of social and institutional kinds.

Consider the cases of Adam Smith, Karl Marx, Maynard Keynes and Milton Friedman. These scholars are, without doubt, among the best known of all economists, but, because of their radically different epistemological, theoretical, and political stances there is much disagreement among economists about their respective worth. It is the similarities in their methods of data analysis that concern us here, not their differences.

First, all four were primarily concerned with secondary and tertiary methods of data analysis. While it is undeniable that they all participated in and observed the economies they were writing about, these were casual empirical observations and not rigorous ethnographic analyses. Keynes, for example, had an intimate knowledge of the City of London, but he never wrote specifically about this; instead, he wrote in the very general form found in *The General Theory of Employment Interest and Money* (1936).

Second, all four developed highly abstract theories of money and price, but in all cases the simplifications developed were based on a detailed knowledge of the historical complexity of the relations between money and price. Friedman and Schwartz's *A Monetary History of the United States 1867-1960* (1963) which is concrete and historical, stands in direct contrast to Friedman's *Price Theory: A Provisional Text* (1962), which is abstract and ahistorical. The former is an example of a secondary data analysis and the latter an example of tertiary data analysis. The two books have money and price as their empirical object, but what distinguishes *A Monetary History* from *Price Theory* is the degree of simplification. The collected works of Smith, Marx and Keynes contain similar examples of this oscillation between secondary and

6

tertiary methods of data analysis. For these writers, then, there was a necessary relationship between secondary and tertiary data analysis.

Primary, secondary, and tertiary data methods of analysis, then, are interdependent, but irreducible. This three-way division is, of course, a simplification. Between the concrete category 'my father' and the abstract category 'being' there are a number of intermediate abstractions such as 'male', 'people', and 'animal'. These complications serve to remind us of the complex nature of the relationship that unites abstract theory with concrete theory. For ethnographers to believe that abstract theory can be operationalized and applied, or, conversely, to believe that ethnographic analysis can falsify an abstract theory, is to fail to understand the nature of the relationship. Conversely, for abstract economic theorists (especially development economists) to believe that concrete ethnographic theory is irrelevant to their concerns is similarly false.

Among lesser known economists there is a marked preference for tertiary methods of data analysis using advanced mathematical techniques. This preoccupation with the imaginary and hypothetical in the economics profession has reached such absurd heights that it has even been decried by mathematical economists such as Nobel Prize winner Wassily Leontief (Kuttner 1985: 78). The objective and impersonal approach of such economists to human studies stands in direct contrast to the emotional and moral issues ethnographers experience when conducting fieldwork (Rabinow 1977). While economists have a tendency to over-emphasize scientific objectivity, ethnographers frequently over-emphasize personal experience. The goal, of course, is to understand the relationship between science and experience as elements of a totality. This is not an easy task. As Marx put it: 'There is no royal road to science, and only those who do not dread the fatiguing climb of its steep paths have a chance of gaining its luminous summits' (1867: 30).

ECONOMY AND OTHER DISCIPLINES

The ethnographer engaged in the collection of primary data on the economy has to count people, measure land, observe different farming techniques, classify and count plants and animals, record transactions, observe the effect of the movements of the sun and moon on ritual and economic activity, and learn about metals, tools, and machines. While doing fieldwork, the arbitrary and abstract nature of the academic division of labour between sociology, demography, linguistics, accountancy, geography, and the natural sciences becomes painfully apparent. Undisciplined fieldworkers will find themselves running in all directions pursuing first this line of inquiry then that; disciplined fieldworkers will find that arbitrary decisions about where, say, economy ends and linguistics begins have to be made constantly. This is because any concept of the economy is merely a perspective on human reality. It intersects and overlaps to various degrees with the perspectives of, among others, linguistics, geography, religion, and natural sciences. The boundaries that an ethnographer has to draw will depend upon the circumstances of the particular economy being investigated and the problem being posed. Just as there is no 'correct' definition of the economy, there is no 'correct' method for drawing artificial disciplinary boundaries. An ethnographer such as Fox (1977) who is interested in ecological change uses geography and history in his analysis; someone like MacFarlane (1976), interested in population and migration, uses demography.

In other words, ethnographers interested in understanding the human quest for food, clothing and shelter must free themselves of any preconceptions about the defining characteristics of the 'economy'; they must define a problem and/or a theme, select a research population, and decide, if possible, what technical knowledge needs to be acquired in order to do the research properly. The purpose of acquiring technical knowledge is not to become a technical expert, but to learn how to ask socially significant questions about technical matters. As Evans-Pritchard notes

> That the Azande are unable, whether they would wish to or not, to keep domesticated animals, other than dog and fowl, on account of *tsetse morsitans* is obviously a fact important to know, but knowledge of the pathology of the trypanasomes is not going to shed much light on the social effects of what they do.
>
> (Evans-Pritchard 1976: 249-50)

8

Fieldworkers who are unhappy about having to define the economy for themselves have a number of existing definitions from which to choose. These include Marx's (1857) definition which assigns primacy to material production and conceives of the economy as the material base upon which a superstructure arises. Alternatively, there is Polanyi's definition which sees the economy as 'embedded and enmeshed in institutions, economic and uneconomic' (Polanyi 1957: 250). Or there is the more orthodox approach, which defines economic behaviour in terms of unlimited wants and scarce means (Robbins 1932). The choice of definition is of crucial importance, not because of what it explains, but because of what it excludes. In other words, definitions determine the scope and limits of an investigation. Obviously the aims and purpose of a study will influence the choice. The definition we have used above (p. 1) was developed in order to limit the scope of this book and to give readers some idea of what they can expect to find. We do not consider it to be superior or inferior to other definitions; it is simply the one we have found most useful for our purpose of writing a book on methods.

THE DIRECT OBSERVATION METHOD

Ideally the direct observation method of ethnographic analysis involves the synthesis of a number of apparent contradictions: it is a disciplined scientific approach, but one that allows for undisciplined exploration and experiment; it employs statistical data collection techniques, but pays special attention to non-quantifiable relationships; it is concerned with the indigenous point of view, but takes an outsider's perspective; it is theoretically informed, but free of theoretical preconceptions; its methods are inductive and empirical, but also allow for deductive reasoning; and it is politically informed, without engaging in uncritical advocacy. Finally, direct and indirect methods of anthropological research form a dialectical unity: direct observation of the particular is the basis of general analysis, but general theories also inform direct observation.

The central concern of this book is with general methodological principles. It is neither possible nor desirable to outline procedures which will cover every possible empirical contingency. Every field situation is unique in some respect, and it is this uniqueness which provides the fieldworker with the opportunity to collect new data, to generate new ideas, and to develop new research methods. But this diversity is meaningful only in the context of the unity of humankind. People are the common objects of all research in the human sciences. The very fact that people everywhere eat, drink, sleep, copulate, talk, and think makes writing a book on general methodological principles possible.

The foundations of some general principles of ethnographic research were laid down by Malinowski (1922) on the basis of his work in Melanesia. These have guided the research practices of thousands of anthropologists who have, in turn, modified and developed them in the light of different situations and changing historical circumstances. Malinowski is often criticized for his theoretical over-generalizations (e.g. Nadel 1957). However, few people, apart from himself (Malinowski 1935: 452-82), have been able to fault the general principles of the method he developed (Malinowski 1922: 1-26). The methodological essays by Evans-Pritchard (1976) and Whyte (1955), for example, which were based on their experiences in rural Africa and urban America respectively, do little more than restate in a slightly different form the principles laid down by Malinowski. These general principles can be summarized as follows:

a. The method of posing questions and formulating hypotheses;
b. The method of making recordings of, and, where possible, participating in, the daily life of the people being studied;
c. The method of description, classification, and quantitative analysis.

What are the implications of these principles for the study of the economy in general?

Posing questions and formulating hypotheses. The general principles involved here have been succinctly summarized by Evans-Pritchard:

> One cannot have the answers without knowing what the questions are. Consequently the first imperative is a rigorous training in general theory before attempting field-research so that one may know how and what to observe, what is significant in the light of theory. It is essential to realize that

facts are in themselves meaningless. To be meaningful they must have a degree of generality. It is useless going into the field blind.

(Evans-Pritchard 1976: 240-1)

Good training in theory does not mean having preconceived ideas. As Malinowski (1922: 9) noted, 'Preconceived ideas are pernicious in any scientific work, but foreshadowed problems are the main endowment of a scientific thinker'.

Does this mean that the ethnographer interested in the economy must have a rigorous training in general economic theory? In our opinion it is necessary that ethnographers have some knowledge of economic history, but it is not essential to know the intricacies of abstract economic theory. In other words, while it is necessary to be familiar with the historical works of scholars such as Smith, Marx, Keynes, and Friedman, it is not essential to comprehend their more abstract theories. This is because economic history is both more important for the ethnographer and more accessible. A classic theoretical text such as Sraffa's *Production of Commodities by Means of Commodities* (1960) could take an ethnographer many months, even years, to understand even though it is only ninety-nine pages long; this effort would generate few, if any, foreshadowed problems to be investigated empirically. An ethnographer's pre-fieldwork time is best spent studying relevant contemporary political and economic history, because the rewards in terms of research direction will be much more valuable. Economic history, a form of secondary data analysis, is the closest neighbour of economic ethnography; furthermore, abstract theory, a form of tertiary data analysis, will only ever make sense if approached from the historical perspective.

History is a form of comparative analysis where the connection between the past and the present works both ways. As Bloch noted, 'Misunderstanding of the present is the inevitable consequence of ignorance of the past. But a man may wear himself out just as fruitlessly in seeking to understand the past if he is totally ignorant of the present' (Bloch 1954: 43). This two-way connection also holds when the comparison is spatial: the ethnographic 'other' cannot be understood without knowledge of the ethnographic 'self' and vice versa. The issues here are not merely philosophical. The growth and expansion of capitalism has created a global

11

economy consisting of many nation states. While this has created a certain degree of economic homogeneity, it is the persistence of economic diversity and economic inequality that needs to be explained: draught animals still coexist with tractors in many parts of the world today; rice is cultivated here by long fallow swidden methods, there by triple cropping on irrigated lands; some workers are bonded and receive their wages in kind while others are salaried and earn more in one day than the bonded labourer earns in a year.

Posing questions and formulating hypotheses of an economic nature presupposes a thorough grounding in anthropological theory, a knowledge of economic history, and an awareness of contemporary political developments in the world economy.

But what about Malinowski's functionalism? A distinction must also be made between a functionalist theory of explanation and a functionalist approach to method. While the former is problematic, and now somewhat out of fashion, the latter is, and always will be, an extremely useful methodological approach. Functionalist questions can and should be asked in the field; so too should questions concerning structure, evolution, and diffusion. In other words, a fieldworker should ask questions such as: What is the function of the traders? What is the structure of marketing? How has the marketing system evolved? How has it spread?

Recording and participating in daily life. The need to learn the local language, to collect linguistic data illustrating the 'native's point of view', to record minute, detailed observations of the 'imponderabilia of actual life', and, where possible, to participate in the daily life of the people is so well accepted that no elaboration is needed. Indeed, it is perhaps necessary to de-emphasize the importance of this principle because, for some anthropologists, it has almost become the only principle of ethnographic research (Werner and Schoepfle 1987).

The advantages of working with an interpreter also need to be admitted. While Malinowski and Firth provide role models, it must be recognized that their linguistic abilities were exceptional, and that the languages used by the people they studied were relatively uncomplicated. Gregory, by way of contrast, undertook fieldwork in a small town in central India where migrants from many parts of the sub-continent had settled. Having set up house in a small neighbourhood of seven households, he discovered that a different language was spoken in each: Urdu, Chattisgarhi, Malayalam, Punjabi, Gondi, Halbi, and Hindi. Hindi was the *lingua franca* and Gregory obtained a rough working knowledge of this language; but the assistance of a multilingual interpreter proved essential.

Description, classification, and quantification. Fieldwork is an interpretative process that involves description, classification, and quantification using techniques such as watching, defining, recording, comparing, contrasting, inferring, summarizing, timing, counting, measuring, weighing, valuing, cross-checking, and computing. Quantitative analysis both presupposes and facilitates description and classification. They are both aspects of what Malinowski called the method of concrete, statistical documentation.

> The collecting of concrete data over a wide range of facts is thus one of the main points of field method. The obligation is not to enumerate a few examples only, but to exhaust as far as possible all the cases within reach; and, on this search for cases, the investigator will score most whose mental chart is clearest. But, whenever the material of the search allows it, this mental chart ought to be transformed into a real one; it ought to materialise into a diagram, a plan, an exhaustive, synoptic table of cases. . . . The method of reducing information, if possible, into charts or synoptic tables ought to be extended to the study of practically all aspects of native life. All types of economic transactions may be studied by following up connected, actual cases, and putting them into a synoptic chart; again, a table ought to be drawn up of all the gifts and presents customary in a given society, a table including the sociological, ceremonial, and economic definition of every item.
>
> (Malinowski 1922: 13-14)

A 'mental chart' is a conceptual framework and the fieldworker interested in the economy will obviously need a concept of the economy. This book is organized around a logical and universal conception which stresses relations between elements of a whole. For example, we see production as opposed to consumption; within production we oppose inputs to outputs. Mental charts of this type are neither right nor wrong; but some concepts are more useful than others for suggesting questions, revealing gaps in data collected, and for generating methods for cross-checking. It is important to remember that mental charts of this type are not ends in themselves; they are instruments which have to be fashioned to cope with the task in hand.

One of the paradoxes of Malinowski's work is that while he talks about the need for statistical documentation, neither *Argonauts of the Western Pacific* (1922) nor *Coral Gardens and their Magic* (1935) contains a single statistical table. However, in an appendix to the latter book entitled 'Confessions of ignorance and failure', he writes:

> Another important inadequacy refers to what might be called the quantitative assessment of certain material aspects of gardening. Thus only a very approximate estimate of the extent of the garden lands of a community will be found. The sizes of fields and plots might have been measured even without the help of surveying instruments. Again, what theoretical vistas this would open, it is difficult to say. But were I able to embark once more on field-work I would certainly take much greater care to measure, weigh and count everything that can be legitimately measured, weighed and counted. The weight of a typical basketful of yams would have been easy to estimate. I failed to do this. The number of basketsful produced by an average gardener I have roughly estimated. ... A far more precise study would not have been difficult. The consumption of taytu [yams] per day would have been extremely interesting. There is no reason why this should not have been ascertained and I simply have to mark a gap.
>
> (Malinowski 1935: 459)

This extremely important methodological self criticism has been quoted at length because, apart from some prominent exceptions like Raymond Firth and Polly Hill, most anthropologists would agree with Evans-Pritchard's claim that 'Statistics have a very limited value even when the required numerical data can be obtained' (1976: 246). This unsubstantiated assertion is based on a misunderstanding of the relationship between description and quantification. A similar misconception, in mirror image as it were, is to be found among economists where quantification and computation has almost become an end in itself (Bliss and Stern 1982).

The necessary relationship between description, classification, and quantification can be illustrated by considering briefly the standardization, scaling, and equivalence processes which measurement presupposes.

Standardization. Quantification is a process of standardization which involves conceptualization, conventions, and politics. Ideally, a standard should have an invariable value. As this is an ideal which is impossible to achieve in practice, conventions have to be established by common consent. Some standards, like the gold standard of world prices, emerged because of the natural properties of gold; others, like the US dollar standard, emerged when the USA replaced the UK as the major world power.

The fieldworker not only has variable international standards to contend with, but also a bewildering variety of national and local standards. More often than not, these standards tell us more about social relations than about quantification. In Java, Islamic law prescribes that a male's share of inheritance should be twice as large as a female's. This is expressed in the formula *sepikul-segendong*. The former term refers to the two baskets that hang from the shoulder poles carried by men; the latter, to the single baskets women carry. The ideology is that men carry twice as much as women. The reality is much different: the baskets are not of a standard size and the weight in a woman's basket is often greater than that in the two baskets of a man (Hull 1975: 108).

Another aspect of quantification is the fact that most socially significant data are often held under lock and key or in the form of secret codes. This is because knowledge is a source of power and control for those who have access to it. The collection of important socially significant data, then, is not easy and it may bring the fieldworker into conflict with vested interests. The quantitative data which are most readily available are sometimes of trivial significance. Somerville's article 'Umbrellaology, or, methodology in social science' (1941) is a sobering reminder of this fact. He discusses the scientific claims of an imaginary person who collected nine volumes of data on the number, size, weight, and colour of umbrellas possessed by all the inhabitants of New York; and who developed theories such as the 'Law of the

15

Tendency towards Acquisition of Umbrellas in Rainy Weather' using the latest statistical techniques.

Scales. Quantification always involves measuring magnitudes on a scale. Scales are of many different types but the distinctions intensive/extensive and cardinal/ordinal encompass most variations. Price is an example of an extensive scale, while tape measures are intensive; both are cardinal. Failure to be aware of the scale one is using can be a barrier to understanding other economic systems based on different scales. Baric's (1964: 47) insight that the Rossel Island shell currency was based on an ordinal scale ('rank') rather than a cardinal ratio scale ('values') was a conceptual breakthrough in our understanding of this complicated exchange system. This insight did not necessarily explain anything, but it cleared away much confusion and allowed subsequent ethnographers to pose interesting and relevant questions (Liep 1983).

Equivalence. Quantification is only possible if equivalence classes are defined. This involves classification on the basis of identity, synonymy, or equality (Kaplan 1964). Identity is a relation of absolute sameness; equality is where non-identical things are rendered equivalent, and synonymy refers to an intermediate case.

For example, the English and metric systems of weights and measures are similar but not identical. The equivalence of one to the other is described in tables specifying that one yard equals 0.9144 metres, one pound equals 0.4535 kilograms and so on. In other words, the relation of equivalence is based on synonymy.

The proposition 'the price of a loaf of bread is twice the price of a pint of milk' is an example of a relation of equivalence based on equality; two heterogeneous objects are rendered equal. Relations of this type are very different from those based on synonymy. The equivalences of English and metric systems of weights and measures are based on conventions and remain fixed until the conventions change. Price equalities, on the other hand, are variable. The process by which prices are established is very complicated and remains one of the central theoretical concerns of economic theory (see pp. 200-12).

Ethnographers will inevitably be confronted with equivalence in the field and it is of the utmost importance to determine the mode of equivalence. The concept plays a central role in *Argonauts of the Western Pacific*, but, as Firth (1957: 220-1) has correctly noted, there is no systematic analysis of the concept. Firth complains of 'the lack of any precise indication of how relative values of *kula* objects are determined' (ibid: 220). However, this statement presumes that the relationship between *kula* objects is one of equality rather than, say, synonymy. In the absence of any further empirical evidence this presumption can be questioned. It may be, for example, that the equivalence of *kula* objects is determined in a manner analogous to that which prevailed in pre-nineteenth century Europe when standards of weights and measures were subject to a great deal of variability.

To summarize, the direct observation method of ethnographic analysis is an interpretative process. Ethnographers are not machine-like recorders of facts, but sentient beings who collect data using their minds and five senses. Data collection is a selection procedure that is governed by a host of conscious and unconscious postulates, and necessarily involves interaction with the people whose economy is being studied. Every fieldwork situation is unique; but because people everywhere produce, consume and exchange food, clothing and shelter, it is possible to outline general techniques for the collection of data on the economy.

USING THIS BOOK

The remainder of this book consists of one deskwork and seven fieldwork chapters. The next chapter, on theory, is a survey of relevant theoretical debates. The first fieldwork chapter, Chapter 3, discusses the problems of site selection and of defining and enumerating households and populations. Chapters 4 to 6 deal with production inputs. There are literally hundreds of inputs into any production process; we follow the conventional practice of classifying these as environment, labour, and technology. Chapter 7 deals with the techniques of measuring output and suggests some elementary calculations that might be performed in the field concerning the computation and analysis of input/output ratios. Chapter 8, on consumption, discusses expenditure and food consumption surveys, and the religious and cultural dimensions of consumption. Chapter 9 discusses distribution, exchange, redistribution, and the methodological significance of conceptualizing circulation as the mediator of production and consumption. By the end of one's fieldwork a synoptic vision of the economy as a whole, and its relationship to myth, ritual, magic, and the like, should begin to emerge. This chapter suggests ways for developing this synopsis by examining circulation at the household, community, national, and global level, emphasizing throughout the links between the macrocosmic and the microcosmic.

Primary data collection is an analytical process, and interpretation is a constant theme of the fieldwork chapters. While these chapters reflect the fact that fieldwork is primarily concerned with the use of analytical techniques for selecting and recording primary data, they also recognize that some analysis and interpretation must be undertaken in the field. Some techniques for doing this are discussed in parts of Chapters 4, 6, 7 and 9 to demonstrate that data collection and interpretation are inter-dependent.

Direct observation involves the use of a number of techniques and we have selected the following primary emphases for each chapter:

Chapter 2	Theory	Reading, questioning
Chapter 3	People	Defining, comparing, contrasting
Chapter 4	Environment	Watching, describing, summarizing
Chapter 5	Labour	Timing, watching
Chapter 6	Technology	Classifying, counting
Chapter 7	Output	Measuring, valuing, computing
Chapter 8	Consumption	Measuring, valuing
Chapter 9	Circulation	Recording, accounting, interpreting

A feature of the book that must be recognized from the outset is that some chapters like 3, 4, and 9 are of a general nature, while others like 5, 7, and 8 are more specific and emphasize particular, and at times quite technical, methods.

We end our introduction with a cautionary note, especially addressed to the postgraduate student. Do not attempt to use this book as a precise guide for 'doing' an economic ethnography in the field. The range of issues we canvass is far too broad for any one study. If Chapters 3 to 9 were followed religiously, then the fieldworker would need far more than the customary twelve to twenty-four months in the field. So, be selective and decide which of the many data collection techniques discussed in this book suit your purposes. Even then, do not apply them mechanically. The discussions throughout are general. Fieldwork is a creative process and techniques outlined in this book will need to be fashioned to suit particular fieldwork situations and research needs.

Chapter Two

THEORY

THE ROLE OF THEORY

Preparation for fieldwork involves, among other things, familiarization with relevant theoretical controversies (see pp. 9-17). Theories can stimulate new ideas, facilitate the posing of novel, interesting questions and generally guide fieldwork. However, they can also overdetermine field research and be a barrier to the development of understanding. Discovering the fine line between theoretical guidance and theoretical overdetermination – between preformulated questions and preformulated answers – is no easy task.

If a theory is understood as an idea, or set of ideas, supported by evidence, then it is clear that ethnographic research can be part of a creative theoretical process. Direct observation is concerned with the collection of primary data and the testing of concrete ideas; it is complemented by indirect methods of analysis, which are concerned with the collection of secondary data to test more abstract ideas. The broader comparative perspective of secondary data analysis can guide ethnographic inquiry, while primary data analysis can stimulate the development of new general theories.

World systems theory, for example, raised ethnographers' consciousness about the historical development of the global economy and caused them to give more thought, during fieldwork, to situating their studies historically and politically; ethnographers, for their part, have successfully challenged the 'passive victim' assumption implicit in world systems theory (Nash 1981). The history of the theory of gift exchange is another illustration of the complementary relationship between direct and indirect methods of research. Marcel Mauss (1925) developed the general proposition that 'gifts are voluntary but in fact are given and repaid under obligation' and sought to demonstrate it using selected evidence from different places and times. Andrew Strathern's (1971) ethnography on the *moka* gift exchange shows that while Mauss's proposition is not universal, it is, nevertheless, a useful starting point for understanding the particular obligations that make people give and receive gifts in the highlands of Papua New Guinea. Gregory's (1982) analysis of gift exchange in Papua New Guinea builds on Mauss's insights, using ethnographic studies such as Strathern's to develop different general propositions, but these are more historically and spatially limited than Mauss's.

Primary data analysis and secondary data analysis are part and parcel of the intellectual division of labour; the theories produced by each method are complementary but irreducible. The distinction between abstract theory and concrete theory is not a simple bipolar opposition, but a hierarchical order. As one descends from the general to the particular, defensible assumptions made at one level become indefensible at a lower level. When studying an Indian village, for example, it makes no sense to talk about the 'average' household for this construct obscures the fact of economic inequality; the 'averaging' method is, in this case, inconsistent with the comparative method which would suggest, say, an examination of the relationship between landed and landless households. However, if an intercontinental comparison was being made between, say, rice farming in Australia and rice farming in India, then the notion of an average Indian farmer may be justified. If it was found that the average size of rice farms was 200 hectares in Australia and only ten hectares in India, then it would be legitimate to abstract from differences among Indian farmers in order to concentrate on the obvious and significant differences between rice farming in the two countries.

It follows that abstract theories cannot be applied in a mechanical way by ethnographers and, furthermore, that while ethnographers may challenge assumptions and stimulate the development of new general ideas, they can never conclusively disprove an abstract theory. To believe otherwise is to conflate different levels of analysis and to misunderstand the dialectical nature of the relationship between concrete and abstract methods of analysis.

The discussion which follows is intended as a guide to some of the relevant theoretical controversies. The literature is vast; van Gennep's (1911: 32-6) spoof about the young scholar who spent so much time chasing up every known reference on his topic of research that he died in old age before even beginning his analysis is a sobering reminder of the dangers to be avoided.

It is also important to remember that the terminology used below, such as 'political economy', 'economics', 'tribal economy', 'peasant economy', and so on, is not our language but that of the theorists we discuss. Abstract terms of this kind are sometimes helpful in that they suggest the scope and limits of a body of literature and lead to certain lines of enquiry; but they should be used with caution by fieldworkers because they can often hinder the comprehension of concrete situations. Take the term 'peasant' for example. Hill (1986: 8-15) argues convincingly that besides its condescending, derogatory, and even racist overtones, 'it also has cosy, even sentimental connotations which tend to conceal the extremities of individual poverty'.

If fieldwork is conducted in an open-minded, creative way, then new terms, theories, and evidence will invariably emerge; the theoretical literature and its terminology should be seen as one set of inputs among many, rather than as a mechanical tool for generating data.

POLITICAL ECONOMY AND NEOCLASSICAL ECONOMICS

Many of the contemporary debates concerning the economy in the disciplines of anthropology, sociology, politics, and history have their origins in a centuries-old controversy in the history of economic thought. The protagonists in this debate have been labelled 'political economists' and 'neoclassical economists' who theorize about 'political economy' and 'economics' respectively. The terms epitomize two radically different approaches to the analysis of economic behaviour and many of the contemporary debates can be readily grasped if one has some knowledge of the history of this controversy. These terms are used, and misused, in a variety of ways today, but in the nineteenth century the distinction was clear.

Prior to 1870, the political economy approach was the dominant paradigm and its primary concern was with the principles governing the distribution of surplus wealth between the different socio-economic classes of society. This involved an explanation of the process of price determination, and the labour theory of value was developed for this purpose. The method employed was comparative and historical, with theory expressed in terms of evolutionary models of technological development.

After 1870, the economics approach rose to dominance. This was a classic example of a paradigm shift: a new economic problem was posed and different methods, theories, and terms were employed to analyse it. Instead of looking at the social relations of production in a given society, attention was focused on the universal problem of deciding how to allocate scarce resources among unlimited wants. A number of intuitive axioms concerning the marginal utility of consumption were posited and these served as the basis of a new theory of value. The paradigm shift expressed itself in a number of highly significant changes of terminology: 'goods' instead of 'commodities', 'utility' instead of 'use-value', and 'economics' instead of 'political economy'. The new theorists, the 'neoclassicals', as they are now called, saw themselves as being more scientific than their predecessors. They used mathematics to develop predictive universal theories and did not concern themselves with the past. As they saw it, goods must be valued with a view to future utility, not past labour. They distinguished their new science of 'Economics' from 'Political Economy' which they characterized as the 'Science of the Evolution of Social Relations' (Jevons 1871: 20).

The neoclassical paradigm is still dominant today. However, it has suppressed rather than replaced the political economy approach. A small number of academic economists are working to rehabilitate political economy and it has enjoyed something of a revival in the past two decades; but it still remains the concern of a minority and has little academic status.

The reason for the rise to dominance of neoclassical economics in the 1870s is a matter of some dispute, but it is clear that it had as much to do with status and power as it did with logic and evidence. This can be demonstrated by examining some of the major theoretical developments within the history of economic thought.

Adam Smith is often acknowledged as the father of political economy. However, the ideas in *The Wealth of Nations* (1776) did not have a virgin birth. Most of them were developed in opposition to other theorists, and his critiques were inspired by his casual empirical observations of the rapidly expanding commercial economy of his day. Smith's work owes much to the French physiocratic school, but he rejected the physiocratic doctrine that manufacturing was 'sterile' and farmers the only productive class (Quesnay 1759). For Smith, both agriculture and manufacturing were productive, with labour 'the real measure of the exchangeable value of all commodities' (1776: 26). One of Smith's policy conclusions was that all barriers to the development of manufacturing be removed. This policy, popularly known as *laissez faire*, is the centre-piece of neoclassical economics; but this is all it has in common with Smith's labour-theory approach.

Smith's ideas were developed prior to the industrial revolution and subsequent social and technological transformations of the British economy rendered many of his ideas obsolete. Capitalist profits, rather than rents, emerged as the most important component of the surplus product; understanding the principles governing the distribution of this new form of surplus required knowledge of the complex processes by which wages, prices, rents, and profit rates were determined. Ricardo's classic work *On the Principles of Political Economy and Taxation* (1817) developed Smith's labour theory of value by using formal logical models of economic analysis. These were, in turn, further developed by Marx in *Capital* (1867). What distinguished Marx's work was the historical specificity of his formal models and his focus on class conflict between wage-labour and capital. Ricardo, too, focused on class conflict; but in his day the struggle between landlords and capitalists was the central political issue.

Marx's theoretical advances owed much to Smith and Ricardo. He developed their theoretical insights using much the same method. Marx situated his theoretical predecessors historically; he examined the intervening historical record and developed a critique of their work by a process of criticism, modification, and transcendence.

The labour theory of value approach of the political economists was the dominant paradigm during Ricardo's time, but waned quickly thereafter. The economics approach, with its utility theory of value, rose to dominance in the 1870s with the publication of the work of Jevons (1871), Menger (1871), and Walras (1874). The utility theory of value had been around for a long time as a subordinate paradigm and, for some reason, was generally accepted at the expense of the labour theory of value in the 1870s. The revolutionary political nature of Marx's thought was clearly an issue; so too was the discovery by Bohm-Bawerk of a logical contradiction in Marx's theory of value (Meek 1956). But the discovery of this logical error in Marx's work was an *ex post facto* justification for the rejection of the labour theory of value, not a causal factor. Paradigm changes do not occur because of the discovery of logical errors. Sraffa's *Production of Commodities by Means of Commodities* (1960), which resolved the contradiction in Marx's theory of value and exposed a logical error in the neoclassical theory of value, has had virtually no impact on the dominant paradigm.

Neoclassical economic theory has grown dramatically over the past century. The pure theory of value has been developed with the aid of highly sophisticated mathematics. Indeed, the theory has now become so abstract that it is almost a branch of pure mathematics (Debreu 1959). It has been applied to almost every field of human endeavour from the analysis of marriage (Becker 1974) to economic development (Schultz 1964). There are many differences between the various neoclassical theories, but the fundamental axioms laid down by Jevons are common to all.

> The science of economics ... is in some degree peculiar, owing to the fact ... that its ultimate laws are known to us immediately by intuition... That every person will choose the greater apparent good; that human wants are more or less quickly satiated; that prolonged labour becomes more and more painful, are a few of the simple inductions on which we can reason deductively with great confidence. From these axioms we can deduce the laws of supply and demand, the laws of that difficult conception, value, and all the intricate results of commerce, so far as data are available. The final agreement of our inferences with *a posteriori* observations ratifies our method.
>
> (Jevons 1871:18)

In addition to these tautological assumptions, neoclassical economics also uses many simplifying assumptions that are, in some cases, demonstrably false. This fact is well recognized by economists. As Levi notes, 'Ours is a complicated world. To describe this world in a manner we can comprehend, we must forgo some of the detail of the real world' (1981:18). This procedure has been justified in a famous article by Friedman where he argued that theory is to be judged by its predictive power. Thus,

> Truly important and significant hypotheses will be found to have 'assumptions' that are widely inaccurate descriptions of reality, and, in general, the more significant the theory, the more unrealistic the assumptions. . . . To be important, therefore, a hypothesis must be descriptively false in its assumptions.
>
> (Friedman 1935: 30)

By this procedure, neoclassical economists have rendered their paradigm virtually immune from empirically based criticism: the universal applicability of the theory is treated as evidence of its success; all failures to predict accurately are explained away as evidence of 'other things' not being constant; and the fundamental assumptions concerning utility theory are treated as intuitively obvious and, therefore, unproblematic.

The history of economic thought, then, can be understood as the history of the replacement of one orthodoxy by another, of the rise of economics, with its utility theory of value, and the fall of political economy and the labour theory of value. A potted summary of over 300 years of intellectual history in these terms not only oversimplifies the defining characteristics of the dominant orthodoxies, but glosses over the many subordinate heterodoxies. Perhaps the most important of these is 'institutional economics'; a short note on this school is necessary in order to redress the bias, if only symbolically.

This school originated in the United States although it owed much to the German and English historical traditions, the work of Weber (1927) and Hobson (1894) in particular. The institutionalists assert the primacy of the organization and control of the economic system, the institutional structure of power. They have developed critiques of both marxist and neoclassical economics; but, for obvious reasons, are primarily concerned to define themselves in opposition to the dominant neoclassical paradigm (Samuels 1987). They are interested in the formation and role of institutions, the relations between economic, legal, and belief systems; in sum, in all those 'complicating' factors of contemporary life from which neoclassical economists abstract. Some high points in the theoretical development of this doctrine include Veblen's (1899) theory of conspicuous consumption, Polanyi's (1944) history of the 'self-regulating' market system, Myrdal's (1968) inquiry into the poverty of nations, and Galbraith's (1967) theory of the new industrial state.

ECONOMIC ANTHROPOLOGY

Tribal economy

The political economy perspective, interpreted broadly as a comparative and historical approach, has been a dominant influence in anthropology since Morgan's time. Indeed, there is a sense in which the approach was taken over and developed by anthropologists. Engels was one of the first to recognize this, describing Morgan's *Ancient Society* (1877) as 'one of the few epoch-making works of our time' (Engels 1884: 450).

An important difference between the political economists and Morgan is that the former were concerned with the analysis of property transfers in a class-based market economy, whereas Morgan was concerned with the analysis of property transfers in clan-based, non-market tribal economies.

Morgan focused on the relationship between kinship systems and rules of inheritance, and developed a number of evolutionary theories using ethnographic data from different parts of the world. Over the next forty years a vast collection of material was accumulated by various ethnographers. Malinowski's analysis of the Trobriand economy (1922; 1935) was, without doubt, the crucial turning point in the development of anthropological thought. For example, Malinowski's work provided the initial stimulus for Mauss's influential theory of the gift. Mauss adopted a Morgan-type evolutionary approach. For him, total prestation, by which he meant exchanges of courtesies, entertainments, ritual, military assistance, women, children, dances, and feasts, 'constitutes the oldest economic system we know' (Mauss 1925: 68). This was the base from which the second stage, the gift exchange of valuable objects, arose. The third stage, the money economy, 'began in ancient Semitic societies which invented the means of detaching these precious things from groups and individuals and of making them permanent instruments of value measurement' (ibid: 94). Mauss was primarily concerned with the principles governing the gift exchange of inalienable property and with people's obligations to give and receive gifts (Gregory 1987b).

The theoretical insights of Morgan and Mauss have been modified and developed by a number of authors in the light of new ethnographic evidence. Lévi-Strauss's *The Elementary Structures of Kinship* (1949) surveys over 7,000 articles on kinship and marriage and argues that the obligation to give and receive gifts is to be found in the phenomenon of the incest taboo:

> The prohibition of incest is less a rule prohibiting marriage with the mother, sister or daughter, than a rule obliging the mother, sister or daughter to be given to others. It is the supreme rule of the gift, and it is clearly this aspect, too often unrecognized, which allows its nature to be understood.
>
> (Lévi-Strauss 1949: 481)

While Lévi-Strauss was developing his theory of the gift from an analysis of kinship systems, an economic historian, Karl Polanyi (1944), was developing a comparative economic analysis based on ethnographic and historical evidence. Polanyi's principal concern was with the 'extraordinary assumptions' underlying the 'self-regulating market' of capitalism and he highlighted these by enquiring into the principles governing exchange and distribution in non-market economies. He identified the principle of reciprocity, which has its basis in kinship, and the principle of redistribution, which has its basis in the political organization of a tribal society. Capitalism, in Polanyi's view, implies the wholesale destruction of these principles and the establishment of markets for commodities run according to the profit principle. Polanyi's work has had an important impact on anthropology and has served as the theoretical inspiration for the work of people such as Sahlins (1972).

Recent writing on gift exchange has consciously adopted an explicit marxist approach to theory, asserting the primacy of relations of production, rather than exchange (Godelier 1977; Meillassoux 1981). While the rise of neomarxist anthropology has involved a certain amount of theoretical involution, some important contributions have been made. The historical development of the world economy has blurred the distinction between tribal economy and capitalism; new economic classes are developing and the old political economy question (about the principles governing the distribution of wealth between different classes) is becoming increasingly relevant. Questions are also being raised about the mode of incorporation into the world economy (Nash 1981) and about strategies for development (Hoben 1982).

Recent writing in feminist anthropology, some of which is inspired by neomarxism, has re-examined issues such as property relations and the division of labour from the female perspective. Marilyn Strathern's *Women in Between* (1972), a study of gender relations in the highlands of Papua News Guinea, drew a distinction between women as producers and men as gift exchangers, and raised new questions about the nature of exploitation. More recent studies, like Josephides' *The Production of Inequality* (1985), develop this theme by drawing on the theories of Marx and Mauss on alienation.

Peasant economy

Anthropological contributions to peasant economy must be seen in the light of the 'peasant question' controversy. This debate was a burning political issue in nineteenth-century Europe and the subject of much theoretical disputation among political economists. It began in western Europe at the end of the eighteenth-century, moved to eastern Europe at the end of the nineteenth-century, and still rages today in Latin America and Asia where farmers make up the bulk of the population. In nineteenth-century England, the birthplace of capitalist farming, the peasant question was not an issue and was ignored by writers such as Smith and Ricardo. Britain was unique in this respect; in all other European countries the peasantry continues to reproduce itself, albeit in a numerically and politically diminished form.

The 'peasant question' is really a number of questions of a descriptive and prescriptive nature: Is capitalist farming superior to peasant farming? Will the development of capitalism in agriculture lead to the demise of peasant farming? Should this be allowed to happen?

The French physiocrats argued that capitalist farming was superior and should be encouraged; this was hotly disputed by influential theorists such as Sismondi (1847) and John Stuart Mill (1848), who argued that the 'magic of private property' made peasant proprietors of small parcels of land more productive than wage-labourers on capitalist farms. Marx (1894: 802-13), on the other hand, agreed with the physiocrats and explained away the evidence on the superior productivity of peasants as the consequence of overwork and underconsumption, that is, self-exploitation; for him the demise of the peasantry was inevitable. Lenin developed this argument in *The Development of Capitalism in Russia* (1899), a position which was subsequently challenged by Chayanov in *The Theory of Peasant Economy* (1925).

The debate is still unresolved today. Harriss (1982: 153) found a positive relationship between farm size and productivity in India, but Taussig (1978) discovered the opposite in the Cauca valley of Colombia. However, the new empirical evidence of these researchers and others has rejuvenated the debate by posing new questions. The nineteenth-century debate was based on information collected by sample survey questionnaire methods and on theories of peasant differentiation that focused almost exclusively on market transmissions of land. The question of inheritance was rarely mentioned and never seriously investigated. Anthropologists, through the collection of detailed ethnographic data on inheritance, dowries, brideprices and marriage gifts, have been able to provide new insights into the reasons for the continued persistence of poverty and non-capitalist agrarian relations in the developing world.

Work on land tenure and kinship, such as Leach's (1961) on a Sri Lankan village, successfully challenged the validity of previous research based on sample surveys and advanced new conceptions of the meaning of inheritance. He argued that it is the body of assets – the 'estate' – of a society which forms the constant continuing entity: it is people who flow through society from childhood to old age and death and not vice versa.

The work of Harriss (1982) on India, Hill (1982) on Africa and India, and Davis (1973) and Cutileiro (1971) on Europe is just a sample of the many ethnographies that advance our understanding of economic inequality and mobility among farming households; their work builds upon earlier ethnographic work such as that in Firth and Yamey (1964) and Halpern and Brode (1967). This literature has provided the basis for some recent theoretical developments (Mencher 1983).

Research by feminist anthropologists has also helped to repose the 'peasant question' by looking at the relationship between women and property. Sharma, in her *Woman, Work and Property in North-West India* (1980), argued that women's effective exclusion from the inheritance of land was the basis for their dependence upon men. She also questioned the interpretation of dowry as a *pre-mortem* inheritance by examining the relative control sons and daughters acquire over their parents' property; her ethnography shows how dowries are transferred to the bridegroom's parents, rather than the bride, and are often redistributed by them to a wide circle of kin.

Perhaps the best known, and most controversial, general work on peasant economy is Geertz's *Agricultural Involution* (1963), a comparative and historical study of the Indonesian peasantry. This book focuses on harmony rather than class conflict and a central thesis is the notion of 'shared poverty': the claim that as peasants get poorer, through population growth and increased commercialization, they share whatever resources they have among themselves according to traditional cultural practices.

Geertz's book has generated a controversy that still persists (Geertz 1984a). However, because of historical and ecological changes in Indonesia over the past twenty-five years, many of the central propositions of this debate are now obsolete. Recent ethnographic research in Indonesia on the impact of multinational mining companies (Robinson 1986), on the economic life of urban slum dwellers (Guinness 1986) and on women traders (Alexander 1987) suggests that a new general theory is now required.

Formalism, substantivism and neomarxism

Neoclassical economics began to have influence in anthropology following a review of Herskovits's *The Economic Life of Primitive Peoples* (1940) by the economist Frank Knight (1941). Knight's critique of Herskovits was little more than a restatement of the axioms of neoclassical economics laid down by Jevons in the 1870s. 'The principles of economy are known intuitively,' echoed Knight

(1941: 245), 'it is not possible to discriminate the economic character of behaviour by sense observation; and the anthropologist, or historian, seeking to discover or validate economic laws by inductive investigation has embarked on a "wild goose chase."' This led to a number of direct attacks on the Malinowskian orthodoxy (Schneider 1974). Few anthropologists have been convinced by these arguments. Bliss and Stern (1982) type applications of neoclassical theory to ethnographic data are extremely rare, although some formal models of hunter-gatherer foraging strategy have recently been developed (e.g. Winterhalder and Smith 1981; Hill and Hawkes 1983).

The publication in 1966 of an English translation of *The Theory of Peasant Economy* (Chayanov 1925) has stimulated much anthropological research and general theorizing in the areas of tribal and peasant economy (e.g. Sahlins 1972; Durrenberger 1984). Chayanov's work was an early (arguably the first) application of neoclassical theory to the analysis of peasant economy. He argued, *pace* Lenin, that the degree of self-exploitation of labour is established 'by some relationship between the measure of demand satisfaction and the measure of the burden of labor' (Chayanov 1925: 8). This neoclassical argument was elaborated using some geometry and lots of statistical data. Chayanov also developed his own theory of demographic differentiation which owed nothing to neoclassical economics; he argued that the biological nature of the domestic cycle determines family size and the ratio of consumers to workers over time.

Sahlins's development of Chayanov's work focused on his demographic differentiation theory and not his neoclassical propositions. Sahlins's lack of interest in the neoclassical paradigm reflects a general mood in anthropology. The emphasis on empirically based, comparative research within anthropology has little in common with the *a priori*, universalist approach of neoclassical economics; as a result, it has had only a minor impact on ethnographic research.

The ideas of Marx and Polanyi have had more impact than neoclassical theories. The works of Meillassoux (1981) and Godelier (1986) stand out on the marxist side, while Bohannan and Bohannan's *Tiv Economy* (1968) is a classic in the Polanyi tradition. The annual publication, *Research in Economic*

Anthropology, has done much to popularize Polanyi's ideas, especially under George Dalton's editorship from 1978 to 1983.

There has been much debate in the academic journals about the respective merits of the formalist (i.e. neoclassical; see p. 23), substantivist (i.e. institutionalist; see p. 26), and neomarxist schools of thought (Ortiz 1983). There are important differences between the approaches of Marx and Polanyi. For example, Marx stressed the primacy of production, while Polanyi focused on exchange. However, when contrasted with the neoclassical paradigm, the differences between substantivists and neomarxists pale into insignificance and their shared historical and comparative method is amplified. At a more fundamental level, then, the controversy between the formalists and the rest is nothing more than an anthropological version of the economics versus political economy debate; the terminology is different, but the substance is the same.

The followers of Polanyi and Marx do not always see things in this light, though, and are inclined to exaggerate their differences. While some disciples are able to advance the thoughts of the masters in the light of new ethnographic and historical evidence, most take a popularizing and exegetical approach to the sacred texts and important questions concerning the lived experience of people are subordinated to trivial questions concerning status group membership within the academy.

As the arch-Polanyist George Dalton correctly noted in the late 1970s,

> Marxism is burgeoning in all the social sciences and in many
> fields of history, but it seems to me a rather Talmudic
> Marxism, much too much concerned with the words of the
> Master, and much too little with real-world events in actual
> capitalist, communist, and Third World countries.
>
> (Dalton 1978: xi)

Commenting on marxist economic anthropology in a later publication, Dalton and Köcke (1983:41) also observed that, 'In trying to fill Marx's old concepts and conclusions with new context important to the subject of economic anthropology, Marxist anthropologists wind up in utter disagreement among themselves' (Dalton and Köcke 1983: 41). However, they fail to realize that these strictures apply equally to the Polanyi-group paradigm they advocate. The assertion Dalton and Köcke make that marxist anthropologists share only a 'name' while the Polanyists share a 'paradigm' (ibid: 41) is an example of mere name calling rather than constructive analysis. Classifying academics in this subjective manner achieves nothing. It raises no questions of any significance and diverts attention from the real issues such as the analysis of economic inequality and poverty (Gregory 1987a).

MODERNIZATION, DEPENDENCY AND ARTICULATION

Development was a matter of concern for the pre-World War II British school of social anthropology (Hogbin 1957); but it was only after the war that the problem of development emerged as a major political, and economic issue. The rise of the USA as the dominant industrial, political and military power, combined with agitation for political independence in colonized countries, was the major contributory factor.

The USA's response to this political agitation was to use development assistance programmes to stop the spread of communism. It was generally believed by US advisers that this objective 'was consistent with the mutually beneficial expansion of trade between rich and poor nations, the pursuit of humanitarian goals, and the fostering of democratic political institutions' (Hoben 1982: 352).

Modernization theory was developed, in part, as a theoretical justification for the United States' post-war foreign policy. W.W. Rostow, the author of *The Stages of Economic Growth* (1960) – one of the classic texts in modernization theory – was also a presidential adviser to Kennedy and Johnson in the 1960s. The popularity of his book was undoubtedly related to Rostow's high public profile and the 'ideological fitness' (Preston 1982: 95) of his theory. Another influential contribution to the modernization literature was Schultz's *Transforming Traditional Agriculture* (1964), a more theoretically rigorous neoclassical economic treatment of the problem of development.

Variations of modernization theory emerged in a number of disciplines. For example, in sociology, a body of literature developed using the language and concepts of Talcott Parsons (Taylor 1979); while McClelland's psychological approach in *The Achieving Society* (1961) remains widely quoted.

While such theories are expressed in different disciplinary languages, they all share a set of common assumptions. These include a focus on the individual decision maker, the use of a distinction between the 'modern' and the 'traditional', and a prescriptive model of development that has a Eurocentric, technocratic orientation (Hoben 1982: 350). Modernization theory accepts as axiomatic the proposition that industrialization of developing countries must follow the path of the west; furthermore, the periods of colonization and neocolonization are seen as essential prerequisites for modernization (Taylor 1979: 40).

Theoretical controversies within modernization theory concern the defining characteristics of the traditional/modern distinction rather than the validity of the distinction itself. For example, the 'irrational tradition-bound native' model was an early assumption of the school. This was subsequently challenged by the economist Schultz (1964) who also argued that the marginal product of labour in traditional agriculture was not zero, but merely very small relative to modern agriculture.

Modernization theory was also the subject of many external critiques. These came from anti-establishment critics of US foreign policy, many of whom were inspired by marxist theories of capitalist imperialism (Griffen and Gurley 1985). The so-called 'dependency' school of Baran (1957), Baran and Sweezy (1966) and Frank (1967) negated the principal assumptions of modernization theory and produced an alternative 'underdevelopment' model which was the mirror image of modernization.

Power relations between states, rather than endowments of different individuals, are the central basis of dependency theory. A distinction between 'centre' and 'periphery' replaces modernization's modern/traditional distinction; and it is argued that the centre exploits, rather than develops, the periphery. The policy conclusion of dependency theory is independent socialist development.

Dependency theory attacked the dualism of the modernization paradigm by stressing the unity of the world capitalist system. This theme was elaborated by the historian Wallerstein (1974) in his 'world system' theory variant of dependency theory. He traced the origin of the world market and argued that the core areas of the system exploit the peripheral and semi-peripheral areas by a process of unequal exchange.

Dependency theory has had significant political impact, especially among the peripheral countries where it has provided theoretical justification for nationalist struggles against US imperialism (Frank 1974: 8). It has also generated much critical comment from some marxist scholars for defining capitalism in terms of exchange instead of production; for posing conflict in terms more of states than of social classes; and for supposing, undialectically, that capitalism is incapable of initiating development in the periphery (Griffen and Gurley 1985:1112). An alternative approach, called 'articulation theory', emerged as a substitute; this stressed the multiplicity of modes of production in the world economy and the need to study the articulation of these subordinate modes with the dominant capitalist mode (Clammer 1978, 1987; Seddon 1978; Taylor 1979).

The literature on development and underdevelopment has had a major impact on anthropological thought. The political economy perspective taken by Morgan, Mauss and other early anthropologists emphasized the comparative at the expense of the historical and political; they were more concerned with idealized versions of tribal and peasant economies in an evolutionary perspective than with the impact of the expanding capitalist world economy. When colonization was studied it was limited to the classification of cultural traits given and received in the 'culture contact' situation (Herskovits 1938). The need to take power relations and history into account is now widely accepted, not only by economic anthropologists, but also by the 'symbol and meaning' school of interpretative anthropology (Marcus and Fischer 1986). Acculturation theory has been almost completely superseded by underdevelopment theory, save in the area of psychological anthropology where it continues to prosper (Padilla 1980).

The empirical findings of anthropologists have challenged some of the basic assumptions of the theories of development and underdevelopment. The ethnographic evidence has consistently exposed the Eurocentric assumptions of the 'irrational economic man' model of modernization theory (Hoben 1982). Furthermore, anthropologists have shown that many development programmes have failed owing to misunderstandings about indigenous economies; consequently these aid programmes have sometimes exacerbated, rather than ameliorated, poverty (Yorke 1982; Gregory 1988).

Dependency theory was readily embraced by many anthropologists in the 1970s, its acceptance being fuelled, no doubt, by the radical political environment of the time. However, dependency and world system theories embodied new assumptions that were also difficult for anthropologists to accept. The implicit treatment of the periphery as a passive victim of the imposed will of the core states was the most serious of these shortcomings (Nash 1981: 417). A central axiom of anthropology, after all, is that social beings are the producers, as well as the products, of their social and economic environments. Consequently, articulation theory, with its stress on diversity, has become more popular (Kearney 1986). Here anthropologists – the French neomarxist school in particular – have made a significant contribution with the development of the 'lineage mode of production' theory (Kahn 1981). The high point in the influence of the political economy approach to development and underdevelopment is undoubtedly Eric Wolf's magnum opus, *Europe and the People without History* (1982). This book situates the traditional objects of anthropology, the tribal and peasant households, in their global and historical contexts, synthesizing a wealth of anthropological, historical, and theoretical literature in the process.

But dissatisfaction with articulation theory is now growing. Anthropologists are increasingly calling for attention to be given to the superstructure as well as the base. Robinson complains about the overriding concern with the elaboration of formal models of production and makes a plea for anthropologists 'to investigate aspects of cultural and ideological change in the context of changing structures of production in the capitalist periphery' (1986:10). Anthropologists in the interpretative camp echo her call: 'Not only is the cultural construction of meaning and symbols inherently a matter of political and economic interests', note Marcus and Fischer (1986: 85), 'but the reverse also holds – the concerns of political economy are inherently conflicts over meanings and symbols.'

CULTURE AND IDEOLOGY

The question of the relation of culture and ideology to the economy raises the old debate concerning status and power. This debate takes different social forms in different countries. In India, for example, the controversy is about the primacy of caste or class, with theorists such as Dumont (1966) taking the side of caste and religion, and marxists like Mencher (1974) arguing the case for class and the economy.

Weber's seminal discussion of the relationship between status and power remains one of the most coherent statements on the topic. He related both status and power to the economy with the insightful observation that 'classes are stratified according to their relations to the production and acquisition of goods; whereas "status groups" are stratified according to the principles of the consumption of goods as represented by special "styles of life" ' (Weber 1948: 193).

The study of consumption, then, is the study of culture and ideology; it is integrated into the investigation of the economy as a whole via the analysis of reproduction (i.e. production, consumption, distribution and exchange considered in their totality). The cultural dimension of consumption has been relatively neglected because of the dominance of neoclassical economic approaches to the subject. Economists analyse consumption from a utilitarian perspective that emphasizes biological need. This approach has been roundly criticized by Douglas and Isherwood in *The World of Goods: Towards an Anthropology of Consumption* (1978). 'Forget that commodities are good for eating, clothing, and shelter,' they polemicize, 'forget their usefulness and try instead the idea that commodities are good for thinking; treat them as a nonverbal medium for the human creative faculty' (ibid: 62). Douglas and Isherwood conceptualize consumption as a public matter, not a private one; for them 'consumption is the very arena in which culture is fought over and licked into shape' (ibid: 57). This cultural perspective is somewhat extreme, but it does serve to remind that the meaning of the term 'consumption' must not be taken for granted (see p. 197).

Their book has had little impact on neoclassical thought, but it has given rise to a revival of interest in the subject of consumption in anthropology. The collection of essays, *The Social Life of Things*, edited by Appadurai (1986), contains theoretical and ethnographic reflections on the subject; it also contains essays by historians and indicates a trend towards the interdisciplinary study of the economy that is now gathering momentum. Other important studies of culture and consumption have been made by Baudrillard (1981), Bourdieu (1984), and Miller (1987); Douglas (1987) has returned to the subject with an interesting collection of articles on drinking. These books introduce many novel ideas as well as developing the pioneering theories of Veblen (1899) and Packard (1959).

While it is an error to reduce status and consumption to class and production, the question of the relationship of the one to the other raises other controversial issues. Dumont's solution to the problem is that, in India, status encompasses power; in other words, that caste encompasses class. This formulation has been the subject of much debate (Dumont 1966: xi-l).

An alternative formulation is to view status as the expression of power. This is an important theme of the 'subaltern' studies school of Indian history. 'Subaltern' means 'of inferior rank' and it is used by these historians 'as a name for the general attribute of subordination in South Asian society whether this is expressed in terms of class, caste, age, gender and office or in any other way' (Guha 1982: vii). The aim of this school, whose theoretical inspiration comes from the writings of the Italian marxist Antonio Gramsci (1971), is to analyse the 'history, politics, economics, and sociology of subalternity as well as the attitudes, ideologies and belief systems – in short, the culture informing that condition' (Guha 1982: vii). Scholars of this school argue that the experiences of exploitation and labour endow subaltern politics with many idioms, norms and values which separate it from élite politics and ideology. This argument is demonstrated by Guha in *Elementary Aspects of Peasant Insurgency in Colonial India* (1983), which also develops a critique of elitist interpretations of Indian history. But the implications of this book extend far beyond the historical context on which Guha concentrates. Not only does it constitute an implicit critique of both Dumont- and Mencher-type approaches to Indian sociology and anthropology, it also develops a new framework for the analysis of ideology that replaces the worn-out 'base/superstructure' metaphor.

The subaltern studies school is just part of the huge and growing literature on peasant ideology. Kahn (1985), in a recent literature review, speaks of the recent 'discovery' of peasant ideology in agrarian economies. The ideology of working-class people in industrial economies, too, has recently become the subject of ethnographic research. Willis's widely acclaimed book *Learning to Labour* (1977) investigates why British working-class kids get working-class jobs. He conducted an ethnographic study of twelve working-class schoolboys over a period of two years, which included their last years at school and their early months at work. To give his study a comparative dimension Willis visited other schools in different socio-economic areas. Most of his data are presented in the form of transcripts of conversations. He found that working-class boys are not passive bearers of the dominant ideology, but 'active appropriators who reproduce existing structures only through struggle, contestation and a partial penetration of those structures' (Willis 1977: 175). This echoes Guha's (1983) findings for the Indian peasantry of the colonial period, and the observations of anthropologists generally on the condition of peoples in subordinated economies.

Willis-type studies of the industrial working classes have stimulated new approaches to the study of élites in capitalist societies. Anthropologists such as Marcus (1983) have conducted ethnographic research among dynastic families of America using a method that complements the subaltern studies approach; élite ideology is neither assigned a spurious primacy nor is it mistakenly taken to be the ideology of the whole society.

CONCLUSION

I am convinced that the actual evolution of research ideas does not take place in accord with the formal statements we read on research methods. The ideas grow up in part out of our immersion in the data and out of the whole process of living. Since so much of this process proceeds on the unconscious level, I am sure that we can never present a full account of it.

(Whyte 1955: 280)

'What is your theoretical perspective?' is a question a fieldworker is often asked. To the extent that this means 'What ideas are guiding your research?' then the question must be given serious consideration. Some of these can be gleaned from the theoretical literature, but this should not be treated as the only source of ideas, as the above quote suggests. Ethnographers must be theoretically informed, but must also surrender themselves to the experience of fieldwork if new ideas are to be developed. The best ideas have built-in planned obsolescence; they begin to age at the moment of their conception and at a rate determined by daily changes in local and world conditions. Anyone engaging in ethnographic fieldwork must surely give this point paramountcy because it is the *raison d'être* of primary data analysis.

Chapter Three

PEOPLE

INTRODUCTION

Economics is about people; but whereas economists are primarily concerned with people in the abstract, such as the rational economic man of neoclassical economics, ethnographers are concerned with people in the concrete. The Latin origin of the word 'concrete' (*concrescere*, to grow together) is suggestive of the focus of ethnographers on the complexities of the relationships between people living at a certain place at a certain time.

As a general rule, the smaller the group studied the greater the potential for the ethnographer to record the complexities in people's inter-relationships; this is due partly to the greater physical proximity between researcher and subjects, and partly to the greater potential for participant observation. Conversely, attempts to provide wide coverage of a relatively large population require a higher degree of simplification; it is likely that in such field situations there will be a greater distance between ethnographer and subjects. This trade-off not only divides ethnographers from economists, but also differentiates ethnographers from each other. Some ethnographers, such as Freeman in his *Untouchable: An Indian Life History* (1979), study the complexities of the life of just one person; others, like Malinowski and de la Fuente in *The Economics of a Mexican Market System* (1957), study the complex relationships between thousands of people. Clearly the size of the research population selected will govern the methods used and the extent to which standard practices will need to be modified to suit an ethnographer's particular field situation.

This chapter canvasses the main issues that need to be addressed when selecting a location, defining a research population, counting people, and conducting household censuses.

RESEARCH LOCATION

The hallmark of ethnography is the in-depth study of small research populations by direct observation (see pp. 9-17). These populations are rarely randomly selected. In other words, when choosing a community for study, it is unlikely that all communities in a region or country will have an equal statistical probability of being selected. It is more usual for a research location to be chosen by purposive sampling because of some actual or perceived characteristic of its population.

A variety of factors influence the choice of a fieldwork location. There are agglomerations of ethnographies about particular regions like the Trobriand Islands (Leach and Leach 1983) and the Chiapas Highlands of Mexico (Vogt 1974). Such concentration has often resulted from a growing corpus of previous research in the area which provides access to historical and comparative material. However, access to particular areas is also dependent on both political and environmental considerations. It is no coincidence that social anthropology emerged as a discipline in colonial contexts as administrators often provided easy access for ethnographers to research locations (Asad 1973). Similarly, the dearth of ethnographies about groups in other remote regions, like Mongolia, can be explained by politically imposed restrictions on access. As Gregory can attest, after two refusals to carry out research in India, changed political circumstances can render previously accessible regions out of bounds for foreign researchers. Remote or physically harsh environments may also be under-represented in the ethnographic literature, although there are exceptions such as the inhospitable Kalahari Desert (Lee and De Vore 1976) or the Amazon Basin (Hames and Vickers 1983). Practical reasons, like the availability of aerial photographs or the existence of elderly informants with memories of precolonial times, may determine the choice of a location (Hill 1977: xi). Finally, unscientific reasons, such as the personal preferences of an ethnographer, should not be overlooked. Some individuals choose field locations because of a fascination with the 'exotic'; others may be influenced by political, climatic, and methodological considerations or a simple desire for adventure. We will not delve here into the complex psychological make-up of the stylized ethnographer.

Decisions about general research regions are made prior to undertaking fieldwork and are based on literature search and discussions with other researchers; but it is often necessary to spend the first month or so in the field searching for a precise location.

It is not unusual for research plans to change after one begins fieldwork. A range of factors may alter one's carefully made plans, including the absence of expected economic institutions, local resistance to research objectives, state or other political intervention, and so on. It is important that just as the fieldworker should have an open mind about what will be observed, similar flexibility should be maintained with regard to the overall research agenda. So many ethnographies begin with a statement (usually in the preface) along the lines of 'I went to study A, I ended up studying B'. For example, Michael Young prefaces *Fighting with Food* (1971) by stating that his research plans, drawn up in Canberra, were to study local government as an emergent political institution. The project was still-born because, as he notes, 'the [village] council was immature, its role in village affairs was insignificant and local leaders were for the most part unconcerned with its existence. It took some weeks to discover this, of course' (Young 1971: xvii). Young ended up studying ceremonial yam exchanges among Kaluana people. Altman (1987) went to central Arnhem Land to study the economy of an Aboriginal township and its relations with the Australian state and national economy; he ended up by residing with a small band of rural people whose main productive activities are hunting, fishing and gathering.

The reference to research location does not mean that the fieldworker is limited to work at one physical location, or with one group of people; indeed, it is sometimes desirable to work in a number of locations and with different groups. It is often the case that a fieldworker progresses through a number of locations before arriving at the final fieldsite. In foreign countries the stylized progression is from port-of-entry to administrative centre to regional centre to field site. Preliminary data can be collected at each phase of one's journey to the final location. Multi-locale studies are essential when comparative data are required. Gregory's research on rural markets in central India involved travelling with merchants to twenty-two small towns within a radius of 50 kilometres of the central market town; detailed studies of land tenure and inheritance were also made of two contrasting villages. Hill's (1963) study of the migrant cocoa farmers of southern Ghana was carried out in numerous locations over a period of four and a half years. In other cases, the mobility of the research population may require the fieldworker to move. Altman had to live at fifteen different locations over a thirteen-month period when collecting data on the daily hunting round of a highly mobile band of hunters.

RESEARCH POPULATION

A population is usually defined with reference to a particular time and place. A research population is an artificial construct that is always abstracted from a wider universe for analytical purposes. This requires a detailed description of the boundaries that are drawn to delineate research parameters. Defining a research population can be extremely complicated especially as political, administrative, linguistic, cultural and other 'boundaries' invariably overlap. At times, population boundedness may overflow into jurisdictions that are beyond study, like over an international border. It is also important to differentiate *de facto* from *de jure* populations. The former category refers to people who are within a population boundary at one point in time (like during a census), but will include visitors and exclude residents who are temporarily absent. The *de jure* population refers to the usual residents of an area. The distinction is particularly important when studying highly mobile societies or groups with high migration rates (see pp.57-9).

Choosing a research population necessarily involves a broad selection criterion. For example, Marie de Lepervanche in *Indians in a White Australia* (1984) concentrated on a migrant population in Australia. Her research population was the immigrant Punjabi population of a small town in northern New South Wales called Woolgoolga. In 1971, the township had a total population of 1,350 of whom 250 were Indian. De Lepervanche (1984:14-15) observed that Indian people lived in forty-seven houses; the research population was dispersed and from the outside it was not always possible to tell whether a house was occupied by an Indian or Australian family. The majority of the Indian households were engaged in banana farming; 59 per cent of the Indian household heads were self-employed and landowning farmers who sometimes employed others. The determinant of this research population was ethnicity; its size (228 in 1970 and 274 in 1973) made it of manageable proportion for direct observation.

Altman's choice of one outstation group in Arnhem Land, on the other hand, was based on a spatial consideration; his research population was defined as the *de facto* population that utilized a particular geographic area in the food quest. However, the territory used by the Momega band overlapped with areas used by other bands. The choice of one outstation as the research population was made after a regional survey, but Altman had no way of knowing the degree of flexibility in this population until long term residence was taken up. What is of significance is that while the regional survey showed Momega to be typical of an Arnhem Land outstation on a number of demographic and formal economic criteria (see p.47), the one critical variable that could not be measured by cross-sectional survey was the significance of hunting, fishing, and gathering activities over the seasonal cycle.

We must also recognize that it is not only the ethnographer who chooses the research population; the research population also has to accept the researcher and provide its co-operation. Gaining access to a research population is the necessary precondition for doing fieldwork and this permission must be sought from the people themselves. Increasingly, the anthropologist is recognized as a resource or potential mediator, and it is this that often ensures access. An important consideration for the Gunwinggu who accepted Altman as an ethnographer was the access that they would gain to his four-wheel-drive vehicle.

Counting people

The fieldworker has to come to terms with the size of the regional population within which the research population is located. However, there are real limits to the time that a single fieldworker

46

can devote to counting people. Consequently, many ethnographers locate their research population within broader population parameters by referring to official census statistics. This is somewhat paradoxical because ethnographic research invariably throws the accuracy of official statistics into considerable doubt (Hill 1986).

Whether one has the opportunity to count people will largely depend on the size of the research populations. There is no rule-of-thumb here, but it is likely that a population of between 1,000 and 3,000 is manageable for a researcher, with trained assistants, to enumerate by direct observation.

A distinction can be drawn between a population survey and a household census. When Altman went to Arnhem Land, he found that the Australian Census of Population and Housing dissected the administrative region where he was based in half. Consequently it was necessary to undertake a survey of communities in the region. Fortunately, these twenty-five rural communities (called outstations) were small and were visited every fortnight by a mobile store that provided an administrative link with the outside world. Altman (1982a) arranged to be employed in a voluntary capacity on what is locally termed 'the tucker truck' and was able to visit all these locations twice in a four-week survey period. While the aim of this preliminary survey was to collect population information, it was also possible to collect the following data:

The language group affiliations of each group
The location of communities and mode of access
The population by age and sex
The cash income and formal employment at each location
Cash income by source – welfare, employment, sale of artefacts
Production of artefacts for sale
Production of fish for sale
Expenditure patterns (from mobile store sales)
Outstation-owned transport (vehicles, tractors, boats)
The nature of outstation housing

These data were subsequently of importance when Altman chose one of these outstations as a research location, because they allowed it to be statistically situated in the regional economy. However, the original survey undertaken in July and August 1979 had a major deficiency as it did not include the township community. This error was recognized and a year later another survey of outstation populations and of the township was undertaken. In the latter survey, a hinterland population of 595 and a township population of 787 (including 107 non-Aboriginal residents) were enumerated by direct observation in a four-week period with the assistance of four Aboriginal assistants (Altman 1982b).

Population surveys, then, generate a wealth of comparative and historical data; in Altman's case this allowed a comparison between outstations and township (rural and urban settings), between outstations themselves, between households within the township, and between two periods in 1979 and 1980. The last was particularly significant, because during the inter-survey period the Department of Social Security sanctioned the introduction of unemployment benefit payments to outstation residents and this had a marked impact on the regional and household economy.

Altman's population surveys contained elements of a preliminary census and elements of what could be termed a household census. In many field situations it may not be necessary to undertake separate population surveys and household censuses. In others, a household census can only be conducted with a part of the population (see pp.53-4).

HOUSEHOLD CENSUS

The term 'household census' implies that in all societies there are standard household units that remain stable. This is not the case. Just as one can differentiate between *de facto* and *de jure* populations, a similar distinction can be made with households. Furthermore, households change over time (over the domestic development cycle, owing to migration, and to disputes) and the domestic unit varies enormously between societies. Households are extremely flexible among people who hunt and gather, but are usually relatively stable (at least over a period of 12-24 months) with agriculturalists.

To begin with, then, it is important to define the household in any particular research setting: it can be defined with reference to residential, commensal, genealogical, occupational, or other criteria. Frequently a definition that is multi-dimensional must be used.

Freeman (1970:1) begins his book on the Iban of Sarawak by stating that the most salient characteristic of social organization is the practice of long-house domicile. The long-house is made up of a number of independently owned family apartments. Freeman employs the term *bilek* to define the Iban family group: it refers to ownership and occupation of an apartment in the long-house, and also to the normal location for cooking, eating and sleeping (ibid: 2-9). Raymond Kelly (1977) also begins his study of the Etoro of Papua New Guinea with a discussion of the long-house. Among the Etoro, however, the long-house is not divided into sections on a family group basis, but into men's, women's, bachelors', and widows' sections, with a large communal section at the front. The Etoro long-house operates as one production and consumption unit, the average size of each numbering about thirty-five persons. 'Big houses' in Hausaland are different again. While they have a single household head and a single entrance, some of these big houses have networks of paths leading to distinct households and the whole compound, with a population of 200 or more, has the air of a tiny compact village (Hill 1982: 93-5). Among highly mobile foragers, on the other hand, physical shelters are frequently uninhabited for long periods and people may sleep out in the open; the hearth group may be the appropriate unit for investigation.

These examples are presented to illustrate the differences in composition of 'houses' and 'households'. While usually there is some spatially discrete area that is occupied by a family group, the fieldworker must ascertain by empirical investigation and observation what physical structure constitutes the house and the relations between the people who occupy it (see pp.59–60).

Households are key units for study because they are usually the most important economic unit. When a researcher first arrives he or she must find somewhere to reside and to form their own household. They will quickly become aware of the spatial distribution of people, and mapping of buildings (whether occupied or not) is often an important starting point to undertaking a population survey or a household census. Physical structures provide a basis for cross-checking the presence (or absence) of people in a community. The geographical location of houses and other buildings can be greatly assisted by aerial photographs and maps (see pp.64-7).

Household censuses are generally conducted with a schedule, although this is only necessary when numerous questions are to be asked. It is important to differentiate the sort of census conducted by an anthropologist from official censuses. Theoretically, a census should measure the population at one point in time. Official population censuses are usually conducted on a particular day. In Australia, the last census was taken on the night of 30 June 1986; the country was arbitrarily divided into manageable census districts and the total population estimated by aggregating the populations in all districts. Such data are generally collected with questionnaires that are filled in by the household head or some other member of a household; they are based on indirect data collection and an assumption of accuracy in informant recall. This method has many shortcomings, as demonstrated by Bernard *et al.*'s (1984) review; for example, there is no means to cross-check information (see pp.104-9).

Anthropologists on the other hand are usually concerned with extremely small areas and small populations, but they gain a familiarity with the population owing to the long-term nature of their fieldwork. While it is frequently recommended (Barnard and Good 1984) that fieldwork should begin with a preliminary census, this should not be interpreted to imply that the exercise is not to be repeated. Furthermore, the ethnographer should not feel any pressure to undertake a census immediately upon arrival at the research location; from our experience a familiarization period for both the fieldworker and local people is important.

The advantages of continuous direct observation are threefold. First, it is generally accepted that household censuses undertaken by anthropologists generate rich data and are far more accurate than official censuses (Howell 1986). Second, a number of censuses undertaken during a fieldwork period allow historical comparisons, even though the time frame may be limited to a year or two. Third, household censuses allow intracommunity comparisons (of size, wealth, and so on) at the household level.

Most censuses, whether official or ethnographic, are not only interested in the total population at one point in time, but also in a number of biological and sociological features of the population. All official censuses include questions about age and sex, or what McArthur (1961: 3) terms 'the fundamental characteristics' of a population. Official censuses increasingly ask questions about the sociological structure of the population, usually for comparative and policy formation purposes. Sociological questions encompass issues like nuptiality, household structure, ethnicity, employment status, cash income earnings, housing standards, and so on. Sometimes official surveys (usually limited to a random sample of the total population) deal with specific issues like the division of the population by height and weight (in anthropometric surveys) or household dietary intakes or expenditure patterns (see pp.175-87).

Ethnographers can ask similar questions in their censuses, but it is more usual for their schedules to be directly correlated to their particular research problems. Consider the methods used by Alan MacFarlane and Raymond Firth in their respective studies of highland Nepal and coastal Malaysia.

MacFarlane, in *Resources and Population: A Study of the Gurungs of Nepal* (1976), utilized a comprehensive census schedule that was administered to the 100 households of the village of Thak. The schedule was divided into eight sections: *de facto* census, *de jure* census, semi-permanent migration, marital history, fertility history, parental history, recent deaths, and miscellaneous. The census schedule included sixty-seven questions and emphasized demographic issues.

Firth adopted a different strategy in *Malay Fishermen: Their Peasant Economy* (1946: 316-7). His general economic census of 331 fishing households covered the following topics:

Household membership
    number
    sex
    estimated age category
    occupation
    kinship relations
Property
    ownership of boats and nets
    number of coconut palms (or annual yields)
    amount of rice produced or obtained from land share-cropped
    presence or absence of a vegetable patch
    number of rooms in house
Subsidiary information on furniture, income etc.

Firth conducted his census towards the end of his fieldwork when he knew most of the people personally; consequently the information given could be checked from other sources. These data were complemented by the following systematic observations:

1   A complete daily record for six months of the value of the catch from each of 20 lift-nets operating from a stretch of beach about half a mile long.
2   Similar, but less complete, daily data on less important fishing techniques used in the same area.
3   A sample census of rice production on 57 acres of land (222 plots) noting:
       owner
       cultivator
       type of rice planted
       approximate yield
       subsidiary information on manuring, labour engaged, etc.
4   A sample census of vegetable production on 11 acres of land (64 plots) with similar data as for 3.
5   A sample set of budgets from 10 households within the census area taken daily at periods varying from one to five months. (Firth 1946: 316-7)

Firth's data were collected in close collaboration with his wife Rosemary Firth (1966). This joint approach allowed for cross-checking across gender boundaries. As Rosemary Firth notes:

> the advantages of team work possible between husband and wife working together were invaluable. It would have been physically impossible for my husband both to have been out on the beach all day recording fish catches, and to have made the rounds of so many houses for daily budgets. In addition there was the visiting of markets and the census work which we did together. ... Of course every anthropologist has his own way of verifying doubtful information, but two people working together on different but correlated problems have a great advantage. I would almost say that any economic survey ought to be done ideally by a husband and wife team working together, but unfortunately this is a convenience of research for which even the most conscientious anthropologist is not always able to equip himself.
>
> (Firth 1966: 6-7)

52

To summarize, it is important to recognize the shortcomings of household censuses; they provide quantitative information at one point in time, but can be notoriously unreliable for reasons that range from inaccurate informant recall to deliberate under- or overstatement for political or other reasons. A census taken at one point in time will miss the variations that occur over the seasonal cycle. Firth's (1946) strategy of keeping detailed daily records of the most significant economic activities is one way to overcome this problem. Second, if a household census is made during the early stages of fieldwork, then it is important that an attempt be made to repeat it some months after fieldwork has begun; such a repeat exercise may provide important comparative data, or, at the very least, a marker of how the fieldworker's understanding of the economy has grown. Re-survey often convinces the researcher that the schedule approach begs as many questions as it answers, but this provides time for reflection and for re-posing of questions. Finally, household censuses may provide a quantitative skeleton of the economy, but questionnaires provide little opportunity for recording the viewpoints of informants that are the qualitative flesh of the economic system.

Sample selection

Ideally entire research populations should be studied. However, as the Firth example above illustrates, sample surveys are often necessary because of the physical impossibility of collecting all relevant economic data. Selection of a sample within a research population can be chosen on a random, non-random, or purposive basis. Non-random selection is generally haphazard, whereas purposive selection is made with some research purpose in mind.

A statistical problem arises as soon as a fieldworker is forced to choose a sample from within a non-randomly chosen community. If strict randomness criteria were to be applied to a sample of households chosen from a research population, then tables of random numbers could be used to select households. However, because research populations are rarely homogeneous, it is important to divide them into a number of categories before making a choice. This requires that the population be stratified or subdivided. Consider a community of 1,000 households where 950 are cultivators, 30 are fisherfolk, and 20 are traders. A ten per cent sample of 100 households without stratification may exclude all fisherfolk and traders. Stratification of the population into cultivators, fishers, traders could ensure that a sample composed of say 95 cultivators, 3 fisherfolk and 2 traders is chosen (*Notes and Queries* 1951: 57).

Rather than providing yet another extended discussion of scientific sampling procedure, we refer the reader to an excellent chapter on counting and sampling in Pelto and Pelto's *Anthropological Research: The Structure of Inquiry* (1978). But it should be remembered that the best scientific procedures are often developed in the fieldwork situation with the help of informants. The following case, we believe, reflects the experience of many fieldworkers.

Edmundson (1976: 7-10) admits that he went to Java with elaborate plans concerning the selection of a stratified random sample, but soon found that abstract theories of statistical sampling could not always be readily applied in the field situation. He notes that 'while aid could be requested at random, one could not expect random acceptance of the request. A simple knock on the door was not sufficient; formal introductions were necessary to obtain a degree of trust and to add a subtle element of gentle social coercion so important in the Javanese village' (Edmundson 1976: 8). Subsequently, the village chiefs (*lurah*) became instrumental in helping Edmundson obtain subjects. Two days were spent explaining the project to each headman emphasizing the need for a representative sample in which the proportions of rich and poor, landed and landless, high and low social status households were equal to the proportions in each village. Then the *lurah* were asked to prepare a list of twenty village households that were representative of each of the three villages surveyed. Edmundson found that the selected samples were far more representative than those obtained using random requests and non-random acceptance because he was receiving acceptances only from villagers owning relatively large plots of land. Edmundson was able to test the randomness of his sample by comparing average sample landholdings with village averages.

The issue of sampling will be returned to in subsequent chapters as we examine a range of methods for measuring household landholdings, labour utilization, ownership and use of technology, and so on. It is clear that there are no *a priori* means to choose a truly random sample. Households may be representative in population terms, but may be uncharacteristically productive or unproductive: the atypicality of households is often of considerable research interest. Finally, often there is no way of empirically establishing whether households are representative or unrepresentative until fieldwork is completed and data analysed *ex post facto*.

Collecting demographic data

Population statistics are obviously of central importance to any economic analysis because many debates about poverty hinge on data concerning the people/land ratio. Demographic data involve much more than counting heads, but if an anthropologist collected all the information a demographer required then there would be little time left for collecting social and economic data. How far should the ethnographer go?

This was a question posed by Borrie *et al.* (1957) in an article on Tikopian demography which was the outcome of collaborative research between anthropologists and demographers. They list the following minimum requirements:

(1) a record of births, and if possible pregnancies and pregnancy wastage, with cross reference to ages of mothers;
(2) age by sex [using, we suggest, the standard five-yearly categories 0-4, 5-9, 10-14, and so on];
(3) the marital composition of adult males and females, cross-referenced with age;
(4) records of migration by sex, age, and marital status, and whether such migration is temporary or permanent. (1957: 252)

Howell (1986) in a recent review of demographic anthropology notes that anthropologists have had a poor reputation among demographers in the past. The reasons for this are not difficult to fathom. As Howell notes:

Some of the accounts of population generated by anthropologists prior to 1960 are simply preposterous: fertility rates over 100 per 1,000, mean number of children born per

woman of 20, average age of 10 or 80, and reported growth
rates of 20% per year.

(Howell 1986:221)

Notwithstanding this, she is emphatic that anthropological field
methods provide an opportunity to generate extremely accurate
data. Demographers have become increasingly critical of the large-
scale and quick data collection methods of official censuses and
surveys; concurrently, the intensive field methods of
anthropologists have become more highly valued. For the
anthropologist who has limited time to collect strictly
demographic data it is better, as Borrie *et al.* pointed out, 'to gather
a limited amount of data accurately rather than to aim at too much
and to run the risk of inaccuracy' (Borrie *et al.* 1957: 248).

The ethnographer with a specialist interest in demography
should consult works such as Carroll (1975), Lucas and Kane
(1985), McArthur (1961), and Palmore and Gardner (1983) for a
detailed review of research techniques. The most difficult statistic
to collect accurately is age; we use this example as an illustration of
some of the methodological issues that are raised when collecting
demographic data.

Krishnamoorthy and Muthiah (1985: 53-67) suggest the following methods of age reckoning in the absence of birth records:

The historical calendar method. In this method, the birth of a
young person is related to some notable event the date of which is
known with certainty. In the case of an adult, age at the time of the
event may need to be estimated and years since that time added.
This method can be particularly effective if linked to major
religious ceremonies for which initiate's approximate age can be
estimated.

The cohort method. This allows the estimation of age for a group
that go through an event (like a rite of passage) together. This
method can be particularly useful for events that are held
regularly.

The family history method. This uses information (often collected
by the genealogical method, pp.59-60) on relationships, birth order, puberty and marriage for all persons in a family or household;
age estimates for each member are based on this information.

Community comparative method. This extends the family history
method to all members of a research population or community.

This method is feasible only with small research populations and can be greatly assisted by a community meeting where age grade relationships, seniority rights, and ritual or other status are discussed.

Methods using components of age. This allows a reconstruction of age when information on components of age (like age at marriage and duration of married life) are known. This method is usually used to estimate the age of married women.

Use of official documents (other than birth certificate). Official documents may not be particularly accurate because a fictitious age may have been entered for a variety of reasons. The age on an official document may be based on an estimate, but this may be of use because age estimates for children are generally more accurate than for adults.

Eye estimation method. This involves a great deal of subjectivity and is the method of last resort; however it can be reasonably accurate for infants and children especially if a check on tooth development is allowed.

MOBILITY AND MIGRATION

Research populations are never fixed; not only are there births and deaths over an observation period, but even in sedentary farming communities there will be movement of people beyond the fieldworker's arbitrarily defined research boundaries. The very nature of ethnographic research tends to emphasize residence at one location and the ethnographer may sometimes be the least mobile member of a community. As a general rule, it is perhaps better not to conceptualize any population as sedentary, but to assume that mobility is the norm.

Different economies can be distinguished by the degree of mobility. Among groups where high mobility is the norm, the fieldworker faces a host of complex methodological problems which can be resolved only in particular field settings; as we noted at the start of this chapter, economics is about people and if the population is fluctuating this must be adjusted for in analyses of production, consumption, and circulation.

We would make two general statements about mobility. First, it is important that ethnographers strive to capture the complexity of situations of high mobility through careful examination of particular cases. People always move for a complex mix of economic, social, cultural, and individual psychological reasons; the ethnographer, as Kearney (1986) notes, should attempt to grasp this complexity rather than apply the highly abstract theories of migration that economists have developed. Second, the more mobile the research population the greater the need for regular censuses.

When working with contemporary foragers in north Australia, Altman found it necessary to undertake daily counts of the population, so high was mobility during the dry seasons. He frequently observed the population change while conducting the daily count as a vehicle from another community arrived and people were off-loaded and new people boarded the departing vehicle. During the mid-dry season, the research population divided into three groups and Altman had to decide with which group to co-reside. During the wet season, on the other hand, there was a constant departure of people to the regional service centre. This departure occurred via a boat that visited every fortnight; Momega was a net loss community, and by the end of this season the majority of the research population was residing in the township. Altman faced a dilemma: whether to remain at Momega and face the possibility that he would ultimately be its only resident, or whether to move to town. This dilemma was resolved when the seasons changed and people returned to the outstation.

A check-list of methodological issues that could be addressed in examining mobility includes the following:

Data collection methods. The genealogical method and household censuses will indicate if there are sections of the total population missing. Data on migration and employment histories can be collected from informants. Census data may be useful, especially if historical records are available. Official records may be of use where people cross administrative boundaries or international borders. How mobile should the fieldworker be? This is an issue that can only be addressed in particular field circumstances. Certainly among research populations that move seasonally, the fieldworker will also have to shift residence. A fieldworker can undertake multi-locale studies by first looking at the locational origin of the migrant and then the destination, or vice versa (Strathern 1975). Often the need to do work of this

58

nature does not become apparent until near the end of one's first fieldtrip. While doing research on markets in central India, Gregory discovered that almost all of the wealthy merchants came from a single district in Rajasthan and the need for a second fieldwork trip to the place of origin of the merchants became obvious. Historical methods are essential for migration studies. Polly Hill's classic study *The Migrant Cocoa-Farmers of Southern Ghana* (1963) is an exemplary account of how to combine anthropological, geographical and historical methods; it is essential reading for anyone interested in making a serious study of migration from an economic perspective.

Units of study in migration. What are the appropriate units in migration studies? Should the emphasis be on individuals, families or other groupings? What are the defining characteristics of migrants? Ethnicity, language, kinship, class, age grade or some combination? Are new groups created in the migration process?

The spatial dimensions of movements. What distances are travelled within a given length of time? Do these movements have political ramifications? A five-kilometre international trip may be of far greater social significance than a 100-kilometre domestic trip.

Temporal dimensions of mobility. Is the migration cyclical or irregular? If cyclical, what is the periodicity? Is it daily, weekly, monthly, seasonally, annually, or longer?

The economic nature of the migration. Do people move in order to produce or to sell? Are these movements related to ecological or seasonal factors? Are the migrants wage labourers, merchants, land colonizers, or refugees?

The economic impact of mobility. What economic links do migrants keep with their place of origin? Are remittances sent? How are these used? Are there any reciprocal flows of goods and services?

GENEALOGICAL METHOD

The genealogical method has proved of such value in anthropological research that it is now considered an essential technique of sociological investigation (*Notes and Queries* 1951: 50). As a previous volume in this series has dealt with the technique in detail (Barnard and Good 1984) there is no need to elaborate here. We merely note that genealogical data can serve as the basis of synoptic tables of great utility for economic analysis. This is especially so in labour-intensive agricultural communities where land is normally transmitted via inheritance (see pp.85-7). Gregory found that large quantities of economic data on demography, migration, inter- and intra-household structure, residence, inheritance, and the division of labour can be summarized using genealogies. However, it is also important to note that genealogies may be of limited significance in certain circumstances. Altman found them of much less use than he anticipated when doing research among the Aborigines of northern Australia. This was partly due to the extremely high mobility of the population and partly because there was little differentiation between actual (consanguineal and affinal) and classificatory kin in economic relations. It is important not to equate 'doing genealogies' with 'doing fieldwork'. The genealogical method is just one instrument among many in the ethnographer's tool-kit; it should only be used when it is needed.

Chapter Four

ENVIRONMENT

INTRODUCTION

Environmental factors are of the greatest importance in all economies because they govern the limits of productive activity, but, as Anthony Forge (1972: 367) has noted, 'the important question is how narrow are those limits?' This is an empirical question and the answer will vary from place to place. The issue is not a simple one of opposing natural and social factors, but one of comprehending the complex interaction between them (Alexander 1982: 141).

The environment provides a host of natural energy inputs into any production process: wind, rain, sun, soils of various types, lakes, rivers, streams, sea water, flora, fauna, and so on. However, when these inputs are used they become partially transformed through cultivation, grazing, logging, pesticides, introduced plants, fire, habitation, and the like. In other words, the environment is both natural input and social output; but as the outputs of one process are the inputs of another, a clear distinction between natural and social environmental forces becomes difficult to maintain.

The efficiency with which environmental inputs are used depends on knowledge of the habits of fauna, the phases of the moon, the movements of the tides, the planetary cycles, and the sequence and duration of the seasons, among other things. This knowledge, which will vary from person to person, will obviously affect the complex nature of the interaction between people and the environment in any given research situation.

If the collection of primary data on the economy necessarily involves simplification and generalization (Malinowski 1916: 248), then how is the ethnographer expected to grasp complex relations between people and the environment? This chapter will attempt to confront this issue by introducing a number of general techniques for grasping complex wholes in a systematic and synoptic way; subsequent chapters will elaborate on the general technique discussed here.

PHYSICAL ENVIRONMENT

What are the economically significant elements of the physical environment? What products do these elements yield? What are the ecological consequences of production? The answers to these questions will provide a means for understanding the systematic relationships between the elements of the environment and the research population (see pp. 69–80). As the fieldworker's initial aim is to get a synoptic view of the economic dimensions of the ecosystem, general features rather than minute details must be the focus of attention. Thus, one should be concerned initially to assess the relative importance of, say, farmlands *vis-à-vis* the forests and waters, rather than the details of indigenous systems of classifying flora and fauna (see p. 89).

The following check-list, which is adapted from Lourie *et al.* (1981: 413–24), may be of use in obtaining this overview.

Relief type
    flat
    undulating (0-200m)
    hilly (200-1000m)
    mountainous (more than 1000m)
Coast-line
    rock
    beach (boulder, shingle, sand, shell)
    mud
    coral
    ice
Freshwater
    swamps
    ponds
    lakes

    springs
    rivers
    streams
Soils
    saline
    ferritic (e.g. laterite, ferritic brown earth)
    organic (e.g. peat, fen, bog)
    well-drained
    poorly-drained
Vegetation
    forest
    woodlands
    desert scrub
    scrub
    savanna
    grass
    meadows
    sparse vegetation
Fauna
    mammals
    birds
    reptiles
    amphibia
    fish
    insects
    others
Climate
    temperature
    barometric pressure
    relative humidity
    solar radiation
    rainfall
    air movement
Human impact
    cultivation
    drainage
    other soil disturbance
    grazing
    selective flora disturbance
    logging

plantation
hunting
pesticides
introduced plants and animals
fire
permanent habitation
recreation and tourism
other

Human geographers, such as Mitchell (1973), have developed sophisticated techniques for collecting these sorts of data and fieldworkers with a specialist interest in ecology should refer to works of this kind for guidance. The following sections outline some relatively simple techniques for fieldworkers whose primary concern is with economic analysis.

Maps, aerial photographs, and Landsat images

A good collection of maps is an invaluable aid for studying the physical environment. Indeed, they are a necessity, because without them many important data on the economy cannot be collected. They facilitate orientation in an unfamiliar physical environment and enable the bumbling fieldworker to determine, for example, that 'Hirapur' is the name of a town rather than a kinship term.

In many parts of the world accurate small-scale maps do not exist, in which case they will have to be made. In most cases simple sketch maps will suffice, especially when used in conjunction with larger-scale maps. Sketch maps of various degrees of accuracy can be drawn. These include rough sketches from visual observations, rough maps drawn from pacing out distances, and those drawn from more exact measures of distance and direction. A simple method for drawing accurate sketch maps has been developed by Bryant Allen (personal communication), a human geographer with extensive fieldwork experience in Papua New Guinea. His 'clockwise-around-the-circumference-method' requires one to be equipped only with a compass and a tape measure. Standing at point A, one takes the bearing of point B, where an assistant is standing, and measures the distance. The assistant moves to point

C with the tape, the compass reader to point B, and new readings are taken. This process is repeated until point A is reached again. It is important to use a plastic tape to avoid magnetic distortion. Another useful hint is to record bearings as figures between zero and 360 degrees, rather than using compass points. The information can then be plotted on graph paper according to a set scale (say 1:1,000) and, if the recording is done accurately, the last line drawn should meet up with point A. Errors invariably creep in and small ones can be handled by distributing the error around all points equally. For example, if a ten-degree error was made in a ten-sided plot, then a one-degree adjustment to every angle will have to be made. In the event of a large error, the plot will have to be remapped. The area of a plot can be quickly estimated by counting the squares on the graph paper enclosed by the plot. Where the land is steep a clinometer reading can be made at each point and the direction of fall of the land shown on the map. More accurate methods require some knowledge of surveying techniques and some specialized equipment. Mitchell (1976: 150–3) used highly sophisticated equipment and techniques in his study of land use among the Nagovisi in Bougainville. However, his methods are too expensive and unnecessarily complicated for most anthropological needs.

Aerial photographs are an extremely valuable research tool, especially in those areas where maps are either not available or of poor quality. While anthropologists (and archaeologists) have been utilizing aerial photographs for several decades, the potentialities were greatly increased in the 1960s with the introduction of new types of cameras, improved high resolution (and colour) film, and new techniques of photogrammetry. Aerial photographs have proved very useful for analysing settlement patterns and for mapping land use and ownership. The Harvard Chiapas Project (Vogt 1974) used aerial photography extensively and found it to be extremely helpful for these purposes; they were even able to generate indices of social change by comparing their photographs with old ones and noting differences, such as the materials used for roofing houses.

Another example of the extensive use of colour aerial photographs occurs in Australia where anthropologists have used them to investigate the nature of burning regimes, the locating of camp sites, and in mapping different ecological zones among groups who continue to hunt and gather. As Aboriginal-owned land must be mapped when mining companies make applications for exploration licenses, applied anthropologists use aerial photographs to identify named sites and to map clan boundaries so that landowners are identified for consultation. Aerial photographs are also used in land claim research.

Conklin's remarkable work *Ethnographic Atlas of Ifugao* (1980) stands as a monument to the value of maps and aerial photography in ethnographic research. For him, maps and ethnographic map-making became not a means to an end but the end itself. His ethnography is presented in the form of fifty-seven maps, covering various aspects of Ifugao environment, culture and society, supplemented by 184 photographs and a 40,000-word text.

The launching of the satellite, Landsat 1, on 23 July 1972 has revolutionized the study of the relationship between people and land. Landsat was designed to collect information about the earth's resources on a systematic, repetitive, medium resolution, multispectral basis. This satellite, which remained operative until 6 January 1978, was followed by the launching of four more. As each orbit takes 103 minutes and achieves a global coverage every eighteen days, literally millions of images of the earth's surface exist on a periodic basis for a period of almost two decades. These data have many uses. In agriculture, Landsat images provide data which allow estimates of land use, crop types (where it is possible to recognize major crops with a 90 per cent accuracy in fields of only hectares), crop area and yields, seasonal variations in land use, crop damages, and plant diseases. In the soil sciences, they enable soil-type classifications, estimates of actual and potential soil erosion, and soil degradation. In forestry, they facilitate land-cover classification, plant-species identification, provide evidence of overgrazing, and assist flood-plain management. Landsat images also have research applications in the fields of geology, mining, oceanography, meteorology, and cartography.

A significant feature of Landsat images is that they need 'ground-truth' data, that is, fieldwork, before they can be interpreted with accuracy. The potential research applications in anthropology are obvious. A recent atlas of satellite imagery (Mueller-Willie 1984) gives some idea of the possible applications. For example, a 1:1,500,000 image charts the main thrust of economic development in the southern Mato Grosso area of central Brazil. It distinguishes tropical rain-forest, transition forest, tree savanna which is used for isolated traditional cattle ranching, areas of recent agricultural expansion, established small landholding areas, and modern cattle ranching. Larger-scale maps of 1:50,000 enable one to distinguish the roads, parks, houses, and factories of urban development.

Anthropologists with an interest in human ecology have been quick to exploit the research opportunities offered by Landsat (Conant 1984), but their potential use extends far beyond this sub-discipline. In Australia, Cane and Stanley (1985) used Landsat images to map fire patterns in central Australia where Aboriginal people live at desert homelands. Cane and Stanley used images from 1981 and 1983 and were able to highlight recent and old burns. They concluded that Aborigines continue to use fire for economic reasons, especially to stimulate the growth of flora that are subsequently utilized as food. (There is also a growing body of scientific evidence that indigenous floral species are far more productive following fire.) Cane and Stanley go so far as to coin the term 'match stick farming' when referring to contemporary Aboriginal use of fire (ibid: 181-7). What is significant about their use of Landsat is that they found that relatively cheap black and white images were suitable for their research purposes (Scott Cane, personal communication).

However, Landsat images have their limitations. The size of a Landsat recording element, called a pixel, is 80 metres by 80 metres, or 0.64 hectare, which means that is difficult to differentiate objects within this area. Furthermore, cloud cover cannot be penetrated. This is a special problem for a place such as Papua New Guinea which has one of the highest cloud cover rates in the world. Finally, the purchase of a temporal series of maps for any one area can be costly, especially if colour images are needed. Landsat images will not, therefore, replace aerial photographs as a research tool. Rather, they are an important addition to the 'view from above' tool-kit.

Seasonality

The migration of the zenith sun between 23°N and 23°S is the principal determinant of seasonal variation in the climate. The sun crosses the equator on 21-2 March (the spring or vernal equinox), reaches its northernmost point on 21-2 June (the summer solstice), crosses the equator on 22-3 September (the autumn equinox) and reaches its southernmost point around 21-2 December (the winter solstice). As the Eurocentric names for these periods suggest, the four seasons found in mid-latitude zones of the northern hemisphere are based on them. However, in many other parts of the world only two seasons - wet and dry - are experienced. This is because the seasonal migration of the sun is accompanied by a general northward and southward movement of the tropical anticyclone belts. In the tropical regions these disturbances sometimes bring about two wet and two dry seasons.

These seasonal variations are likely to be considerably modified by local effects. For example, a slope tilted towards the midday sun receives the intensity of radiation appropriate to a lower latitude, though the length of the day is obviously not affected. Anthropologists frequently reside in communities that are remote from official weather stations and the collection of information on the local 'microclimate' can be important. At a minimum it is advisable to take daily recordings of rainfall, maximum and minimum temperatures, and wind direction and velocity. These can all be measured with a relatively cheap and simple tool-kit consisting of a plastic rain-gauge, min/max thermometer, and small plastic wind-gauge. Other information like humidity, evaporation, and hours of sunshine can be measured with slightly more sophisticated equipment.

Such local measurements of climatic conditions are extremely useful because they provide a quantitative data base to compare with local definitions of the seasons and calendar. In many societies, but especially among people who hunt, herd, fish and gather, seasonal changes are recognized on the basis of weather conditions, wind directions, and visible changes in flora and fauna. There can be significant variations from year to year between calendar months and locally defined seasons depending on weather conditions.

Information on local climatic conditions is essential for comparative and historical purposes. On one hand, assumptions are frequently made about particular locations on the basis of the nearest official weather station (if one exists), but there can be marked variations within small areas. On the other hand, it is all too easy to make assumptions based on observations during a year or two in the field and to find particular annual patterns. It is important to compare climatic conditions during fieldwork with any existing historical records to illustrate the typicality or atypicality of the observation period.

One should not expect to find a regular annual cycle or indeed any cycle at all. In the longer run seasonal variations are also likely to be affected by climatic cycles of variable length and other factors about the earth's climate that are not yet understood (Lamb 1982: 722).

PRODUCTION SYSTEMS

The *Concise Oxford Dictionary* defines 'system' as 'complex whole, set of connected things or parts', and, second, as 'method... (principle of) classification'. We employ this dual meaning of the term here. Thus, a 'production system' can be defined as 'the complex relationship between various economic elements of an environment and research population'; second, the analysis of production systems presupposes a method, a principle of classification. The aim of this section is to outline a system of classification with the aid of some illustrative examples drawn from our own fieldwork.

The first steps in describing a production system are to identify the economically significant elements of the environment (see pp. 62–4), to observe the inputs and outputs of each element and the ecological consequences of its use, and then to specify the systematic input-output relationships between the elements. The complexity is handled by beginning with the most general observations and proceeding to the particulars in a series of ordered stages.

Consider the case of Torand village in central India where Gregory worked. At the most general level, the key environmental elements in Torand are the village farmland, the cattle, a stream that flows through the village, an iron ore quarry, and the surrounding forest. The forest is exploited for marketable products and is illegally cleared to make farmlands; the quarry is mined illegally for ore to be converted into steel tools by the blacksmiths; the stream is dammed to provide irrigation water and is also fished; cattle provide manure and milk; and the farmlands provide foods (mainly rice) and other marketable products. The consequences of environmental use in this village are that forests are being destroyed as the population grows; but, simultaneously, the quality of farmlands is being improved and/or maintained. Migration is an economic necessity for villagers: some go for long periods, others for short periods of up to ten days on wage labour contracts. Some of the produce of the village is sold at the weekly market where many household necessities are also purchased.

A simplified version of the production system of which these environmental elements are part is depicted in Table 4.1. This shows the relationships of economic inputs to outputs in the

Table 4.1 The production system of Torand village

Elements of environment	Economic inputs	Economic outputs	Ecological consequences
people	labour, fish, manure, milk, food, cash	labour	population growth, migration
forest	labour, tools	farmland, market products	degradation
quarry	labour, tools	iron ore	depletion
stream	labour, tools	water, fish	water conservation
cattle	labour	manure, milk	breeding
farmlands	labour, forest, water, manure, tools	food, market products	land degradation, maintenance, improvement
secondary industry	labour, iron ore, steel, tools	tools	
tertiary services	labour, market products	steel, cash	

Source: Gregory (n.d.)

context of primary (disaggregated into various ecological components), secondary, and tertiary activities.

This table restates the description of the village economy given above. It records the fact that every economic input into a process is also the output of another process and clarifies the nature of these complex input-output relationships. The advantage of synoptic tables of this form is that they can provide a perspective on the economy as a systematic whole and, as such, facilitate organized research. Take labour for example. Who performs the household labour inputs (e.g., cooking)? Who performs household labour outputs (e.g., farming)? How much time is spent on each? How is the labour organized? Does it involve co-operation or coercion? What is the division of labour by age and gender? This table also poses questions about technology, output, consumption, and circulation which are dealt with in subsequent chapters.

Having obtained this highly simplified overview, the fieldworker's next task is progressively to sharpen the focus to bring new problems into sight. By continually changing the resolution of the focus from broad to narrow and back again, and by shifting the object of the focus from one input to another, all particulars will be covered and systematically related to the whole.

It is clear from Table 4.1 that the villagers of Torand engage in foraging, hunting, mining, fishing, and farming. Each of these activities defines a separate sub-system which has to be investigated. In this particular case the farming sub-system is the most significant economically and demands closest attention. In other societies, fishing or hunting may be more important; in yet others, trading activity in the tertiary sector could be central. The relative importance of an activity will not always be obvious at the beginning of research. Indeed, in some cases, it will only become so at the end of a research trip after the data have been analysed. For example, Altman's research showed that the Aborigines of northern Australia with whom he worked were not as reliant on welfare pension cheques as many people believed. He showed that, while cash from social security payments is important, hunting, fishing, and gathering activities remain of foremost economic significance (Altman 1987).

Table 4.2 The Torand farming sub-system

Farmland	Water source	Product
lowland terraces	irrigated by stream	vegetables
lowland terraces	rainfed irrigation	rice
upland terraces	rainfed irrigation	rice
undulating fields	dry area	cereals

As an illustration of what is meant by 'sharpening the focus' on particular inputs, consider the case of the Torand farming sub-system. Some obvious questions suggested by Table 4.1 are: What are the different types of farmlands used for? What particular food and market products are associated with the different types of land? Table 4.2, a lower-level simplification, provides the extra details.

General comparative and historical questions can be asked with data presented in this form: What is the relative importance of each mode of farming? What is the history of land use for each category of land? These questions can be answered by observation, land measurement, and questioning of informants.

Gregory was given access to land records and these were checked by pacing the fields with various informants. The total area of the village was 192 hectares of which 150 hectares were farmland. Irrigated land accounted for one per cent of total farmland area, rice lands for 60 per cent, and dry lands for 39 per cent. Vegetables were grown on the manured, fertile soils next to the stream; the rice on soils of different qualities and elevations; and the cereals (e.g., *Panicum miliaceam*) grown on poor quality soils bordering the forest. The poor quality soils have to be left fallow for various periods to restore soil fertility. In some neighbouring villages, where forest land is plentiful and the terrain more mountainous, the fallow period is very long (up to twenty years or more). In Torand, by way of contrast, the clearing of land is the first stage in the creation of terraced rice fields; in the sixty years to 1981, some 76 hectares of village forest land were cleared.

These different farmlands, then, support agricultural cycles of varying lengths depending on the fallow period. In theory, farming sub-systems should harmonize the different cycles, but this ideal is rarely met in practice. In Bastar, the government forestry department developed scientific plans for self-reproducing forests but corrupt guards often sold off access rights to the highest bidding illegal contractor; villagers too could buy 'encroachment rights' to grow millet. Issues of this nature are, we suggest, the rule rather than the exception, and they must be carefully investigated if the ecological and economic consequences of different farming systems are to be understood.

The following is a check-list of issues to consider when collecting data on agricultural cycles in general:

1 Field preparation
2 Sowing
3 Growing
4 Harvesting
5 Transportation
6 Storage
7 Distribution and exchange
8 Consumption

Each section can be broken down into a number of subsections in the study of environmental issues. For example, the issues to consider under field preparation could include:

a clearing
b levelling
c fencing
d water conservation
e irrigation
f drainage
g trees
h fallow period
i crop rotation
j rotation with animals
k ploughing
l fertilizing

Preliminary observations concerning the labour and technology used at each phase of the cycle should be made. Is ploughing done by hand, draft animal, or tractor? Is sowing done by hand, transplanting, or seed drill? What methods of weed, pest, insect, and water control are used in the growing season? Is the harvest performed with finger knives, sickles, or combine harvesters? Is transportation by foot, ox cart, truck, rail, or boat? Are these different methods combined in any way? What factors determine the choice of technique? (see pp. 116–19).

Depending upon the nature of the problem to be investigated, it may be necessary to sharpen the analytical focus once more to examine the precise details of each agricultural cycle in use. An almost infinite variety of different forms of sub-sub-systems of farming can be distinguished. The length of the fallow period (or land intensity) defines one continuum, and the relative use of labour and machines defines others. If land, labour, and machines are thought of as points on a triangle, then the area within the triangle represents the infinity of possible types. Thus, a long fallow system of farming that uses relatively small amounts of unassisted labour could be described as relatively land-intensive; triple crop, wet-rice cultivation of the type found in Java as labour-intensive; capitalist farming of the type found in England as machine-intensive; and the helicopter-assisted pastoralism of northern Australia as somewhere between the land- and machine-intensive systems. Clearly, it is impossible to discuss all these permutations and the particular methods for studying them. However, as an illustrative example of the attention to detail needed, we include a check-list for studying long fallow farming systems. This list, which has been adapted from Conklin (1957), will obviously need to be modified to suit particular research requirements:

A Selecting

    1 What taboos apply to the felling of certain areas or trees?

    2 What is the distance of swidden sites from the pivotal settlement?

    3 What are the rules governing the selection of sites?

    4 Has the land been used before? When? For what purpose?

    5 What climatic factors effect site selection?

    6 How is soil classified? Which types are excluded as unsuitable?

    7 How important is the terrain?

    8 What is the state of vegetation cover?

    9 What discussions take place among households?

    10 How are conflicts resolved?

    11 What determines the timing of the commencement of activities?

12 Are sites tested for auspicious omens?
13 How do households mark their site?
B Cutting
    14 What labour-saving techniques are employed in felling?
    15 What soil-preserving techniques are used when slashing?
    16 Is the debris spread evenly over the floor?
    17 How are domesticates protected?
    18 What forms of labour are used? Individual? Reciprocal? Paid?
    19 What tools are used?
    20 Are all large trees felled? If so, how?
    21 What is the division of labour?
    22 Is the debris levelled to ensure optimum burn?
    23 How long is debris left to dry?
C Burning
    24 Are firebreaks made? How?
    25 What determines the timing of burns?
    26 Are there any rituals?
    27 What firing techniques are used?
    28 Is uncontrolled burning common?
    29 Is there any secondary and tertiary burning?
D Cropping
    30 Is there intercropping of grains, root crops, and trees?
    31 What is the incidence of different crops?
    32 What is the planting time?
    33 Where are different crops planted?
    34 What planting technique is used? Dibble? Planting stick?
    35 Are there any specially designated ritual plots?
    36 Are plots fenced?
    37 Are watches kept over the sown crop?
    38 What is the regularity and technique of weeding?
    39 Are rituals obligatory at harvest?
    40 What technical and social techniques are used when reaping?
    41 How is the harvested product transported? Threshed? Dried? Stored?
E Fallowing
    42 How is the length of the fallow period measured? Years? Plant association?
    43 Do different areas have different fallow periods?

Long fallow farming of this type has been called 'swidden', 'slash and burn', and 'shifting cultivation'. We would advise field-workers not to worry about these terms and others until fieldwork has been completed; a definitional and terminological method has little to recommend it. Farming sub-systems are complicated and the use of a single term to describe a complex dynamic process obfuscates rather than clarifies. The general analytical approach we suggest involves moving from the general to the particular, from one particular to another, from comparative states to dynamic processes, and then from the particular to the general. As these analytical moves are made the parts should always be analysed in relation to the whole. Concrete reality is complex and unless a mental chart is used to inform data collection it is very easy to become bewildered and to lose direction (see p. 93). Trade-offs between simplification and detailed analysis have to be made continuously. For example, Gregory collected detailed data on the farming systems and sub-systems of Torand, but very little on the sub-sub-systems. This is because his research at Torand was part of a larger rural marketing study. It was neither possible nor desirable to spend extra time collecting such fine-grained data because other aspects of the Torand economy, such as the tenure system, needed investigating.

Non-farming sub-systems

In order to illustrate the generality of the methodological principles outlined above it is useful to consider how an analysis of a non-farming economy might be carried out. The example used here is Momega outstation in northern Australia where Altman resided between 1979 and 1981.

A synoptic view of the Momega production system is shown in Table 4.3.

A comparison of the production system of Torand (Table 4.1) with that of Momega (Table 4.3) highlights both the similarities and differences between them. Both economies involve simple mining, manufacture of art and craft, fishing, and trading; the major difference lies in the mode of land use. In Torand, 300 people farm 190 ha; at Momega thirty people forage over an area of approximately 600 square kilometres (parts of which are shared with other bands).

Table 4.3 Production system at Momega

Elements of environment	Economic inputs	Economic outputs	Ecological consequences
band	labour, food, ochres, pigments, tools, cash, welfare	labour	reproduction, mobility
land	labour, tools	food, bark	regeneration by burning, tree depletion
quarry	labour, tools	ochres, pigments	depletion
secondary industry	labour, bark, pigments, tools	tools, bark paintings	
tertiary services	labour, bark paintings	cash, welfare	

Source: Altman (1987)

A closer examination of the foraging sub-system at Momega reveals that the land can be divided into four broad ecological zones: tidal river margins, flood-plains, lowlands, and uplands (plateaus and hills). These are visited at different times of the year for purposes of food collection. Table 4.4 is a synoptic view of this sub-system.

The methodological questions raised by a synoptic table of this form are obviously different from those of Table 4.2. For example, the relevant measurements that need to be made here are

Table 4.4 Foraging sub-system of the Momega band

Residential zone	Season	Main kilocalorie source produced	Main protein source produced
lowlands	early-wet	bird-life	bird-life
lowlands	mid-wet	mammal	mammal
tidal	late-wet	fish	fish
flood-plains	early-dry	bird-life	fish
lowlands	mid-dry	mammal	fish
uplands	late-dry	mammal	mammal

distances and travelling time rather than area: What was the ground distance travelled? What was the mode of transport? How long did it take? This case also raises more detailed questions about the modes of hunting and fishing.

Fishing. Altman found that Momega people combine detailed knowledge of the tides, the seasonal cycle, the breeding habits of the silver barramundi *(Lates calcarifer)*, and net-making to trap large quantities of fish during the early-dry season. The nets are large conical traps that are used in conjunction with fences made from local materials and built across tidal creeks. The immediate fish-surpluses that can be produced by a small group of men provide sustenance for relatively large ceremonial gatherings during this time of year (Altman 1987).

This particular example raises a number of general methodological issues. For example, this nature-intensive system requires that the ethnographer has some knowledge of the movements of the tides. Tides are periodic and related to the motion of the earth, sun, and moon. At most coastal areas tides are semi-diurnal, which means that the interval between successive high waters is about 12 hours and 25 minutes – about half the time of the moon's apparent revolution around the earth. However, in some areas, such as the China Sea, tides are diurnal and the interval is approximately 24 hours. The height of the tides varies from day to day. The highest tides – the spring tides – occur shortly after the new and full moons each month, while the lowest tides – the neap tides – occur shortly after the moon's first and third quarters. The maximum height of tides varies greatly around the globe and the relative positions of the sun, moon, and earth can produce some unusual effects such as the long period tides that can last for up to nineteen days. Intimate knowledge of local tidal variations significantly reduces the risks and uncertainties and is essential for successful fishing. People at Momega, who lived 30 kilometres from the sea, only trapped fish during spring tides; movements to the trapping locations, 15 kilometres away, were made on the basis of observations of the moon.

Economic theories of fishing discount the importance of local knowledge and are based on the false assumption that fish can be caught blindly (Christy and Scott 1965: 88). However, as Cordell (1974: 379–80) has noted, 'there is little appreciation of how, and to what extent, fishermen make use of environmental clues to predict the behaviour and movement of different species'. His study of canoe fishermen who work the estuaries and mangrove swamps of the Brazilian coast provides another example of the importance of local knowledge. He shows that a lunar tide calendar is closely adhered to: 'it synchronizes boat movements, the choice of fishing methods, and the availability of fishing spots according to bi-weekly and daily tide fluctuations' (Cordell 1974: 391).

Relatively labour-intensive and machine-intensive fishing systems must also be situated ecologically. In Gahavalla village, on Sri Lanka's southern coast, there are three ecological niches and three distinct fishing methods. In one section of the bay, beach-seines are used to catch anchovies and other shoal fish; the area of the bay outside the range of beach-seines is fished using traditional boats, nets, and lines; on the edge of the continental shelf tuna are caught using motorized craft. The beach-seine consists of a cod-end, a large body, wings, and hauling ropes; it is about one kilometre in length and weighs about two tonnes when wet. The average net takes about three hours to launch, set, and haul. Each net has a permanent crew of nine, but in the last stages of a big catch as many as fifty men participate. This labour-intensive method of fishing provides two-thirds of the village's income and is the major source of livelihood for a majority of households (Alexander 1982). Fishing systems of this kind raise issues that are discussed in greater detail in subsequent chapters on labour, technology, and output.

Hunting. This also depends on an intimate knowledge of the local environment. In order to study this nature-intensive sub-system, Altman had to sharpen the focus of his study even further to get beyond the simplifications contained in Table 4.4. He found that successful hunting within each broad zone was only possible with a detailed knowledge of the many small ecological niches within each. In the early-wet, for example, hunters walked to swamps where birds were known to be concentrated at this time of year. At other times, people would shift their camping location to exploit other seasonal concentrations of game. These seasonal movements, of up to 12 kilometres distance, were often made without reconnaissance owing to people's certainty about the breeding habits of indigenous fauna.

Hunting of some form or other occurs in almost all economies, but whether or not it is a subject worthy of careful investigation will depend upon the particular circumstances. In the Momega case, hunting was a core economic activity and Altman devoted considerable research time and effort to the subject, collecting data on a daily basis. In the Torand case, Gregory observed that hunting was a peripheral economic activity and no attempt was made to collect systematic data. But was this the right decision? Questions of this type are raised all the time during fieldwork. They cannot be avoided and occur just as often in a research population of thirty as they do in one of 3,000.

Any data collected will necessarily involve generalizations of one form or another; the only choice the fieldworker has concerns the level of generalization, and the research problem will determine at what point along the general-to-particular continuum one should concentrate. This is why it is important to have a theme to guide one's research; a method for deciding whether or not a particular line of research is relevant is absolutely essential. The advantage of long periods of fieldwork is that the boundaries of research can be pushed in whatever direction necessary. Gregory started off by confining his research to market relations; but, as the months went by, he found it necessary to collect data on production and land tenure in two contrasting villages in order to develop a better understanding of the rural marketing system. Altman's subsequent research in northern Australia has focused on the impact of land rights and mining (1983) and tourism (1988) on the Aboriginal economies of northern Australia; but his detailed knowledge of the economic life of just one small group gave him many insights that were invaluable in his regional studies.

TENURE SYSTEMS

Whereas a production system can be defined as the systematic relationship between the different physical elements of an environment and a population, a tenure system can be defined as the relationship between different social elements of a research population with respect to scarce natural resources such as land and water. These are two different aspects of the same system; however, when conducting fieldwork it is advisable to take as many different perspectives on the same subject as possible.

Land tenure systems can be extremely complicated. Their elements include mythology, kinship, marriage, religion, rank, law, social groupings, history, and economics. The degree of organization of the system is greatly influenced by political relations between people inside and outside a region. Tenure systems are very difficult to study because, unlike production systems, most of the elements are invisible; they are also much more diverse than production systems because political winds, unlike monsoons, are not governed by regular natural forces. The only valid generalization that can be made about the land tenure systems found in places such as southern Ghana (Hill 1963), the Trobriand Islands (Malinowski 1935), Ponam Island (Carrier 1981), Aboriginal Australia (Peterson and Langton 1983), white Australia (Huber 1977), and southern Italy (Davis 1973) is that they all involved complicated relations between people and land (or water). What are the general methodological implications of this complexity and diversity?

Malinowski's discussion on 'The method of field-work and the invisible facts of native law and economics' (Malinowski 1935: 317–40), one of the few articles on methods for studying land tenure, contains many useful hints. The task, according to him, is to arrive at simplicity and unity by a laborious process of unravelling contradictions and placing facts in their living relationship. As Malinowski noted, 'The maxim that you cannot understand the rules of the game without a knowledge of the game itself describes the essence of this method' (ibid.: 320).

Malinowski called his method 'functional', but 'systematic' or 'methodical' is, perhaps, a better description of his classificatory procedures. He prepared synoptic tables consisting of numerous columns and rows (i.e., matrices) and examined particular issues by forming sub-matrices and sub-sub-matrices in a manner similar to Tables 4.1 to 4.4. His analysis of Trobriand land tenure, for example, was based on a table that contained myth, kinship and marriage, magic, and rank as its rows; and social groupings and law/economics/politics as its columns. Tables of this kind, Malinowski (1935: 339) reminds us, are merely convenient summaries; it is essential not to make a fetish of them. Working in this way is a useful habit to adopt because, as Audrey Richards noted, the scheme.

leads to a consideration of the same data consecutively from a number of points of view, such as the environmental, the structural, the normative, the technological and the dogmatic, and hence forces the field-worker to a fuller collection of field material and also results in new hypotheses which spring out of the empirical data.

(Richards 1957: 26)

Rather than summarize Malinowski's article here, we intend, instead, to focus narrowly on some of the methodological implications of the contemporary world economy and nation states for the study of land tenure. These factors do not determine the structure and form of indigenous land tenure systems, but they do constrain and modify them. Like the sun and moon, the influences of the world economy and the nation state will vary from place to place; consequently, these influences and their impact can only be assessed empirically.

Private property and the market

Private property gives an individual alienable rights over land registered in her or his name. When this land is sold, or leased out for agricultural purposes, questions such as 'What determines the price of land?' and 'What determines the rent of land?' are raised.

This has been a central issue in economic theory from the time of Adam Smith. However, a striking feature of this body of theory is its almost exclusive concern with the so-called 'pure theory' of rent. This involves the positing of a number of assumptions (e.g., profit maximization, perfect competition, etc.) and deducing the formal logical relations between rents, prices, profits, and wages. Sraffa's (1960: 74-80) discussion of rent is a highly sophisticated example of this form of theorizing.

While such work is important for clarifying the nature of economic relationships, it cannot be operationalized because of its highly simplified assumptions. In any case, the fieldworker is usually more concerned with the determining influences of social and cultural factors that economists invariably assume away.

For example, pure theory says that the price of land is equal to the capitalized value of differential rent. Thus, if rent equals \$100 per hectare, and the going interest rate is 10 per cent, then the price of land will be $1,000. (This is merely a technical way of saying, 'this hectare costs ten years' purchase of the average annual income it brings', which is how farmers usually talk about the price of land.) However, this formula rarely works in practice; the reasons for this are often of great sociological significance and need to be fully investigated.

Huber (1977), in her ethnography of Italian migrants in western New South Wales, Australia, reports that these people were anxious to buy horticultural farms as close as possible to their relatives living in the town of Griffith. With the rapid increase in the number of migrants coming to the area in the 1950s and 1960s, the demand for these farms rose and sent the price to a highly inflated peak in 1969. However, near Leeton, some 60 kilometres away, similar farms could be bought for half the price. When a real estate agent pointed this out to a prospective immigrant buyer he replied: 'I've already migrated once; I don't want to migrate again' (Huber 1977: 70).

Another illustrative example is given in de Lepervanche's (1984) ethnography of Punjabi migration to Woolgoolga in northern New South Wales (see pp.45–6). Here, small banana plantations of around four hectares were selling for between $4,000 and $6,000 in the 1950s when bananas fetched $14 a case. By 1970, plantations were costing in excess of $10,000, even though the price of bananas had crashed to between $3 and $4 a case. When the price of bananas began to fall, Anglo-Australian farmers were unable to run their farms as profitable enterprises and sold them to the newly arrived Punjabis. These migrants remained solvent by hard work, pooling labour, sharing resources, and undertaking supplementary work such as seasonal cane-cutting. As one observer put it, 'while the Indians were off at the cane earning good money to pull themselves through, the Australians were crying into their beer at the low prices they were fetching for bananas' (de Lepervanche 1984: 101).

Land prices are often below the capitalized value of rent. In these situations it is necessary to pay particular attention to the motivation of sellers. As Hill (1972: 88) has noted, it is often a conjunction of unfavourable circumstances which causes selling. Thus, she continues, to ask a farmer 'Why did you sell?' is almost as ridiculous as to enquire 'Why are you poor?' Such questions often cause great embarrassment and the information is best obtained from others. Indebtedness and/or inability to meet obligatory expenditures, like marriage, are usually important contributory causes. Other factors to investigate include extreme poverty, migration, ill health, old age, excess land in relation to resources, and domestic disputes.

Nowadays the state attempts to influence the market for land in various ways. This fact raises questions such as: What are the laws relating to land and are they enforced? If not, what strategies do people adopt for getting around them?

In the Murrumbidgee Irrigation Area of Australia, the Water Conservation and Irrigation Commission of New South Wales controls sales of land and water supplies. The area is divided into small horticultural blocks of around 20 hectares and large area farms of around 200 hectares. The former can only be used for fruit and vegetable production, and the latter for rice cultivation. No person can own more than a certain amount of land and subdivision is not permitted. Regular aerial surveys and prosecution of any offenders ensure that these regulations are observed (Huber 1977: 66). Laws of this type make for an active land market and generate reliable records of obvious value for the fieldworker because they facilitate informed and directed questioning of informants.

This situation is in striking contrast to Bastar district in central India, where Gregory undertook fieldwork in 1982-3. Here laws exist relating to maximum landholdings and rules for subdividing land equally between male and female offspring. These laws are rarely observed and consequently official records alone are of limited value. In some cases they are merely out of date, while in others legal fictions are entered by corrupt officials. These records, then, are of interest only if one can get the people to explain the real situation. Gregory managed to obtain fairly accurate data for two villages, but only after overcoming numerous bureaucratic obstructions and undertaking extremely time-consuming work correlating the genealogies of tiny holdings of subdivided plots of land with the genealogies of the people in the villages (see p. 60). Thirty-one land transactions over the period 1921 to 1981 were recorded. Five of these involved encroachment on to forest land, six were sales, and the remainder were inheritances.

Private property, inheritance, and marriage

Family relations determine the shape of many non-market transfers of land, especially those concerned with marriage and inheritance. Numerous laws exist to prevent the fragmentation of land through inheritance. Many of these laws are based on the belief that fragmentation of land is caused by the mindless application of inheritance laws, but this doctrine has been repeatedly shown to be incorrect by ethnographers (Davis 1973: 111). Rules are made to be broken and the task of the fieldworker is to record the strategies different families adopt in the light of factors such as wealth, phases in the domestic cycle, gender relations, marriage, individual initiative, and the like. The importance of luck, rather than order and regularity, is another common theme in inheritance studies (Leach 1961: 143; Hill 1972: 181–7). Thus, some useful questions to guide research on this topic include: What strategies do families adopt to accumulate and transmit land? How do they avoid fragmentation of family lands? What is the role of luck?

Elite families often employ legal experts to organize generational transitions. Marcus (1983) draws attention to this in his study of American family dynasties. He notes that as a wealthy family ages generationally, and begins to take on charitable roles, it becomes potentially weakest as an organized entity. The family must create a transcendent, controlling version of itself if it is to achieve a coherence of organization. 'This coherence does not come as much from commitment made by its members to their common lineage, as from the application of law and the work of fiduciaries whose primary responsibility is to protect the founder's legacy from divisive family quarrels' (Marcus 1983: 223).

Research among élite families is obviously very difficult because wealthy families have their secrets and are reluctant to grant access to nosy researchers. This fact is, no doubt, one of the reasons anthropologists have concentrated much of their research effort on colonized, illiterate people where access is relatively easy (see pp. 43–5). Marcus's work, is therefore, a long overdue step in a new direction and some useful methodological clues can be gleaned from his research. He notes that some dynasties are more knowable than others. The less famous and financially more modest dynasties are often more accessible; so too are the dynasties which have been through the final stages of dissolution (which was the case with his subjects). From direct observation of these families, and the secondary literature on other families, it is possible to draw up plausible hypotheses about the workings of the less accessible families. This was the method he employed to analyse the Hunt family and their effort (which was almost successful) to control the world economy by cornering the silver market (Marcus 1985). An additional source of information was the subsequent US government enquiry into the Hunts which made public much information about the family that would have otherwise remained secret.

Within poor agrarian families, mini-dynasties are often built up by a patriarch through careful marriage strategies. These extended families, like those of the ultra-élite, are also at their most vulnerable when they reach the peak of their wealth and power. They are, of course, unable to afford the services of a fiduciary and often dissolve at this point. Davis (1973: 120–3) reports the case of Vincenzo Capece from Pisticci in southern Italy who inherited 2.87 hectares, but subsequently expanded his holding to 14.40 ha over the next thirty years, through marriage (4.59 ha), purchases (3.75 ha), and renting (3.19 ha). He was, at the time of Davis's fieldwork, the 71-year-old head of an extended farming family that included three sons, one of whom worked as a clerk in the city. The unity of the family was dependent entirely on the strong will of Vincenzo.

This case illustrates the close attention one must pay to the distinction between the ownership of private property and the control of family land acquired through marriage. Vincenzo's first wife brought in 1.83 ha. When she died Vincenzo got a life interest in the whole, but property rights to only one-twelfth of this plot, with the remainder going to his sons. His second wife brought 1.11 ha and to keep this in the family he married his youngest son off to his second wife's daughter. Finally, by marrying his second son to his paternal cousin's daughter he reunited land that had been previously subdivided. Thus Vincenzo controlled 4.59 ha of family land acquired by marriage, but owned only 0.15 ha of it.

The ownership/control issue also raises the question of women's rights. Mundy's (1979) report, that Muslim women in highland Yemen were not gaining control of the distinct share of the patrimony to which they had rights under Islamic law, echoes a theme found in much recent writing. This has led to a questioning of the theory of dowry and bridewealth developed by Goody and Tambiah (1973) who conceive a dowry as a form of *pre-mortem* inheritance. Clearly, what is at issue here is the question of power. This involves getting beyond the general male/female dichotomy in favour of an examination of particular relationships between, for example, husband/wife, father/daughter, mother/daughter and mother-in-law/daughter-in-law. Mundy's (1979: 170) argument that it is 'not that woman's claim to property is questioned or denied but rather that she needs an agent to fight for her and to work, protect and control the land' is suggestive of the lines such an enquiry might take. Terms like 'inheritance' and 'dowry' can be an obstacle here; as mentioned above, we suggest an approach that focuses on the comparative details of intra- and inter-household relations rather than on definitions and terms.

In summary, when collecting data of this kind, it is necessary to have genealogies, land maps, or aerial photographs showing the distinct plots, and charts and tables that link the two. Another useful strategy is to construct 'genealogies' of plots of land, showing their areas, subdivisions and consolidations, and changing uses and ownership over time.

Customary land tenure, the market, and the state

'Customary' land tenure refers to the neo-traditional land tenure systems developed in ex-colonial countries. Colonization led to the outright alienation of land, often by brute force, in many parts of the world. Some neocolonial states have tried to redress the worst excesses of colonization by either granting land rights to dispossessed groups, or by recognizing indigenous land rights through the implementation of 'customary' land law. The effect of this new legislation has been to create large data bases showing the genealogies and landholdings of the people concerned.

An interesting example of such state intervention has occurred in the Northern Territory of Australia with the passage of the federal *Aboriginal Land Rights (Northern Territory) Act* 1976. This legislation transferred all land previously reserved for Aboriginal people to inalienable communal title. It also established a claims process whereby traditional Aboriginal owners could claim crown land. Traditional Aboriginal owners were defined in the legislation as 'a local descent group who have common spiritual affiliations to a site on the land ... and are entitled by Aboriginal tradition to forage as of right over that land'.

Over the past decade, Aboriginal land ownership has increased from 19 to 33 per cent of the Northern Territory, or to nearly half a million square kilometres. Anthropologists have been instrumental in preparing land claim documentation presented to the Aboriginal Land Commission; the regular appearance of anthropologists in the courts has resulted in a new branch of applied anthropology that could be termed 'forensic anthropology'.

The Land Rights Act has also provided Aboriginal people with statutory rights to limit access to their lands. For example, Aboriginal owners have the right to veto mineral exploration on their land. The mining industry has been a vocal opponent of this provision in the legislation, but Aboriginal interests argue that it is an essential feature of effective land rights. This example illustrates how intervention by the state can radically alter property relations and the political economy of a region (see Peterson and Langton 1983; Maddock 1983; Altman and Dillon 1988). Similar state intervention has occurred in North America (Berger 1985; Salisbury 1986).

The other key factor to consider is the role of cash cropping. It should not be assumed that customary land tenure is a 'barrier' to development; rather, one should investigate how tradition is manipulated in the modern context. This was the approach taken by Rodman (1987) in her analysis of traditional land tenure in Longana, Vanuatu. She used aerial photographs to provide the basis of a land tenure map with a scale of 1:5,000. Using superimposed acetate sheets she composed a map. This was supplemented and cross-checked by walking the boundaries of nearly all the plots and enlisting the aid of informants who became skilled map readers. She discovered that 5 per cent of Longanan landholders controlled almost one-third of the plantation land. These men did not break with tradition in acquiring the land. To the contrary, they are 'masters of tradition' who skilfully manipulated the flexibility of the customary land tenure to their own advantage. They did this by selectively using bonds of kinship to manoeuvre around heirs.

Recent historical developments such as these suggest that many of the old debates about the inapplicability of western property concepts to non-western systems of land tenure have to be reconsidered. The issue now is how these systems have modified and changed each other. Land tenure relations, it should be remembered, are never solely economic. Land is a space that is lived, not just perceived. People become emotionally tied to it and project their personality into it; personal and group identity are defined with reference to it. In Longana, Vanuatu, the people say, 'There can never be a Longanan who has no land' (Rodman 1987: 38).

INDIGENOUS CLASSIFICATION SYSTEMS

Indigenous classification systems can sometimes be very useful in economic analysis. Gregory used the indigenous classification of soils in his analysis of Torand land use (see p.72); Altman used the Gunwinggu division of the seasonal cycle into six parts (see p.77); Alexander (1982: 38) found that the three class divisions the Gahavalla people use accurately represent the distribution of wealth. Indigenous classifications of labour, technology, output, and consumption can also be of great analytical use to the observer.

However, indigenous classification systems of plants and animals are extremely complex and it is possible to spend all one's research time gathering ethnobotanical and ethnozoological information. This has become a specialized sub-discipline in anthropology (Berlin *et al.* 1973) and the economically inclined ethnographer should approach the subject with caution. If plants need to be identified, then photographs can be taken. Where this simple method proves inadequate, more scientific procedures, like collecting samples, will have to be adopted; ethnobotanical guides, such as Sillitoe's (1983) and Womersley's (1976), should be consulted.

Indigenous classifications of time are likewise very complex, but their basic principles should be mastered because they can be of great economic significance. The following section outlines some basic features of a number of different calendrical systems. The purpose of this discussion is to provide some basic information and to highlight the general importance of understanding the role of conventional standards in any measuring system (see pp. 208–10). We also use a discussion of calendars as an illustration of the diversity and complexity of indigenous classification systems.

Calendars

'Social life', notes Mauss (1904: 78–9), 'does not continue at the same level throughout the year; it goes through regular, successive phases of increased and decreased intensity, of activity and repose, of exertion and recuperation.' The periodicity of these cycles is governed, in part, by the movement of the sun and moon: calendars were developed to measure it. The word 'calendar' comes from the Latin *calendarium*, meaning interest register or account book, itself a derivation from *calendae*, the first day of the Roman month, the day on which future market days, feasts, and other occasions were proclaimed.

Calendars are either solar, lunar, or lunarsolar. Solar calendars, being seasonal, are usually of the foremost economic importance. Lunar calendars are used mainly for religious purposes, although they are also important for fishing activities (see pp. 78–9). The days that a religious calendar declares taboo for labour and eating are clearly of economic importance and fieldworkers will frequently need to be familiar with both solar and lunar calendars.

Calendar-making is best seen as the attempt to resolve two insoluble problems. The first is that neither the solar year nor the lunar year is made up of complete days: the solar year consists of 365.24 days, while the lunar year consists of 354.37. The second, and related, problem is that no simple relation exists between the daily cycle of the sun and the monthly cycle of the moon, which is 29.53 solar days long (Ronan 1982).

The solution to these problems involves the arbitrary addition and subtraction of days and months. The large number of solar, lunar, and lunarsolar calendars that exist reflects the different arbitrary conventions established in different societies.

Solar calendars. The obvious unit for a solar calendar is the day, measured either from sunrise to sunrise, from sunset to sunset, or in some other arbitrary way (e.g., midnight to midnight). Multiples of the day have often been used to develop weekly calendars. In west Africa for example, there is a standard 'market week' of three, four, five, six, seven, or eight solar days which governs the periodicity of markets in a given locality. The names of the days in the calendrical week in some districts of west Africa are often the actual names of the main places in which a market is (or was) held (Hill 1966). Weekly calendars of this type do not require any adjustment for the obvious reason that they do not use the seasonal year as a unit of measurement.

The most widely used annual solar calendar is the Gregorian or Christian calendar. This calendar dates from 1582 when the Julian Calendar was reformed during the reign of Pope Gregory XIII. This calendar is based on a 365-day year. The extra 0.24 days are made up in leap years when an extra day is added to the month of February. Leap years occur in those years that can be divided by four, but not in those centennial years that cannot be divided by 400. Thus 1700, 1800, and 1900 were not leap years, whereas 2000 will be.

This calendar was adopted by Britain in 1752 and its current widespread acceptance by business and governments is a legacy of British imperialism. Its primary use is for secular economic and political affairs. Even though it is a Christian calendar, it provides no simple means for determining the date of Easter which is determined by the lunar cycle and the vernal equinox and whose calculation requires the use of complicated astronomical tables.

Lunar calendars. The Muslim calendar is an example of a widely used lunar calendar. This is based on twelve months of thirty and twenty-nine days alternately. This amounts to 354 lunar days, which is 0.37 days short of the actual lunar year. This problem is overcome by adding a day to one of the months at regular intervals. However this correction ignores the fact that the lunar year is some eleven days shorter than the solar year. The result is that the Muslim lunar months slowly regress through all the seasons. An important time in this calendar is the ninth month of Ramadan, which is observed as a month of fasting by Muslims (Ziadeh 1982).

Lunarsolar calendars. Lunarsolar calendars attempt to overcome the problem inherent in lunar calendars by adding lunar months now and again in order to bring the lunar months and the seasons back into line.

Some of these calendars are ingeniously simple. For example, the Yami fishing community of Botel-Tabago Island near Taiwan use a calendar based on phases of the moon. Around the time of the vernal equinox in March they go out in boats with lighted

91

flares. If flying fish appear, the fishing season is allowed to commence, but if the lunar calendar is too far out of step with the seasons the flying fish will not rise. Fishing is then postponed for another lunation, which they insert in the calendar, thus having a year of thirteen instead of twelve lunar months (Ronan 1982: 598).

Other lunarsolar calendars are extremely complicated. In India a highly complex lunarsolar calendar has been in use for thousands of years (Freed and Freed 1964). The lunar element of this calendar is made up of a lunar year of twelve lunar months and 360 lunar days. The lunar day (*tithi*) is a theoretical abstraction which is defined as the time for the moon to move eastward by 12 degrees (i.e., 360 degrees divided by thirty). Because of the elliptical form of the orbits of the earth and moon, as well as other complicating factors, the lunar day is sometimes shorter and sometimes longer than a solar day (*divisa*). On average, though, it comes out shorter at 23 hours and 37 minutes. This means that a lunar year of 360 lunar days is equal to about 354 solar days. Thus, six lunar days must be deleted from the calendar each year so that the number of days in the lunar and solar years are equal. But on the long lunar days, when the sun rises twice, a lunar day must be added. Finally, in order to bring the lunar year of 354 days into accord with the solar year of 365 days, lunar months are added and deleted.

These additions and deletions obviously create problems for ceremonies that are due to be held on these days or in these months. What usually happens is that a ceremonial day that has been deleted is held on the preceding day while an added day may result in the ceremony being repeated, especially among wealthy high-status people (Freed and Freed 1964: 78–80).

To make matters even more complicated, different variations of the system are used in different parts of India. In northern India, where the *purinmanta* system is used, the moment of the full moon ends the lunar month; while in southern India, where the *amanta* system is found, the new moon ends the month. The result is that many similar pan-Hindu holidays appear to occur a fortnight apart (Freed and Freed 1964: 71).

To make matters even more complicated still, these calendars coexist along with the Gregorian calendar and the Indian National Calendar. The latter, a solar calendar, has seven months of thirty days and five months of thirty-one days. A day begins at sunrise and ends at the following sunrise, but a given date on this calendar always falls on the same date on the Gregorian calendar. These calendars affect those people having urban jobs and those having business with the courts or other government offices. The ancient lunarsolar calendar still determines almost all religious ceremonial dates and the social rhythm of millions of rural dwellers.

The moral of this extended discussion of calendars, then, is that a fieldworker who plans to work in an Asian country is well advised to become familiar with the calendrical system of the area in question, preferably even before fieldwork begins.

SIMPLIFYING COMPLEXITY

The motto 'Seek simplicity, but distrust it!' quoted in Devereux (1967: 31), is a very useful guiding principle. An open-minded approach to fieldwork necessarily involves some anxiety because it often takes a long time to comprehend unfamiliar forms of economic behaviour; in other cases, the simplicity of a familiar act can be unnerving. As Malinowski and de la Fuente noted,

> The ethnographer becomes easily lost at first, and fieldwork
> in a market place is by means easy. The difficulty consists in
> the chaos of the general picture, combined with the appalling
> simplicity of each concrete transaction. The chaos makes it
> difficult to see the wood from the trees. The triteness and
> finality of each individual act short-circuits any full
> development of problems, and in a way paralyses observation.
> (1957: 64)

In general, the more anxiety a phenomenon arouses, the less the fieldworker seems capable of observing it correctly and of evolving adequate methods for its description (Devereux 1967: 3). Understood anxiety, on the other hand, 'is a source of psychological serenity and creativeness, and therefore of good science as well' (Devereux 1967). The Malinowskian method of systematic classification used throughout this book is one means to reduce anxiety by transforming 'chaotic complexity' to 'manageable documents' (Malinowski and de la Fuente 1957: 65). But in utilizing this approach always remember the above motto!

Chapter Five

LABOUR

INTRODUCTION

Labour is a process whereby people interact with the environment to produce useful products for the purposes of human reproduction. It is a social activity that requires the expenditure of time and energy, and involves the transformation of raw materials inputs into outputs using various techniques; labour also includes the work involved in reproducing people. The analysis of labour raises many issues: What proportion of the population works? What is the relationship between producers and non-producers? How is the labour process organized? What is the length of the working day? How is labour divided? What is the productivity of labour? What is the social significance of changing technology? Do children work? How is labour compensated?

Labour is obviously a broad topic. Indeed, there is a sense in which this whole book is about the analysis of labour because an ethnographic approach to the economy must, by definition, give primacy to the analysis of the social relations between people. In a rice-growing economy, for example, the agronomist studies the seeds a farmer uses, the engineer the mechanics of a farmer's tools and machines, while the ethnographer studies the labour process in the context of the society as a whole.

In order to narrow the scope of this chapter the principal emphasis will be on the measurement of labour time. While some methods for describing and classifying labour relations will be outlined, the emphasis is on quantitative methods. Our justifications for doing this are twofold.

First, as already pointed out (see pp.17–19), in order to avoid unnecessary repetition we emphasize different methodological techniques in different chapters. The last chapter, for example, stressed the need for careful general observation and outlined some procedures for classifying data in a systematic way using synoptic tables. It is assumed that these and other qualitative procedures will also be creatively applied by the fieldworker in an analysis of labour.

Second, in recent years a number of new techniques have been developed for collecting quantitative data on labour time. These methods, while they have their problems, provide a relatively simple means for making systematic observations. It must be recognized that there is often a marked divergence between what is actually happening in an economy and what the ethnographer thinks is happening on the basis of impressionistic observation. Time allocation studies provide a means for getting beyond mere impressions and statements of the following types are increasingly common in the literature:

> after months of being with the Machiguenga in a variety of settings, I came to believe that the women were idle much more of the time than the men. [My data reveal] that there is no significant difference in idleness between adult males and females.
>
> (Johnson 1975: 309)

> It also surprised the observers that the men spent the same amount of time at work as the women, for it seemed to them that the women were far more active than the men.
>
> (Erasmus 1955: 331-2)

Evidence of this type suggests that, at the very least, time allocation methods of data collection should be given serious consideration. The analysis of the labour process will necessarily involve some time measurement. The main question is how precise should these measures be. Gregory found that days and weeks were sufficient for his purposes when studying markets in central India, although he did make some detailed hourly observations on some market activities; Altman, on the other hand, despite some early scepticism, found that a careful record of daily time use proved invaluable in his analysis of an Aboriginal economy in north Australia.

LABOUR RELATIONS

A labour relation can be defined, in general terms, as an agreement between employers and employees for the performance of certain tasks. When collecting data on concrete cases the following check-list of questions may be of assistance:

What is the duration of the contract?
Where is the work to be carried out?
What tasks are to be performed?
How is payment determined?
Does this payment take the form of labour, products, money?
What are the rights and obligations of the employee?
What are the rights and obligations of the employer?
What is the social and economic status of the employee?
What is the political-legal context of the contract?
What power and control does the employer have over the employee?
What is the basis of this power?
What power does the employee have?
Does the contract involve individuals or groups?

Description and classification should proceed simultaneously and synoptic tables of the different types of labour relations be prepared. The terminological distinctions used by the indigenes is

Table 5.1 Types of swidden labour in Hanunóo

Name	Translation	Main characteristics
sadili	self	self
arawatan	swidden-unit	reciprocal, complete
darayanan	adjoining-swidden	reciprocal, partial
pasapnun	communal	nonreciprocal, feast, nonritual
pamgas	planting	nonreciprocal, feast, ritual, without harvest shares
pagani	harvesting	ditto but with harvest shares
pinakyaw	job	nonreciprocal, pay, by job (without meals)
siniran	day	nonreciprocal, pay, by day (with meals)

Source: Conklin (1957: 54)

96

a useful starting point for further investigation. Consider Conklin's classification of the types of swidden labour used by the Hanunóo as shown in Table 5.1.

Tables like this pose new questions to be investigated such as: How important are these different forms of labour? On what basis is reciprocal labour organized? Kinship? Residence? Age grading? What are the harvest shares? How are they set? What is the purpose and function of the rituals? What beliefs are they based on? Who cooks the food?

In agrarian societies of the type Conklin studied, kinship relations are obviously very important. Relations such as those between husbands and wives, brothers and sisters, parents and children, elder and younger siblings, and among affines are obviously important for understanding the division of labour, the rights and obligations of workers and employers, disputes, and the like. We refer the reader to Barnard and Good's *Research Practices in the Study of Kinship* (1984) for further methodological guidance when studying these matters.

In economies characterized by extreme inequality in the distribution of property, special attention needs to be given to the nature and role of coercion. Power of one form or another is a feature of all labour relations, but it is the exercise of this power which distinguishes different types of labour. Unfree labour of the slave-labour type, for example, differs from reciprocal labour in that the power relation is asymmetrical. But what is the basis of this power? How is control exercised? What is the origin of the relationship? How has it changed over time? Answers to these questions vary from place to place, and time to time, highlighting the need, once again, for a comparative and historical approach to the study of labour relations. The politico-legal context of labour contracts must be emphasized, too, because of the importance of the state in the economic lives of people today.

Hill's (1977) discussion of farm-slavery in rural Kano (Nigeria) is an illustration of how historical methods and fieldwork can be combined to produce new understanding of this important subject. Using oral, genealogical, and literary sources, she was able to reconstruct the social context of farm-slavery by detailing the rights and obligations of slaves and slave owners; her method also enabled her to collect data on the transition to a community of free farmers.

The Hausa had a form of labour called *bawa*, which translates roughly as 'slave'. Terms like this are only ever first approximations and the task is to elaborate as fully as possible the relations of domination and control. In west Africa, farm-slaves had many rights, including that of self-ransom and the freedom to follow remunerative occupations when not required to work on their owner's farmland. They often worked alongside the slave owner's married sons under the authority of a slave foreman. Slaves had a right to marry and the owner was obliged to help them find spouses. The slave owner's freedom to sell any slave living with his family was severely constrained by local opinion which held that children should never be separated from their parents unless the owner became impoverished. This institution continued to flourish during the first twenty years or so of colonization, disappearing by about 1930. As the system of farm-slavery declined, day labouring developed. These people, who cannot find work all year round, resemble the slaves in being obliged to supplement their day-labouring income by farming or non-farming work on their own account (Hill 1977: 219).

Unfree labour of this 'slave' type is not a thing of the past of course. In contemporary India debt-bondage is still a very widespread form of labour. Money borrowed to pay for marriages is the origin of many of these bonded-labour contracts. The Indian government has declared debt-bondage illegal. While the policy has been successfully implemented in some parts of India, such as Bastar where Gregory worked, it still persists in a variety of illegal and semi-legal forms throughout the sub-continent.

Many contemporary forms of unfree labour have their origin in international relations. Traffic in children is big business in Asia and other parts of the world where quasi-legal agencies sell children for purposes of adoption and prostitution to rich countries. The analysis of this topic calls for special methods and the reader is referred to the pioneering work by Ennew (1986) for further guidance.

WORK-PLACE INDUSTRIAL RELATIONS

Industrial work-place studies raise special methodological problems because, in most cases, the work-place and the household are separate economic entities. The following check-list of points are some of the issues to look for when observing the working conditions of labourers:

What is the payments system?
What are the daily work routines?
What is the division of labour?
What are the personnel and management practices?
Is there any sharing of information and consultation?
What is the incidence and structure of on-the-job training?
What is the nature and effect of technological change?
Are working conditions safe and healthy?
How are trade unions structured and organized?
What is the relationship between wages, prices, and profits?
What beliefs and ideologies have the workers developed?

Collecting data of these kinds requires careful observation, discussion with both workers and managers, and, where possible, participation as a worker. June Nash's (1979) study in a Bolivian tin mining town is an exemplar of how the direct observation method of ethnographic analysis might be modified for the purposes of research of this kind. The following is a brief discussion of the problems she confronted and the methods she employed.

'Conditions of work within most [Bolivian] mines', says Nash (1979: 171), 'can without exaggeration be described as inhuman.' There are no conveniences such as latrines or drinking water; the temperature can vary from 10 to 41 degrees Celsius within a few yards; all miners get silicosis; deaths from accidents and massacres often occur. In the year (1970) Nash worked in the mining community five men died in accidents; after she left the field protest action brought about the murder of over a hundred people in the Cochabamaba Valley in 1974 and scores of miners in 1976 (1979: xi). Depressing conditions of this type make 'participant' observation impossible and pose the ethical and political questions of fieldwork in the starkest possible form.

Nash, being a woman, faced particular difficulties. She wanted to observe the conditions of work firsthand, but was initially refused access by the engineer in charge on the grounds of the workers' alleged suspicions that women in mines bring bad luck. The workers she consulted, however, were anxious to have her enter the mine. She eventually got permission and spent five full day-shifts in the mine. Her direct observations enabled her to frame new questions to put to both workers and management.

A feature of her method is the skill with which she is able to relate micro and macro factors. Consider her analysis of the impact of changed technology which came about after the nationalization of the mines in the 1950s. Formerly, work teams had been organized in groups of six to a dozen under the leadership of an 'empirical engineer' (*tecnico empirico*), a man of long experience, skilled in gaining the co-operation of the men who worked with him. The men were paid according to the mineral content of the load they produced, and each team distributed the returns among themselves according to set proportions. The effect of this was to create intra-group solidarity and inter-group competition. After nationalization, the teams were broken up into partnerships and workers received a basic wage plus a bonus which was calculated according to the cubic metres mined rather than the mineral contained in the ore. This broke up work team solidarity but broadened the ties between all workers. The 'empirical engineers' were replaced with trained technicians who remained aloof from the miners and with whom the miners were often in conflict.

The working of the payments systems is illustrated with case studies. For example, a contract driller earned $2,292 in October 1970: of this 16 per cent was his basic wage, 65 per cent his contract earnings, 8 per cent his incentive, 3 per cent a family subsidy, and 8 per cent a share of profits (Nash 1979: 227). However declining productivity of ores, combined with increasing costs for an enlarged bureaucracy, has caused the company to operate at a loss since 1965. 'There is,' notes Nash (ibid: 210) 'a delicate balance between wages, prices, and profits which, if tipped, sets off a wave of protest and political action or of repression.' The dependence of the workers and managers of the mine on world conditions beyond their control was put succinctly to Nash by one of the supervisors she interviewed:

> Four times the owners of this mine have tried to close it. First it was closed when the silver was exhausted; then tin was found to have value, and it was reopened, but in 1946 when Hochschild was the owner, he wanted to close it after he had capitalized Colquiri with the profits of San José, but the Banco

Minero took it over to keep workers employed. In 1957 the
nationalized mines wanted to close it, but then they got better
machinery to concentrate the ores and it was kept open. Now
they are talking about closing it again because it is a marginal
mine. But in time they are going to find other methods of
concentrating the minerals and the mines are going to live.
No technician can say that the mine is marginal. Oruro ought
to live for a hundred years.

(Nash 1979: 251)

Studies of this type illustrate the necessity to link local economic
conditions to the wider historical and political environments.

MEASURING LABOUR INPUTS

The practice of collecting data on labour inputs has its historical
origins in the industrial revolution and the associated widespread
shift to wage-labour in France and England (Minge Klevana 1980).
The emphasis was on how factory workers used time; the aim of
management was to use paid labour as efficiently as possible. From
the mid- and late nineteenth century there was increased pressure
to reduce the long working hours of factory workers; this resulted
not only in state intervention that specified who could be
employed (hence effectively eradicating child labour in factories
and mines), but also in the establishment of a regulated working
day. This state intervention in industrial countries coincided with
the institutionalization of the union movement. With the advent of
mass production in early-twentieth century USA, time and motion
studies were developed to observe the work practices of factory
workers and to increase both labour productivity and returns to
workers (Friedman 1987).

Fieldworkers have used similar techniques to observe labour
inputs in agrarian societies. As in the factory setting, such
observations tended to focus on particular production processes.
Alternatively, indirect techniques like questionnaires have been
used to gauge labour time expended. In some cases a sample plot
of land was used in experiments to measure labour use (e.g.
Godelier and Garanger 1978). In others, observed activities were
assumed to be 'average' and were then extrapolated to the entire
research population (for a summary of such studies see Bronson

1972). In general, these studies have been concerned either to assess the efficiency of non-industrial production processes or to examine changes resulting from the introduction of new technology (see pp.158–60 and 168–71).

Hill and Hawkes (1983), for example, used direct observation to examine the hunting behaviour of the Aché of eastern Paraguay. These people reside primarily in a mission settlement, but spend about one third of the year in the jungle hunting and gathering. Hill and Hawkes collected data on subsistence activities on sixty-six observation days between March and July 1980; the study population consisted of fifty-four men over the age of ten. The emphasis was on hunting returns and different technologies; extremely detailed data on labour inputs in different phases of hunting were generated.

Hayami *et al.* (1978) collected data on the daily activities of a sample of eleven households in the rice growing village of Barrio Tabuan, Languna, Philippines. Data were collected by indirect means; respondents, who were all literate, were required to fill in a prepared questionnaire on daily activities over a year-long survey period. However, the questions on time utilization were restricted to 'productive work' and, in particular, to labour use in rice production. Again, extremely detailed data were collected on all aspects of rice production, including time spent in land preparation, planting, weeding, harvesting, and processing. These labour inputs were also classified according to the season, the economic class of the farmer, and the type of labour. Hayami *et al.* (1978: 36-7) also concentrated on 'how family members allocate their time among different jobs in terms of average number of working days per working member'.

Collection of data on productive labour inputs alone will invariably result in the need to define activities prior to collecting data. This particularist approach, termed 'specific focus studies' by Grossman (1984b: 445-6), has a major shortcoming in that it presupposes that 'productive' labour inputs can be distinguished from 'non-productive' labour inputs before the study begins. Specific focus studies are frequently of limited comparative use because different fieldworkers use different definitions of work, as well as different definitions of the labour force. Carlstein (1982) and Borgerhoff Mulder and Caro (1985) criticize the over-emphasis in such studies on Eurocentric conceptions of what constitutes productive labour. Pahl in his comprehensive study *Divisions of Labour* (1984) suggests that the emphasis on such work outside the home (usually by men), rather than on domestic labour, can be directly linked to the onset of the industrial revolution in early nineteenth century England.

TIME ALLOCATION

Historically, three anthropological studies using time allocation techniques stand out. The earliest example is Audrey Richards's (1939: 382-405) approximate work diaries kept for Bemba adults in two African villages, Kasaka and Kampamba, during two short periods (eighteen days and nine days) in 1933 and 1934. In 1948, McCarthy and McArthur (1960: 145-94) collected detailed time diaries for two periods totalling nineteen days for two small groups of Australian Aborigines at Fish Creek and Hemple Bay. This study was experimental as subjects were requested to subsist on 'traditional' foods and not to consume shop foods that were available at the time. Finally, Erasmus (1955: 322-33) collected detailed data between July and September 1948 at Tenía, a village of 200 inhabitants in Mexico. Erasmus used a radically different technique from Richards and McCarthy and McArthur; instead of continuous observation of activities, he used a random observation approach. As Erasmus and his wife moved around the village each day conducting their general ethnographic inquiries, they recorded the activities of each villager seen, and the time at which the observation was made. Over a three-month period, 5,000 observations were recorded, of which 2,500 were on adults, 2,000 on children, and 500 on the aged. These observations were coded into three broad categories – economic activities, household activities and leisure – and thirty-six smaller categories. Erasmus continually reviewed his data base to ensure that all villagers and all times of day were receiving similar coverage; if some were deficient, visits around the village were planned to compensate for discrepancies. Erasmus was surprised by his results:

> The fact that Teníans spent as much time at work as they did
> came as a surprise to the observers. Had they made an
> estimate based entirely on their impressions, they would have
> arrived at a figure substantially lower than that indicated by

the quantitative data. When a large proportion of the
population can be observed at leisure at almost any hour of
the day, a strong impression of indolence may result. This in
itself might easily account for the strength of the 'coconut
tree' picture of primitive work habits in the past.

(Erasmus 1955: 331)

Richards and McCarthy and McArthur left their data largely
unanalysed; it was later anthropologists, like Sahlins (1972) and
Minge-Klevana (1980), who used the data to develop general
propositions about 'original affluence' and to test whether labour
time declines with industrialization.

Apart from these three pioneers, time allocation techniques
were rarely used until the 1970s when Erasmus's spot check
technique was further refined by Johnson (1975). The relative
efficiency of this technique has seen a rapid growth in the use of
time allocation in ethnographic analysis over the past decade.
Comprehensive analytical surveys of this literature have been
prepared by Nag *et al.* (1978), Minge-Klevana (1980), Gross
(1984), Grossman (1984b) and Borgerhoff Mulder and Caro
(1985). These surveys document the various techniques for doing
time allocation studies, as well as the advantages and shortcomings
of these methods. The following three sections outline these
techniques with a particular emphasis on their role in the study of
the economy.

Survey techniques

There are four broad techniques that can be used in time
allocation studies: continuous direct observation, random spot
checking, informant recall, and the diary method.

Continuous direct observation requires the fieldworker to observe
continually the activities of subjects during a particular time frame
(like 6 a.m. to 6 p.m.). This technique is rarely used because it is
extremely time consuming and can generate data on only a limited
number of subjects. This technique was first used by Richards
(1939) and recently by Edmundson (1976) in East Java.
Edmundson and three assistants continuously observed the
activities of fifty-four sample members for fourteen hours
each day; each subject was observed for six days, yielding a data

base spanning 324 researcher days of continuous direct observation.

The random spot check technique was developed by Erasmus (1955) and considerably refined by Johnson (1975). It is now frequently referred to as 'Johnson's technique' or 'the Johnson method'. The key to this technique is randomness. A random sample of the population is chosen for investigation and the sampled people are visited at randomly determined times and dates. All the activities of all household members are recorded as soon as observed. In Johnson's study of Machiguenga Indians in the Upper Amazon of south-eastern Peru, thirteen households with a total of 105 members were regularly visited. In this study, the population was not strictly random because the sampled population only included households within reasonable walking distance (forty-five minutes) of the anthropologist's residence. Sample households were visited during daylight hours (6 a.m. to 7 p.m.) with visiting hours selected in advance with random tables. Visits were made on 134 days over a ten month period and generated 3,495 observations of individuals. Activities observed were recorded in eleven activity codes. Observations of particular activities (like eating, food preparation, child rearing) were divided by the total number of observations and revealed patterns of time expenditure. The number of hours per day spent on each activity was calculated by multiplying the percentage of total time allocated to the activity by the thirteen hour observation period. Two critical features of this technique are that all members of a designated household must be found within the hour randomly allocated to them, and the activity first observed must be recorded.

Informant recall entails a researcher inquiring about the activities undertaken by all members of a household during a preceding period, usually twenty-four hours. White used this technique in his study of production and reproduction in a Javanese village (1976). White's data were collected in six hamlets with a total sample of ninety-two households in Kali Loro during 1972–3. In each hamlet two or three part-time assistants were recruited as interviewers. The sample households were visited every sixth day to eliminate bias that may have been introduced by the local use of both the seven-day week and the Javanese five-day week (see pp.90–3). Visits took place between 5 p.m. and 6 p.m. and a complete record of all activities undertaken by each household member aged six and over during the previous twenty-four hours (from 5 p.m.) was made. This method generated sixty full days of information per household over a year; approximately 17,000 complete person days of time allocation data were collected, coded for seventy-five different activities.

The diary method, also called the time budget approach, requires participants to record all activities during a specified period (usually twenty-four hours) on a prepared diary form. A version of this method was used in a comprehensive twelve-country study in which a member of each of 25,000 randomly selected households (stratified by income class) kept a twenty-four-hour diary of thirty-seven categories of activities (Szalai 1972). A respondent was notified in advance that he or she would be required to report all activities during a stipulated twenty-four-hour period on a pre-circulated form. The data recorded included time, types of activities, locations, and other people present. After the day in question, the interviewer visited the respondent, checked the diary for completeness and coherence, and added any clarifications or corrections needed (Szalai 1972: 37).

The major difference between these techniques is that the first two are based on direct observation while the latter two are based on informant recall. While these four techniques are quite distinct, some combination is invariably used in practice.

The two direct observation techniques will always require some informant recall: in the continuous observation technique this will be necessary for periods (however short) when the observer is absent or unable to observe subjects directly; in the random spot method the observer may be unable to locate subjects during the randomly allotted hour. For example, in discussing her methodology, Sexton (1986: 145) notes that when household A was selected during the hour 2.30p.m. to 3.30 p.m. she attempted to find all members of that household within the hour. If a person could not be found, she visited the person in the evening, or early the next morning, to ask about his or her earlier activities. The data for the observation in question were recorded as missing if a person could not be questioned by the next morning.

Similarly, each indirect method is rarely used in isolation. In Szalai's *The Use of Time,* where the respondent was unable or unwilling to furnish a self-recorded diary (illiterates, invalids, people having scruples about filling in printed forms, and so on), interviews were required (Szalai 1972: 37-8). Hence the informant recall and diary methods were used together.

The random spot check technique appears to be the most popular for a number of reasons. First, the random spot check technique is very economical of observer time. Gross (1984: 540) provides the following hypothetical example with a village of 1,500 people with 200 households. If the observer visited seven randomly selected households per week to make spot checks, spending an average of twenty minutes per visit (including travel time), 2,730 person observations could be generated over one year with investigator time expenditure of only 121 hours. Second, direct observation generates the most accurate data; there is growing evidence that informant recall data can be extremely inaccurate (Bernard et al. 1984; Borgerhoff Mulder and Caro 1985). Third, the random spot check technique is especially useful in the study of agrarian economies where most work is carried out in the vicinity of the home. Pedersen (1987), for example, found this technique suited to the study of plantation labour in the Seychelles where houses were located on coconut plantations. However, a disadvantage of this approach is that direct observation can influence work behaviour. Nag et al. (1978: 300) found this a particular problem when studying child labour.

Time allocation techniques will need to be modified to suit particular field situations and research problems; it is likely that some hybrid of the four techniques described above will be used (although the diary method is obviously of no use with illiterate research populations). The fieldworker faces a trade-off in choice of technique between the in-depth study of a few people possible with continuous observation and the broader coverage provided by spot checking. Another trade-off is between the accuracy of direct observation and the potential for inaccuracy in informant recall.

Johnson (1980: 292) suggests three rules of thumb that should be followed when collecting time allocation data. First, strict sampling procedures should be used to guarantee the representativeness of the sampled population and the sampled time (of day, of year). Second, research should cover all activities rather than operate with preconceived notions of what constitutes 'productive labour'. Third, raw data should describe activities in technical detail and in social context. If these rules are followed, then the data collected can be interpreted by the fieldworker and reinterpreted by others according to differing theoretical interests. Furthermore, we recommend that a time allocation study is only undertaken after the fieldworker has spent several months in the research community and has a degree of familiarity with the economy.

When planning to undertake a time allocation study, a host of methodological issues must be addressed. Many are discussed by Gross (1984) and Borgerhoff Mulder and Caro (1985). We draw attention to the following:

The sampling universe has already been discussed in some depth (see pp.45-57). Ideally, a fieldworker would collect time allocation information for the entire population, but in reality this is extremely difficult unless one is working with a small and stable population like Erasmus's (1955) village made up of 200 individuals neatly divided into thirty-two households. A randomly chosen stratified sample is the statistical ideal; but, as Johnson's choice of sample, based on the practical consideration of travel time, shows, this may not be possible. Purposive sampling may be justified by the nature of the research problem. For example, if the researcher wants to make inter-household comparisons, it will be important to collect details about a few households, rather than attempt community-wide coverage (see pp.53-5).

The coding of activities is so important that it cannot be overstressed. Johnson (1975: 304) recommends coding time, place, person, and activity. The primary activity codes used by Johnson in his study included eating, food preparation, child care, manufacturing, wild food getting, garden labour, idleness and recreation, hygiene (laundry, bathing, defecation), visiting, school, and wage labour. A more detailed subdivision into twenty-one activities is also provided (Johnson 1975: 308). In more recent studies there has been a move to increase activity subdivisions. Grossman (1984a: 268-75) divides the activities of Kapanara villagers of the Eastern Highlands Province of New Guinea into nine main categories and thirty-two sub-categories; Sexton (1986: 143-55) uses nine main categories and seventy-nine sub-categories. The problem with such fine divisions is that the number of observations for many sub-categories may be statistically insignificant.

108

The sampling unit used in time allocation studies is almost always the household, but this unit is always problematic (see pp.48-9). The advantage of the household is that a single informant can assist in the reporting of the activities, or whereabouts, of other household members. However, the household will be of limited use in situations where there is rapid change in household composition during the observation period; in such cases the unit of analysis will have to be the individual.

The observation interval can vary enormously from an instant to varying periods of continuous observation. With the random spot check technique, only a brief observation period is required. However, as it is important to get a feel for work rhythm, it is advisable that some prolonged periods are spent observing and recording various activities.

The observation period should ideally be twenty-four hours (see pp.113-14); but users of the time allocation method have tended to limit daily observations to a maximum of fourteen daylight hours. Erasmus (1955) and Johnson (1975) made random visits over a thirteen hour day; this made their data directly comparable (Erasmus 1980). It has become standard practice to observe activities over one seasonal cycle, or a twelve-month period. Johnson (1975) chose days randomly, but Grossman (1984b: 452) notes that it is sometimes preferable to stratify the year by months and to pick an equal number of days within each month randomly. This modification will ensure that a disproportionate number of days do not occur in any one month. In some field situations alternative intervals beside calendar months may be preferable for stratification.

A case study

Lorraine Sexton, in *Mothers of Money, Daughters of Coffee* (1986), uses time allocation data in her description and analysis of gender relations in the Yamiyufa economy of Highlands New Guinea. Her study illustrates how this quantitative method can be used to analyse social relations in a rigorous comparative and historical manner. We consider it in some detail to provide the reader with a concrete illustration of how this method might be applied.

Sexton (1986: 143-55, 170) chose to use the random spot check technique as developed by Erasmus (1955) and Johnson (1975). She rejected the continuous observation method because she believed it would be too labour intensive; the informant recall method was not used because she doubted the accuracy and objectivity of people's recall. This concern was justified at a later date when Sexton used the informant recall technique for two fortnightly periods; she found that people under-reported work and over-reported leisure. Sexton chose a stratified random sample of eleven of the forty-nine households at Kiyamunga village; subsequently one of the households was dropped because lack of rapport made it difficult to collect accurate data. She provides information that contrasts her sample of households with all village households. A particular problem in her field situation was the fluidity of household composition due to male labour emigration, extended visits to kin, changes in marital status and so on. People were either deleted or added to Sexton's sample as they joined or left a household for more than a month. Her original sample began with fifty-seven, but ultimately a total of seventy-nine individuals participated in the survey.

Sexton observed activities throughout the year. She selected a random sample of ninety-one observation days (a 25 per cent sample for the year) and completed eighty-three days; information on the monthly distribution of observation days was presented; only one month, April 1977, was under-represented (with three days' observation rather than the average of seven) because Sexton was absent from the village for two weeks. Observations were made during daylight hours between 6.30 a.m. and 6.30 p.m. Each day was divided into ten randomly chosen hours; sample hours were chosen with substitution to ensure strict randomness. Initially, households were selected on a similar strict random basis; but, after a few days, Sexton selected households without substitution so as to avoid bothering people more than once per day. Sexton notes:

> During the hour assigned to find them, I or a research
> assistant located all the household members to record what
> each person was doing at the moment he or she was first
> observed. For example, after 2:30 p.m. and before 3:30 p.m. I
> found each of the four members of household A and noted

110

the following information for each person at the moment I
saw him or her: household number: person's name; date;
hour; specific activity, such as harvesting sweet potatoes,
chopping wood or sitting by the hearth; name of other people
present and whether they were participating in the same
activity; and location.

(Sexton 1986: 145)

In eleven tables, Sexton (1986: 147-55) provides raw data on her
observations for activities of adult males and females. Data on the
activities of juveniles are not presented because preliminary
analysis of the data showed that people under 18 years of age
spend little time working (ibid: 37). As her emphasis was on
changing gender relations, she used time allocation data to
establish the sexual division of labour and co-operation in
production. She was also concerned with questions like: Do
women work harder than men?, and, What changes have occurred
in their relative productive roles in the colonial and
post-independence periods? She found that, on average, women
allocate 46.2 hours per week to the domestic economy
(subsistence, household tasks, cash cropping, commercial
activities and wage labour) to which men devote only 29.3 hours
per week. On the other hand men spend 8 hours per week on civic
activity in contrast to women's 2.2 hours.

Sexton contrasts her data with Richard Salisbury's (1962) for
the nearby Siane, despite a number of difficulties. The main
problems were: first, that Salisbury used a combination of
continuous observation and informant recall in his 1953 survey
whereas Sexton used random spot checks; second, he collected
data for men only; and finally, he used days and half days of work
as the measurement unit rather than hours. Nevertheless, the
existence of Salisbury's data made historical comparison
irresistible, especially as Sexton was able to fit her extremely
refined data base into Salisbury's broad categories of activities.
Hence Sexton was able to present Salisbury's reconstruction of the
1933 pre-contact economy and his data on the Siane economy in
1953 alongside those of the linguistically and culturally related
Yamiyufa for 1977–8.

With these data Sexton (1986: 56) concluded that the
incorporation of the Yamiyufa in the world economy has resulted

in a substantial decrease in the time allocated to subsistence activities. This decrease, however, has not been evenly spread; today women bear the major responsibility for subsistence work. Sexton argues that this transformation is partly responsible for the development of a savings and exchange system called *Wok Meri* (or 'women's work' in Pidgin).

Some caveats

It is not easy for an anthropologist in the field to come upon an Abelam unawares. Since I did not want to record 'greeting anthropologist' as a frequent activity when people were first observed, I often had to reconstruct what people were doing immediately before I arrived.

(Scaglion 1986: 540)

Richard Scaglion's comment indicates just one problem that may arise in a time allocation study. Our recommendation is not to try to sneak up on your subjects because they will invariably get the jump on you; it is preferable, if not essential, to have subject co-operation in a time allocation study. This may mean that in certain field situations such studies will not be possible, or that methods will need to be devised that are 'diplomatic'. Altman conducted daily surveys with a group of Australian Aborigines in Arnhem Land over a 253-day period. According to these people's practice, enquiries about activities and production levels were counter to social norms, but these were initially tolerated from an outsider. As fieldwork progressed, and Altman became increasingly incorporated into the local community, it was important to treat information collected as strictly confidential. On a number of occasions people attempted to use him as a means to gain access to information about the politics of food distribution.

There are a number of other possible shortcomings in the use of time allocation; it is important to understand these if time allocation techniques are to be used effectively. The following are the most important caveats:

Representativeness of the observation period is of critical importance. The growing emphasis in time allocation studies on a year-long observation period allows the fieldworker to give due consideration for short-term seasonal fluctuations. However, the onus is also on the fieldworker to establish that the observation period is representative (in climatic, political, economic terms); if the fieldwork period is unusual then the researcher must not only mention this, but must also attempt to gauge how special considerations may have influenced data collected.

Ambiguities in categories can result in definitional problems. If two children are observed in a random spot check herding their mother's goats and playing on the job, should this be categorized as work or leisure (Erasmus 1980: 289)? A more complex example of this problem is raised by Borgerhoff Mulder and Caro (1985: 327). A woman found chasing a chicken may be: a) visiting and about to take the chicken as a gift; b) engaged in a cash-gaining activity and about to sell the chicken; c) involved in a stage of food preparation; d) protecting her sleeping infant from disturbance; or e) forestalling the chicken's defecation on dishes. Problems of interpretation are raised by issues of this kind. The commonsense response to problems of ambiguity is to ask the subject. When the actor's interpretation of an activity differs from the ethnographer's, it is important to record this. Borgerhoff Mulder and Caro (1985: 328) suggest that a binary code that describes the physical task and its social context and purpose is used.

Work density is a term used by Erasmus (1980) to refer to how hard people actually work. Time allocation uses a temporal measure which assumes that everyone works with the same intensity. Montgomery and Johnson (1977) provide a solution to this problem by combining calculations of energy expenditure (as a measure of how hard people actually work) with a time allocation study. Energy expended at different activities is measured by indirect calorimetry, that is, by determining calorie expenditure from oxygen consumption measured with a respirometer and oxygen analyser (see Norgan *et al.* [1974] and Edmundson [1976] for further elaboration). This combination of time allocation with energy expenditure measurement and analysis provides extremely accurate data on work density; it is also an extremely complicated and relatively expensive research method that can only be justified in particular circumstances.

Night-time activity can be important, as Scaglion (1986) demonstrates in his one month exploratory study among the Samukundi Abelam of Papua New Guinea; Scaglion is the only researcher who has used the Johnson direct observation method for an observation period of twenty-four hours. Not surprisingly, Scaglion found some marked differences between time allocation based on thirteen hours (of daylight) and those based on a twenty-four-hour period. In particular, ritual, hunting, and visiting were significant night activities for the Abelam; over three-quarters of all observations of ritual occurred at night. Scaglion found that only about 74 per cent of night-time hours were spent sleeping. While this preliminary study is important, we stress that making random spot observations throughout the night may not be acceptable in most field situations. However, where night-time activity is public, there may be a case for making some night-time observations; Scaglion (1986: 543) suggests 10 per cent of total observations would maintain adequate statistical confidence levels. Recording night-time activity is extremely important in situations where people regularly fish all night (Firth 1939: 367-70).

Mobility and migration are two factors that complicate all economic analysis (see pp.57-9). Time allocation methods have to be adapted when used among people who hunt, fish, and gather because such activities frequently result in the dispersal of producers. Altman (1987) found that a combination of continuous observation, interviewing and random spot checking had to be used with Australian Aborigines. Furthermore, it was essential to check activities that he did not directly observe with hunting returns that were also recorded at the end of each day. Cross-checking activities with output is always desirable, although it is limited to materially productive activities with visible returns. Similarly, in situations where people commute to work on a daily basis it may be difficult to ascertain what they are doing at a specified time. Records from, and interviews with, employers and employees may provide the necessary data.

CONCLUSION

It is obvious that labour time cannot be measured without simultaneously observing, describing, and classifying labour relations. Indeed, using the disciplined observational techniques that time allocation studies require, it is possible that qualitative data on labour relations may be of a better standard. In any case, time allocation studies should always be seen as only one method among many. Their results should be cross-checked with quantitative data on production (see pp.144-55), consumption (see pp.181-94), and circulation (see pp.199-203); and reconciled with normative data on division of labour by age, sex, ritual status, and specialization.

Chapter Six

TECHNOLOGY

INTRODUCTION

Technological inputs are of a mechanical, biological and chemical kind and include such things as tools, machines, plants, animals, fertilizers, and pesticides. The efficiency with which these inputs are used depends upon the knowledge of the producer and the social organization of production. These factors will affect the method by which land, labour and technology are combined and the choice of technique. It is this interaction of the technical and social which is of primary concern; this requires that the fieldworker have some technical knowledge, but only that which is necessary to ask socially informed questions (see pp.7-9).

The preceding chapters, which examined the productive process from the perspective of the household, the environment, and labour, have, of necessity, raised the question of technology in general terms. When conducting a household census (see pp. 48-57), data on the technical inputs owned and/or controlled by a household are gathered; when studying the environment the impact of machines, pesticides, and fertilizers is noted; when examining labour, observations about the use of tools, machines, and technical knowledge are recorded. This chapter, then, examines the productive process from yet another perspective that enables more detailed questions concerning technology to be posed.

A recurring theme of both the ethnographic and economic literature concerns the analysis of choice of technique: Why do some farmers choose oxen rather than horses? Why do some potters use a wheel and others their hands? To what extent are choices freely made? What are the economic, social, and cultural

116

factors that constrain choices? The ethnographic approach to this issue has been clearly spelt out by Layton in his analysis of choice of technique in a French village community:

> Most technological innovations introduced to Pellaport in recent years have proved advantageous in certain respects, but disadvantageous in others. The tractor, for instance, is more powerful than a horse or ox, but it needs to be controlled more rigorously. This may necessitate actually increasing the size of the farmer's labour force. If we are to understand the farmer's motives in accepting or rejecting this and other innovations we need to look at the way in which he himself has perceived the new trait; for he may be deterred by its manifest disadvantages, fail to exploit its benefits as fully as he might, or even be so overwhelmed by manifest benefits that he fails, until he has adopted the innovation, to recognize its drawbacks. We need also to study the circumstances in which the farmer reaches his decision; for what appears advantageous in one context may not seem so in another.
>
> (Layton 1973: 503)

Layton's approach – a particular version of the comparative social method advocated in this book – is also useful for analysing the related issue of the coexistence of different technologies in a given social setting. What has to be explained is not the evolutionary progression from 'inferior' to 'superior' techniques, but the fact that movement is often 'sideways', 'backwards', or in two different directions at once. The Roti Islanders have 'regressed' to gathering, but, as Fox (1977) notes, they are better off because of it; in the Maghreb, north Africa, hand-coiled and wheel-spun clay pots continue to be produced side by side (Balfet 1965).

The comparative/social method of analysing technology, then, is to be distinguished from the evolutionary/technical approach. The latter method, which ranks technologies in a hierarchical order of supposed evolution, is the dominant orthodoxy in many of the social sciences, including both neoclassical and neomarxist economics. In many versions of this approach it is assumed that tractors are 'obviously' superior to horses, that horses are obviously superior to oxen as traction animals, that sickles are obviously superior to knives, and so on. Assumptions like this, to the extent that they are based on *a priori* reasoning or casual empirical observation, are unjustified. Fieldworkers must constantly be examining the unconscious assumptions that inform their own work and that of others. If this chapter does nothing more than cause the reader to be aware of these unconscious assumptions then it will have achieved an important task.

The analysis of technology poses special problems of measurement and these must be understood if useful data are to be collected and if the many theoretical controversies concerning technology are to be adequately addressed. The basic problem is that technology consists of a heterogeneous collection of inputs that cannot be reduced to a single measure analogous to hectares in the case of land or hours in the case of labour. A collection of different machines and draft animals can be measured in horsepower terms; but to ask 'What is the horsepower of pesticides?' is clearly meaningless.

It is possible to overcome some of these measurement problems by labelling technological inputs 'capital', assigning them a monetary value, and adding up the numbers. But this raises other theoretical and conceptual problems because 'capital' is an abstraction rather than a physical thing. There is also the practical problem of deciding which values to use. Should one use average daily prices or average monthly prices? Should these averages be based on national prices or international prices? Whether this strategy is adopted or not – a somewhat less problematic exercise today given the global nature of the world economy – the fact remains that a full inventory of technology must be prepared whatever method of measurement is used. However, counting cannot proceed unless the technical inputs are grouped according to their similarities. A central methodological issue here, then, is classification. But it is pointless to begin classifying and counting without some purpose or question in mind.

This chapter, it should be noted, considers technology only from the perspective of an input into the production process. While it discusses 'new' inputs such as tractors, high yielding varieties of grain, and fertilizers, the particular problems involved in studying the impact of technological change are discussed in the next chapter. This is because change raises questions about efficiency, intensification and the variation of output over time. Furthermore, for ease of exposition, only simple counting methods of quantification are discussed in this chapter; other more complicated issues concerning weighing, measuring, and valuing are discussed below (see pp.144-55).

TOOLS

Describing the technology used by a group of people, and understanding why they choose it, requires that meticulous attention be given to the comparative details of the cases in hand. The simple-minded collection of data on inventories can quickly degenerate into umbrellaology (see pp.15-16) unless the comparative significance of what is being collected is kept in mind. An ill-informed hunch, or even the belief that the issue being investigated may turn out to be important, is better than having no ideas at all to guide research. Questions that can guide fieldwork in this area include the following: Who owns what? What use do they put it to? What advantages does A get from using tool x over B who uses tool y?

In economies that use land and labour intensively the most important natural energy source is human labour. Tools in these economies usually take the general form of levers, wedges, and screws, and the particular form of hammers, axes, adzes, knives, etc. An inventory of tools should be prepared and questions concerning their origin, function, and social use asked. How are the tools acquired? Are they home-made, produced by a local artisan, or bought at the market? Are they privately owned or shared? What functions do they perform? What are the advantages and disadvantages of using different techniques for performing the same task? What social factors govern the choice of technique? The methodological procedures to be adopted when answering these questions are best illustrated by considering an example.

In many south-east Asian societies both the finger knife – a small blade with handle that enables a reaper to harvest paddy with one hand – and sickle are part of the cutting tool inventory and both instruments continue to be used today despite the seemingly 'obvious' technological superiority of the sickle. The persistence of the finger knife is, from the point of view of many European observers, evidence of the hold religion has over choice of technique. This argument has been criticized by Miles (1979: 239) who argues that 'the final explanation for the finger knife's survival among millions of Asians with access to the sickle resides less in an understanding of their notions about the supernatural than in a comparative analysis of agricultural systems that utilize the tools'. It is useful to review his discussion briefly because it illustrates the meticulous attention to detail needed if erroneous ideas based on casual empirical observation are to be avoided.

Miles's argument is based upon direct observations made among the upland Yao of northern Thailand. They grow opium poppy, maize and rice and use the finger knife to harvest rice. Only after observing the cultivation of all three crops over a period of two years did Miles realize the tool's crucial contribution to the complex system of agricultural production that operates among the Yao. He noted that rice was harvested with finger knives just before the end of the wet season when 'the panicles they cut were not only green and immature, but also dripping with moisture from the regular downpours of the year's wettest month' (Miles 1979: 229). The neighbouring lowland Thais, by way of contrast, began harvesting rice with the sickle about six weeks later in the dry season after the crop had matured. The stems of rice panicles cut with the finger knife, he also observed, were short, of equal length, and capable of being readily stored on specially constructed drying racks. The stems of rice cut with the sickle, on the other hand, were of vastly uneven length and could not be rack-dried in the same way during the wet season. In addition, reaping with the sickle lops both weeds and rice, whereas use of the finger knife enables the reaper to select rice panicles only. This fact enables the Yao to spend less time on the prior weeding of their grain swiddens, releasing labour for work on the maize and opium crop at a crucial time of the year.

The key to understanding the Yao use of the finger knife, then, is that the upland Yao farmers grow opium whereas the lowland Thais do not. Because rice and opium are normally harvested at the same time of year, the Yao have had to develop a strategy for coping with the excessive demands this places on their labour. By harvesting with a finger knife they are able to move the date of the rice harvest to a time which does not coincide with the opium harvest. If they used a sickle to harvest rice they would have to choose between rice production or opium production. Thus their choice of input technique is governed by their decision to produce both rice and opium as outputs.

On the basis of this directly observed comparative analysis, Miles makes a number of inferences about the use of the finger knife in southeast Asia as a whole. The details of his argument cannot be considered here; it is his exemplary method of analysis we have been concerned to highlight. The other moral of this story is that what often appears as 'obvious' to an outside observer who views technology using a European evolutionary/technical model is quite often wrong. Strong hypotheses about behaviour should be formulated only after careful attention has been paid to the comparative empirical detail of the issue in contention. Unfortunately, erroneous hunches based on casual empirical observation all too often harden into truths before they are investigated thoroughly; sadly, it is always much harder to dislodge misconceptions than it is to have a new idea accepted.

Archaeologists, who must, perforce, take an evolutionary/ technical approach to the subject of technology, have long realized the value of ethnographic analysis in the study of prehistory; some have carried out anthropological research and made valuable contributions by continually switching from one mode of investigation to another. Hélène Balfet's analysis of contemporary Maghreb pottery is a case in point. She studied a situation

> where at the present time there are to be found side by side pottery vessels that differ so much from each other that they could certainly pass for examples from different epochs *if one were to study them out of context.*
>
> (Balfet 1965: 161, emphasis added)

One set of pots is shaped on a wheel and fired in a kiln while another type is shaped by hand and fired by heaping fuel and pottery together in the open. Little time is spent working on the surface finish or decoration of the wheel-shaped, kiln-fired pots, but the technological inferiority of the hand-made pots contrasts with the extraordinary care put into the minute details of finish and decoration.

Balfet decided to collect comparative social data on the different production processes in order to solve the puzzle of why two such different techniques coexisted. She found that the production of hand-shaped pots was a normal feminine domestic chore. In each home, an annual domestic workshop, organized under the direction of the 'mistress' of the house, is set up to replace those vessels which have been chipped or broken throughout the year. The process supplies the family with vessels for the preparation and serving of meals, for carrying and storing water, and for preserving yearly provisions. As the vessels are on display on shelves, adornment is important because it is proof of the foresight, care, and ability of the 'mistress' (Balfet 1965: 163).

The wheel-shaped pots are produced by full time male specialists for exchange rather than domestic use. The consequences of this mode of production have been outlined by Balfet in the following terms:

> When we come to the level of the artisan-specialist, a closer relationship can be observed between the producer and his product, since his whole time is devoted to his work. The frequency of the operations establishes such a routine that the chain of movements becomes mechanical. This freedom from technical awareness together with the repetition of experiences favors critical reflection. This, under the impulse of qualitative needs from the clientele and quantitative demands for productivity, spurs the search for improvements, attempts at rationalization, and adaptation of tools and of new procedures. To these conditions favorable to progress can be added the internal cohesion of the profession, proven by the uniformity and standardization ... which permits the rapid diffusion of innovations and their conservation and accumulation by the whole group.
>
> (1965: 170)

Between the part-time women potters and the full-time male artisans, there are a group of semi-specialized women potters who, through force of economic circumstance, are obliged to produce for sale as well as domestic use. This complication only serves to remind us that comparative analysis must focus on ambiguity as well as opposition.

MACHINES

As the information sought by a measurement process is always a comparison of the thing measured with another reference quantity of the same kind, the quantification of the concept 'machine' must be operationalized before it can be counted. This involves the systematic disaggregation of the concept by an ordered series of operations that progresses from the abstract general to the concrete particular. When studying technology the fieldworker will be confronted with an almost infinite variety of machines. The traditional anthropological concern for minutiae can easily degenerate into ethnographic particularism unless some method of grasping the part in the context of the whole, and for distinguishing the significant from the insignificant, is employed. The following discussion outlines one possible way of doing this.

A machine can be defined as a device that transforms natural energy into mechanical energy for the accomplishment of a physical task. Machines are either simple or compound. Simple machines include levers, wedges, screws, pulleys, and wheels; compound machines include prime movers, generators and motors. The natural energy sources they use are human, animal, chemical (e.g., coal, petrol), thermal (e.g., air currents, flowing water), electrical, and nuclear; and the physical tasks they perform have uses in agricultural, industrial and other processes. These distinctions can be summarized as follows:

Machine
    a simple
       levers
       wedges
       screws
       pulleys
       wheels
    b compound
       prime movers
       generators
       motors
Natural energy
    a human
    b animal
    c chemical
    d thermal
    e electrical
    f nuclear

Physical tasks
  a agricultural
  b industrial
  c other

It is clear from this taxonomy of machines, which is the standard one used by mechanical engineers, that what we refer to as 'tools' are really simple machines of one form or another; that some tools are combinations of simple machines; and that some machines are combination of other machines. Tools such as hammers, axes, adzes, knives, drills, saws, files, chisels, planes and the like are all simple tools of the lever, wedge, or screw class; ox carts and ploughs are made up of simple machines of all five types; while cars and tractors are combinations of simple and compound machines.

We have included this taxonomy here, not necessarily as something to be applied, but as an illustration of a method of classifying. If each machine type is subclassified by type of energy used and task performed, then some 144 logical possibilities are generated (8 times 6 times 3). If the physical tasks are more precisely defined under each heading – e.g., cutting, digging, carrying, food preparation, etc. – then it is clear that the possibilities for multiplication of categories are greatly expanded. However, a definitional and deductive method of classification of this type is only useful if it is modified and adapted as fieldwork proceeds. In other words, it must be used in conjunction with the inductive, empirical method. Having decided upon a relevant framework, the items within each category can be counted and other relevant physical characteristics of the objects concerning durability, use, source of production, and so on, noted.

With compound machines the relationship that holds between energy input and the output of physical tasks is mediated by prime movers, generators, and motors. This can be illustrated diagrammatically as follows:

energy —> prime mover —> generator —> motor —> operator —> task

Prime movers are machines that receive their energy input from a natural source such as air currents, moving water, coal, petroleum, or uranium, and transform it into mechanical energy. Examples include windmills, watermills, turbines, steam engines, and internal combustion engines. Through use of mechanisms such as linkages, cams and gears, simple machines can perform force-amplifying and motion-modifying tasks much more efficiently, but they require more mechanical energy. This can be provided by a combination of prime movers, generators and motors. Complicated machines of this type are called compound machines. A diesel-electric locomotive is an example of a compound machine where all these transformations occur within one object. An electric washing machine, by way of contrast, contains only a motor, and requires the output from another machine located elsewhere which contains a prime mover and generator (McCarthy 1982).

When machines are used to amplify force or modify motion the work they do can be measured. Work, in this mechanical sense, is defined as the force (in kilograms or pounds) times distance (metres or feet); and the power of a machine is measured by the rate of work it does. If a lift can raise a 10 pound weight up to 12 feet in 30 seconds, then its power expenditure is 120 foot-pounds per 30 seconds, or 240 foot-pounds per minute. In English-speaking countries the unit of power is horsepower which equals 33,000 foot-pounds per minute. The horsepower of this lift, then, is equal to 240 divided by 33,000, or 0.00727 hp (McCarthy 1982: 232).

Horsepower allows for the heterogeneity of machines to be reduced to a single measure and compared. In this sense it is analogous to the hectares which provide a measure of land. Horsepower can also provide a useful quantitative means of analysing technological changes over time. If fieldwork is being conducted on a farm that uses a number of tractors and combine harvesters, then horsepower can be used to reduce the various machines to a single statistic whose changing values over time can then be analysed.

This particular conception of a machine is suggestive of a range of important issues on which the fieldworker could collect data. Information on the different sources and uses of available energy flows is clearly of central importance for understanding the operation of any economy and every effort must be made to get measures of energy flows and, most important of all, their cost. The appropriate research methods will vary from place to place, but always involve paying close attention to many non-quantifiable matters. In village India, for example, rural electrification has given many villages a new energy source but at a cost many people cannot afford. The result is that some people get access to electricity by throwing two extension cords over the power lines and stealing it. This places excess demands on the system and, along with many other factors, causes frequent blackouts. This energy source is, therefore, too unreliable to be used for productive purposes in many places and is used mainly for domestic lighting at night. Many poor farmers in India still rely on water- and animal-driven prime movers to perform most of their lifting, cutting, and percussive tasks.

When analysing the comparative merits and demerits of different machines, it is important to get the actor's viewpoint. People from different socio-economic groups will have different views and it is important not to conflate these perspectives. The bad anthropological habit of asserting that 'the X say this' must be avoided at all costs. Every society has its divisions into men and women, young and old, rich and poor. It is true that different people sometimes speak with one voice, but it is always in particular contexts and careful observation of these special circumstances should always be analysed comparatively.

Scott's *Weapons of the Weak* (1985) illustrates the importance of collecting data on the contrasting views of the rich and the poor. In Sedaka village in Malaysia the size of farms defines two distinct classes who have very different views about the efficiency and profitability of the combine harvesters that are now used in their village (Scott 1985: 154-64). All agree that the introduction of combines benefited the rich and hurt the poor, but the assessment of the magnitudes of the costs and benefits is another matter. The rich farmers note the speed with which the combine gathers and harvests the crop; they believe that the yield is increased and considerable money saved because of lowered labour costs. They say they are pleased to be relieved of the management and supervision problems involved in recruiting harvest labour; however, they are silent about the change from being enmeshed in a series of customary social ties and obligations to an arrangement in which only a single contract with a machine broker is necessary. The poor contest most of the claims of the rich and cite other drawbacks of machine harvesting. They point out that yields are probably lower because the machine often jams and spills paddy when it is turning or when its bin is full, that it often misses rows close to the bund, and that it flattens paddy at the point where the harvester enters the field. They claim it creates deep ruts when the fields are wet and destroys bunds when it passes from one plot to another. Finally, they cite the inconvenience of having to co-ordinate planting times in order to ensure that the machine will have a route through cleared fields to any parcel of land not beside a road.

ANIMALS

The spectacular developments in machine technology over the past 200 years must be seen in the light of the sobering fact that 80 per cent of the world's cultivable land is still tilled by people with the help of animals (Mason 1982: 970).

Draft animals have a variety of agricultural and industrial uses: they pull implements and vehicles, operate stationary machines such as pumps and grinders, thresh grain, and carry loads. Some animals are bred to provide food, clothing and shelter; others are declared sacred and either protected or offered to gods as a sacrifice. These sacred and profane uses vary from place to place and the task of the fieldworker is to document the social context of these uses for the society being studied.

Animals must also be counted. An animal census raises all the problems that a population census does and more. This is because there are hundreds of different types of animal; they often roam around and are not easily identified; they breed at different rates which are not easily determined; they are lent, borrowed, sold, stolen and killed regularly; and so on.

The first task is to develop a preliminary classification of the different types of animal. Having identified the most important categories, careful attention should then be given to developing secondary and tertiary classifications as a prelude to counting.

In India a five-yearly census of animals and farm implements is carried out by the government. This is in the form of a large booklet consisting of 172 labelled columns and thirty-one blank rows. The columns classify animals and farm implements according to a five-level hierarchical order, while the rows are for recording the numbers owned by each household head for a given village. As the rationale behind the classification has been carefully thought out, it is useful to examine aspects of it here because schemes like this can make the fieldworker's job of counting animals easier.

The Indian animal census makes the following primary distinctions between animals: cattle, water buffalo, sheep, goats, horses, donkeys, asses, camels, pigs, dogs, poultry.

A second-level classification distinguishes hybrid from indigenous varieties; a tertiary classification, male and female; and a quaternary classification distinguishes young from old according to different criteria for each animal. A fifth classificatory level for cattle makes other important distinctions as follows:

male
    less than one year old
    from 1 to 2.5 years
    over 2.5 years
        castrated
        not castrated
female
    less than one year old
    from 1 to 2.5 years
    over 2.5 years
        milking on 15 April 1982
        dry on 15 April 1982
        no issue by 15 April 1982

Collecting data of these kinds is a very time-consuming process that tests the patience of both census taker and informant. It is important, therefore, to have a very good idea about which animals are economically significant before beginning a task of this kind. It is obviously preferable to collect reliable data for the most important animals and none for the others than to have rough, unreliable estimates on everything. The method of successive approximations commends itself here. Having identified the important animals, conduct a preliminary census at the primary level of classification. This will give, for example, the number of cattle without regard to sex, age and status. The next time they are counted an attempt should be made to distinguish the sex of the animal. Any discrepancies between the two figures thus far obtained should then be reconciled and a third count made distinguishing both sex and age; some time later, a fourth count distinguishing status can be made. The particular circumstances of the society in question will determine the modifications that need to be made to this method; for example, if the animal population is unmanageably large it may be appropriate to select sample households for the purposes of secondary and tertiary censuses.

The statistics collected in official censuses of this type are highly unreliable and should only be used with utmost caution. This is because census form makers, such as those in India, think carefully about the theoretical structure of a questionnaire but give little or no attention to how the poor, overworked and underpaid, village accountant is supposed to find time to record all the required information accurately. What happens in India, it seems, is that the census taker sits down with the village headman and fills in the blanks with him. In the village where Gregory worked, everybody, including the village accountant, agreed that the figures were only rough approximations. Gregory tried to collect his own data using the census form but found it far too complicated. In the end he settled for aggregate data on water buffalo and cattle. Accurate data were obtained by counting stock penned up at night and cross-checking the data with verbal statements from household heads. These were then checked with official aggregate figures. The comparison showed that official data on household ownership of cattle were accurate in relative terms but inaccurate in absolute terms; rich households were shown to own more cattle than poor, but the actual numbers owned per household were quite wrong. Hill's (1986: 45) experience is much the same. She found that cattle censuses are always unreliable unless they are associated with a practical purpose such as inoculation against rinderpest; and even then age classification presents great difficulty because of the high rates of buying and selling.

As with machines, data must also be collected on the merits and demerits of keeping one animal in preference to another. This raises choice of technique issues, of which the ox versus the horse controversy is the best known. This is a 500 year old debate that is still going in Japan (Mason 1982); it was also a debate in eighteenth- and nineteenth-century Europe (Quesnay 1756). Surprisingly, it seems to have never been an issue in south Asia where oxen and water buffalo have been used for centuries. Horses operate best with a wheeled plough and require shoeing, padded leather collars, and complicated harnesses; oxen, on the other hand, do not require shoeing, are able to work in mud, and can be operated with a simple wooden yoke and a single nose rope. Poverty, says Quesnay, forces farmers to use oxen because they cannot afford wheeled ploughs and padded leather collars. Could this be a reason the choice never arose in India? If so, why did rich farmers not adopt horses long ago?

FLORA

When Paul Sillitoe first went to the highlands of Papua New Guinea in 1973 he had no idea of the difference between a sweet potato and a yam. As a result, he had great trouble identifying and understanding the botany of the Wola with whom he worked. His subsequent publication, *Roots of the Earth: Crops in the Highlands of Papua New Guinea* (1983), is intended, among other things, to save future fieldworkers the unnecessary troubles he experienced. It is astonishing that modern-day fieldworkers can go to the field so ill-prepared, but, as Sillitoe notes, he was not 'the ignorant exception, but the ignorant rule' (1983: 4).

The moral of the Sillitoe story is that one should study the relevant botany beforehand or, at the very least, include a botanical handbook as essential luggage. Handbooks such as Purseglove's *Tropical Crops* (1968, 1972) contain information on the uses, origins, cultivars, ecology, structure, pollination, germination, chemical composition, propagation, husbandry, major diseases and pests, improvements, production, and trade for all the major tropical crops. Information such as this is vital when trying to understand the cultural uses to which different crops are put; it enables one to focus on key social issues without being confused by the technical details.

Attention must be given to the classification and handling of wild and domesticated crops, their associations and successions, their use as inputs into the production process, and their use as products for sale or as food and drink for consumption. The following taxonomy may be useful as a preliminary classificatory device:

Horticultural
    fruit and nuts
    vegetables and legumes
    flowers and ornamentals

Cereals
- wheat
- rice
- maize
- barley
- millet

Forest products

Other field crops
- coffee
- tea
- cocoa
- sugar
- tobacco

Special attention should be given to the economic and social consequences of new crops and strains. This raises the question of the 'green revolution', which is really a new term for an ancient evolutionary and diffusionary process called 'agricultural intensification'. The history of agricultural systems everywhere is one of change precipitated by the adoption of foreign crops and the development of new indigenous strains. The growth of machine-intensive farming in Europe and its diffusion to other parts of the world must be seen within this broader perspective if its impacts are to be understood.

The green revolution is a scientific package which includes labour-saving machines such as tractors, combine harvesters, cars, and trucks; new crops such as soybean, sorghum, and sugar beet; new genetic strains of plants and animals; and new chemical and biological methods of pest and crop disease control. No crop is ever 'new' of course: sorghum is new for Europeans in the sense that it was originally imported from Africa, while the newness of soybean is defined by the new techniques which were developed to process the edible oil contained in an ancient south east Asian leguminous plant.

Of particular importance to the developing countries has been the development of new high-yielding strains of wheat and rice. In 1943 the American Rockefeller Foundation entered into collaborative research with the Mexican government to develop new strains of wheat suitable for Mexican conditions. In 1943 Mexico's yields were among the lowest in the world but by 1961 they were among the highest. The transformation was brought about by the release of new high yielding dwarf lines. Encouraged by its success in Mexico, the Rockefeller Foundation established the International Rice Research Institute in the Philippines. This resulted in the development of new high yielding grains such as IR8 which more than doubled yields. The new grains also reduced growing time which facilitated the development of double and trebling cropping regimes and further contributed to higher annual yields. However, to achieve these high yields large doses of insecticides and fertilizer proved necessary. Multinational companies and governments have been the agents of the diffusion of this new technology. Governments have encouraged its adoption through the use of strategies such as price subsidies and the establishment of rural credit programmes.

The green revolution has had a number of unintended ecological, social, and economic consequences that the fieldworker of today cannot afford to ignore when working in agrarian settings. Perhaps the most serious has been environmental degradation. In the period from 1942 to 1962 chemical pesticides were seen as a panacea. But initial optimism turned to pessimism with the discovery that chemicals were upsetting the predator-prey balance among insects. The populations of previously harmless insects exploded and emerged, for the first time, as pests. To control these new pests, chemicals had to be developed; the application of these new pesticides led to the explosion of yet more hitherto harmless insect populations and so the vicious circle went on. The other alarming finding was the discovery of pesticide residues in food, people, and wildlife. The response of the scientific community to this was to develop integrated forms of pest control where all methods, not just chemicals, are used.

While these problems have now been recognized, solutions are still a long way off. In Java, for example, the green revolution has increased yields dramatically. In some areas a treble cropping system yielding in excess of 14 tonnes per hectare per year has become the norm, but the sustainability of this level of production is by no means certain. In 1975 a previously insignificant rice pest, the Brown Planthopper (BPH: *Nilaparvata lugens Stal*), spread throughout Java destroying in excess of 500,000 tons of rice. The Brown Planthopper has a short gestation period of three to four weeks, high fertility, enormous tolerance to crowding, and tremendous mobility because its complex development cycle produces winged progeny every other generation. Females can lay 1,400 eggs in ten days and up to 1,000 insects can survive in one clump of rice sheltered from insecticides. In large numbers they can destroy a green growing crop in a day or two. The problem was initially overcome with the release of new Brown-Planthopper-resistant varieties of rice, but within a year or two new populations of the pest, called BPH Biotype II, burst upon the scene and crop losses in excess of 1.5 million tons of rice occurred in 1979. Yet new seed varieties (IR 36 and IR 38) were developed and there were no further outbreaks. However, these varieties are not suitable for all areas of Java and the recovery was slow in some places. The future is uncertain because the risk of a new BPH biotype remains (Fox 1987).

Another unintended consequence has been linked to the unpredictable nature of the farmers' response to the green revolution. Recent research in India has shown that many farmers find only some part of the package acceptable or practicable, that rich farmers are able to adopt the new technology much faster than the poor, and that relations of dependency between rich farmers and labourers strengthens rather than weakens because of an increased demand for labour (Farmer 1977, Harriss 1982). In Java, research shows that farmers use fertilizers in an indiscriminate and injudicious way, but this is partly because the state subsidizes fertilizers to approximately 85 per cent of their cost (Fox 1987: 13).

This brief review of the green revolution serves as a reminder that many important research questions of an anthropological nature can be generated by familiarizing oneself with the relevant technical literature from different disciplines. Fieldworkers who are ignorant of the history of these issues are placing themselves at an unnecessary disadvantage. The task is not to become a technical expert, but to be aware of relevant issues so that informed sociological questions can be asked (see pp.7-9).

FERTILIZERS

A large range of different measures to restore fertility to the soil are currently in use in different parts of the world. These include:

a burning
b fallowing
c controlled use of fallow
d crop rotation
e application of soil from drainage ditches on to garden beds
f composting
g manuring
h chemical fertilizers and pesticides

Once again, the collection of data on these practices requires close attention to be given to the interrelationship between technical, social, and economic variables within a comparative context. Some indication of what is meant by this can be illustrated by considering the case of livestock manure.

Manure has value in maintaining and improving soil because of the plant nutrients, humus, and organic substances contained in it. However, it must be carefully stored to minimize loss of nutrients; sometimes additional fertilizer, such as phosphoric acid, may be needed in order to gain full value from the nitrogen and potash contained in manure (Stewart 1982). In other words, it must be judiciously managed to derive the most benefit; this presupposes that farmers are willing and able to expend the necessary time and effort to use it, a decision governed by the costs and benefits of alternative fertilizers and the social and economic condition of the farmer.

Manure consists of 0.5 per cent nitrogen, 0.25 per cent phosphoric oxide, and 0.5 per cent potash which means that 900 kgs of manure is equivalent to 45 kgs of 10-5-10 chemical fertilizer. For a wealthy machine-intensive farmer the advantages of fertilizer are obvious: it is relatively cheap, results in higher yields, and the labour cost of handling it is relatively low. However, for a poor labour-intensive farmer the costs and benefits are the other way around: manure is readily available in remote villages at relatively little or no cost; labour is relatively cheap; and the disadvantages of manure as a source of nutrients are countered by its superior value as a mulching material in the prevention of erosion and evaporation.

Cultural factors can play a major role in the decision to use certain types of manure. In India, human excrement is a highly polluting substance and is not used by farmers, but villagers do use cattle dung for a variety of purposes such as manure, fuel, and disinfecting living areas. The widespread use of manure in Asia, Africa, and Latin America stands in stark contrast to the profound lack of interest in the subject on the part of professional agronomists, development economists, and anthropologists (Hill 1982: 177). Could it be that there is an unconscious cultural resistance to the subject on the part of academics?

It should be noted that international development agencies have finally come to see the merits of indigenous techniques of soil conservation. In the Pacific, for example, a US$1.5 million UN Development Programme has been established to 'introduce, adapt or revitalize appropriate technologies that will improve the sustainability of atoll environments' (Madeley 1988: 114). It has encouraged atoll dwellers to use a lapsed practice known as 'pit cultivation'. People dig a pit connected to a fresh water supply, lay organic matter at the base of the pit, and make their own soil which is then used to grow fruit and vegetables. Interestingly, many 'alternative' agricultural communities in western societies are also 'reverting' to similar methods of organic gardening (Sommerlad *et al.* 1985).

INPUT COMBINATIONS

In the previous sections the importance of collecting fine-grained integrated (technical, social, economic) data on the preference of one input over another was stressed. The choice of technique problem also arises when comparing one combination of inputs with another: Why does this household choose to keep more goats than sheep and that household more sheep than goats?

The investigation of this problem requires the fieldworker to pay close attention to the qualitative and quantitative association of one input with others. Once the counting has been done, it is often possible to discover these links and to test preliminary hypotheses in the field by further questioning; alternatively, the data can be used to test native theories about the best combination of inputs.

On the island of Roti in eastern Indonesia water buffalo, pigs, goats, and sheep but no cattle are kept. This presents a striking contrast to the neighbouring island of Timor where large numbers of cattle are kept but relatively few buffaloes, pigs, goats or sheep.

Associated with this is a contrast between the mode of land use: the Rotinese are intensive palm utilizers, the Timorese swidden agriculturalists. Within the island of Roti, the relative proportions of various fauna kept vary from state to state on the island. In the easternmost state of Ringgou/Oepao the proportions are 66 per cent buffaloes, 17 per cent pigs and 17 per cent goats/sheep combined. In the westernmost state of Delha, by way of contrast, the respective proportions are 7 per cent, 65 per cent, and 28 per cent. In other words, Ringgou/Oepao is a buffalo-intensive sub-economy and Delha a pig-intensive sub-economy. These data provide quantitative measures of certain common native observations about different local emphases of the palm economy of the island. Pigs are an indicator of the intensity of palm utilization: like the people, pigs live on a daily diet of palm juice and are the prime means of converting palm juice (rich in calories) into protein. Water buffalo, on the other hand, are an indicator of wet rice cultivation: they are both a source of protein and the main means of working the land. Sheep and goats are an indicator of sparse, relatively poor land: they need pasture and graze on the poorest of denuded rock-strewn land (Fox 1977).

While the Rotinese economy is primarily palm dependent, there are a variety of coexisting peripheral pursuits. This gives the islanders flexibility to adapt to changing circumstances in different parts of the island. 'In any one year, and in any one local area,' Fox (1977: 50) notes, 'the various subsystems may make proportionally different contributions to the subsistence of the population.' There is a discernible long-term trend associated with population increase. The pig-intensive states have the highest population densities and engage in the most intensive form of palm utilization.

When contrasting economies in this way, it is also important to investigate their complementarities and contradictions. For the eastern Indonesian case the situation is one of conflict. The deteriorating swiddens on Timor are providing the basis for the expansion of the Rotinese palm economy. Owing to their fire resistance, palms are the first trees to appear on overworked swiddens; it is to these niches on Timor that the Rotinese have migrated. The sub-systems within Roti, on the other hand, are complementary and provide the Rotinese with a flexibility the Timorese do not have.

An historical example of the political significance of technical input proportions is the Norfolk four-course system of crop rotation. This was established in Norfolk, England, at the end of the seventeenth century and it involved growing wheat on a field in one period, turnips the next, barley undersown with rye grass and clover in the third, and cattle grazing on the rye and clover in the fourth. Ideally, a farmer would divide up his land into four equal sections and have each section at different stages of the cycle. Sheep and cattle were fed off the produce of different fields and provided manure for them.

The Norfolk system became standard practice on newly enclosed farms by 1800, but it required an alteration to the 1000-year-old layout of the unfenced arable fields and common land. It was the practice in those times, as it is in certain parts of India today, to let cattle graze freely over the land after harvest. This made it impossible to have more than one harvest and to grow crops on common land. A precondition for the successful adoption of this practice, then, was the social and political transformation that the enclosure of the commons brought about. Between 1700 and 1845 some 2,400,000 acres of land were enclosed, the majority by private acts of Parliament (Fussell 1982: 333). These acts dispossessed the small farmers of their commons and led to the creation of the English working class. Marx (1867: 667-724) called this process 'primitive accumulation' and argued that it was the precondition for the subsequent development of industrial capitalism in England.

Whether one accepts Marx's interpretation or not, this case serves to illustrate that the state, along with élite groups in society, can play a key role in the process of technical change. The methodological point to be made is that the fieldworker must investigate not only the relations within and between households when studying technology, but also how these relations are affected by relations between the élite and subordinated classes on the one hand and between individuals and the state on the other.

INDUSTRY

Secondary economic activity involves the combination of labour and technology. It is usually divided into handicraft and industrial production. The workers in the former are called artisans while those in industry are referred to as industrial workers.

Artisans can be defined as people with specialist skills who transform raw materials into usable products with the aid of tools and machines. The category includes Arnhem Land Aborigines who manufacture a wide range of products like string bags, spears, fish traps and nets and bark paintings from local materials for both domestic use and for sale (Altman 1987: 75), the craftspeople of India who work with clay, stone, metal, wood, leather, and cotton (Fischer and Shah 1970), and the 'Harris Tweed' weavers of the Western Isles of Scotland (Ennew 1980). What distinguishes artisans from other users of machines is their highly developed manual skills and their technical knowledge of the processes involved in the transformation of raw materials into usable products. The study of artisan production, then, raises special questions concerning the control and transmission of this knowledge from one generation to the next. The following is a check-list of some of the general issues to be investigated:

The role of the artisan
    1 How is labour in the household divided by gender and age?
    2 What social status do artisans have in the community?
    3 Are they perceived to possess sacred power?
    4 Are there any myths that account for their status?
    5 What other social roles do they have?
    6 How do they view the history and future of their craft?
Tools (see pp.19-22)
    7 What tools are used for obtaining raw materials?
    8 What tools are used for transforming raw materials?
    9 What tools are used for finishing and selling the product?
    10 Are tools regarded as sacred and subject to certain taboos?
    11 Are there any myths associated with the tools?
    12 Is it believed that tools possess magical power?
Raw materials
    13 What are the physical properties of the raw materials used?
    14 What language do they use to distinguish these properties?
    15 How are raw materials acquired?
    16 Are the raw materials believed to possess sacred qualities?
Working techniques
    17 What is the geographic orientation of the working site?

18 What are the social conditions of work?

19 How is the working schedule organized?

20 Is the production process punctuated by ritual?

21 Do they wear special clothing?

22 Is the production process governed by seasonal factors?

23 What other occupations do the artisans engage in?

24 Do working techniques vary between different artisans?

Technical knowledge

25 What knowledge is public?

26 What knowledge is private?

27 What special terms are used to express this knowledge?

28 How is the craft learnt and skills transmitted?

29 Are the skills treated as divine gifts?

Output (see pp.144-55)

30 What are the main products?

31 What social function do they fulfil?

32 What are the subsidiary products?

33 Are products with a similar function differentiated?

34 How are relations with customers established and maintained?

35 Are products sold for cash or kind?

Whereas the artisans' place of residence, place of work, and place of education are normally under the one roof, the industrial workers' residence, factory, and school are normally quite separate (see pp.98-101). This fact raises special methodological problems which ethnographers have handled in different ways: Dennis *et al.* (1969) studied the isolated Yorkshire coal mining town of Ashton; Willis (1977) observed a small group of boys as they proceeded through their last two years at school and into the early months at work; Pahl (1984) conducted research in the industrial island of Sheppey in Kent; Metcalfe (1988) focused on class struggle in the coalfields of New South Wales; and Kriegler (1980) on industrial workers' perceptions of their conditions. The general methodological approach of these authors is diverse in that some, like Willis, worked with small groups while others, like Pahl, commissioned large-scale surveys of over 500 households. However, they also have important similarities in that they employed modified versions of the participant observation method.

Consider the case of Kriegler (1980). He wanted to collect biographical information on shipyard workers in Whyalla, South Australia, who exhibited an 'unmistakeable suspicion and distaste for academics, social workers, politicians, members of the media and others seeking to "research", "alleviate", or "report" on the plight of the declining shipbuilding industry' (1980: viii). He ruled out a survey approach because the workers simply would not have co-operated. Instead he adopted the role of a student drop-out and secured a manual labouring job with the company for three months during which time he kept his true purpose for being there secret. His ultimate aim was to interview every employee (including supervisors) with whom he worked. He justified his deception on the ground that by not revealing his true motives he was able to avoid the problem of attracting dissident informants (he does not mention the additional fact that the company might have refused him permission to carry out the research). At the end of three months he drew up a list of twenty-nine men with whom he had made close ties and, in the final week of his employment, asked them if they would be willing to be interviewed in their homes at a later date. All except one agreed enthusiastically. This study illustrates the need for creative methodological thinking when faced with difficulties in a particular fieldwork situation.

SOCIAL CONTROL OF TECHNOLOGY

Investigating the relation of people to technology raises the general methodological problem of how to observe the 'invisible facts' (see pp.80-2) relating people to the means of production. The following check-list, which assumes that relevant inventories of technologies have been prepared, is intended as a guide to some of the issues that should be covered.

Rights
1 What different kinds of rights over technology exist?
2 Who has a right to use this item of technology?
3 Who has rights of control?
4 Who has rights of disposal?
5 Does ownership or use give rights to income or physical output?
6 How are rights established and enforced?

Transmission of property rights

      7 What inheritance rules exist? Are they observed?

      8 Are items of technology bought and sold?

      9 Are they leased?

      10 Are they rented?

      11 Are they given away as gifts?

Ownership

      12 Is the item owned by an individual, a household, or a group?

      13 How is ownership established?

      14 How is ownership safeguarded?

      15 What sanctions are available to an owner?

      16 How is ownership expressed?

Obligations

      17 Does the owner have an obligation to give/share with others?

      18 Does a non-owner have a obligation to receive/share?

      19 How are obligations avoided?

Storage

      20 How and by whom are machines stored?

      21 How and by whom are floral inputs stored?

      22 How and by whom are faunal inputs stored?

      23 What are the safeguards against theft?

      24 How is control over storage exercised?

Disputes

      25 Why do disputes arise?

      26 How are they resolved?

The answers to these questions can provide valuable insights into the ties that bind societies and the conflicts that divide them. However, there is no simple way to collect such information except by exploiting opportunities as they arise over a long period of time. The careful observation of disputes is, perhaps, one of the best ways to collect reliable information. Attention should be given to the language used, to the counter claims about norms that have been violated, to the social relationships of the individuals involved, and to the history of the dispute. Nowadays many disputes are settled in courts of law which keep transcripts and other records of disputes. Data of these kinds are often useful as a means for obtaining oral evidence from informants.

The case study method is useful for understanding the relative importance of different forms of technology and their modes of transmission. In Torand village in central India, oxen used as traction animals are the most important technical input. Wooden ploughs are relatively cheap and the labour of kinsmen and women relatively plentiful. Oxen, on the other hand, are by far the most expensive input and a pair of oxen is an essential condition for farming. A farmer can make do with a reduced labour force but not with a half a team of oxen and farmers will literally trade labour for oxen if necessary. One household head of a poor family swapped his son for an ox with a rich farmer. The son lived with the rich farmer and was at his beck and call until the ox was returned six months later (Gregory n.d.).

The direct observation of the mode of appropriation of newly introduced technology is also revealing of the 'invisible' relations of domination and subordination that operate within a society. Among the Gunwinggu of north Australia, new technology has been adopted and adapted along gender lines. Men, who are the hunters, now use shotguns and rifles and monopolize vehicles whenever available. Women now use metal digging sticks and metal fish hooks, but the improved efficiency of this tool kit over ironwood digging sticks and bone hooks is limited. Men's efficiency on the other hand has increased markedly, not only because the gun is a more efficient means to hunt macropods, but also because new species like feral water buffalo, cattle and pig are now hunted. The situation is further complicated by the ready availability of welfare payments and a range of new foods that are procured. The female role as provider of carbohydrates has been usurped by the availability of cheap alternatives like flour and sugar. On the other hand the male role as hunter has effloresced partly because protein foods are relatively expensive, partly because hunting is now more efficient and partly because hunting continues to have important links with the ritual domain (Altman 1987).

The general questions this example raises include: What does control of technology tell us about social relations? How can the change in the relative significance of male and female economic activities be explained? By individual choice or the monopolization of technology inherent in the division of labour? What role does ideology play in technical change? Some of these issues are canvassed in the next chapter.

Chapter Seven

OUTPUT

INTRODUCTION

The last three chapters have outlined some techniques for collecting data on production from the perspective of inputs. This chapter covers similar ground, but from the perspective of output. The study of output, then, provides an opportunity for the fieldworker to cross-check the accuracy of data already collected, to identify omissions, and to reflect generally upon the lines of inquiry being pursued. Synoptic tables of the type illustrated in Tables 4.1 and 4.3 are very useful for this purpose because they enable questions of the following type to be posed: Has the systematic relationship between primary, secondary, and tertiary economic activities for the research population as a whole been adequately described? Has the relationship between the production system and its mining, farming, fishing, and other sub-systems been grasped? Have the relevant inputs been identified, counted, and measured? Has the division and organization of labour been understood? Have the various social and technical methods for combining inputs been compared and contrasted? Have data on the distribution of property between households been collected?

The identification of 'output' may pose problems because, as Tables 4.1 and 4.3 illustrate, all the inputs for one point in time are the outputs of a process from a previous point in time. In a hypothetical agricultural economy producing one annual rice crop this fact presents no methodological difficulties because a clear distinction can be made between rice output and inputs. However, actual economies are never as simple as this. Joint

143

production is the norm and the harvest cycles are of uneven length and duration: some products, such as milk and fish, are collected daily; others, such as sweet potato, are harvested when desired; while crops such as yams and rice are seasonal. When yesterday's outputs are today's inputs, how are outputs and inputs to be distinguished? Over what time period should the data be collected? Is the calendar year the best temporal measure to use? The fieldworker will have to resolve these difficulties by keeping systematic daily records for some products, seasonal records for others, and whatever is appropriate for products in the residual category.

The collection and analysis of data on output, then, is a continuous process rather than an discrete event. While it is foolish to waste valuable fieldwork time carrying out complicated time-consuming computations, it is wise to spend some time analysing output data because such analysis may suggest interesting new hypotheses to be investigated. In this chapter we provide an example of ways such computations may be undertaken with some Melanesian data. In presenting this example we are not saying that the calculations we make can, or should, be undertaken in all cases. Rather, these data are presented primarily to illustrate the importance of cross-checking and hypothesis formulation and reformulation; and also to clarify the meaning of some general economic concepts such as productivity, relative intensity, efficiency, and intensification.

For ease of exposition the discussion in the chapter is restricted, in the main, to a discussion of primary and secondary production processes; tertiary activities are discussed later (see pp.199-203).

QUANTIFYING OUTPUT

Output is quantified by counting, measuring, weighing, and valuing in a systematic manner. While these objectives can be stated in simple terms, their execution poses great difficulties. There is simply too much happening in any economy of more than one person for the anthropologist to observe: on any one day it is possible that one person will be hunting, another fishing, a third gathering, a fourth harvesting vegetables, and a fifth killing a sheep; on any market day thousands of transactions will be occurring simultaneously, generating thousands of prices which

144

vary not only according to the type of product, but also according to the time of day and year.

Faced with such a bewildering flow of information the observer is forced to be selective. One procedure is to use scientific sampling techniques. While this method has its merits, it requires that the sample be large enough to be statistically significant. As we have frequently mentioned it is unlikely that this condition will be met in most anthropological fieldwork. It is for this reason that we have emphasized the importance of the selective comparative method in this book. This involves selecting, say, a rich household and a poor one and studying them intensively over a relatively long period. This method will not eliminate all counting and valuation problems but it does minimize them.

Measuring and weighing output

The initial questions that a fieldworker must ask when contemplating the measurement of output are: What products should be included in the estimation? and, How can these quantities be measured? The answers to these questions will be provided by the fieldworker's research focus and the nature of the local economy. As an illustration of how the investigation might proceed, we consider two examples: the first deals with an Aboriginal community in north Australia where people primarily hunt, gather, and fish (Altman 1987); the second with a rice village in the Province of Laguna, Philippines (Hayami *et al.* 1978). In both these examples data on output were measured over a long period (296 days in the former, 356 days in the latter), and time allocation studies (see pp.103-14) were used to cross-check data.

In measuring production, the set of sampling issues that have been addressed in earlier chapters recurs. As usual, the fieldworker must identify a manageable sample of households whose output is to be monitored. In the Australian example, the entire community was included in the output survey because its population averaged only thirty-one persons; in the Philippines example, a non-random stratified sample of eleven households out of a village total of ninety-five was chosen.

It is important that the investigator makes an informed decision about measuring standards to be used. The usual options are avoirdupois or metric weight for most crops, hunted game, fish, and so on; troy weight for metals like gold and silver; cubic measure or measures of capacity for liquids and some grains; and numbers for censuses of animals (see pp.127-30). The nature of output will determine the appropriate scale of measurement; for example, it is likely that grain crops like rice will be measured in kilograms rather than in grams or tonnes.

Altman (1987: 31-45) concentrated on weighing all products hunted, gathered, and fished by the Gunwinggu. These data were collected in three main ways. First, the investigator attempted to accompany one production team as regularly as possible to weigh bush foods as they were hunted and collected. Second, when more than one production team set out from camp, key helpers were provided with spring scales and notebooks and were asked both to weigh and to count products. At other times, informants' reports were used to estimate the weight of game. Third, parts of cooked game people brought back to camp were weighed and the total weight was estimated from an ever expanding data base on species and their size. For example, a wallaby hindquarter represented about 19 per cent of the whole animal so total weight could be reconstructed. It should be noted that such practices did not start until Altman was in the field for six months and the Gunwinggu had become quite used to this *balanda* (white man) who wanted to weigh and measure everything. Altman's observations covered the six seasons in the Gunwinggu calendar (see pp.76-80), but there were obvious variations in the accuracy of data over the year. The three wet seasons were low mobility periods, and for this reason data collected during these seasons were probably more accurate than those for the dry, high mobility seasons. In fact during the mid-wet season weighing products was a fairly straightforward exercise because people resided at one location and macropods formed the bulk of local foodstuffs production.

Over the 296-day survey period, conducted during the period October 1979 to October 1980, an estimated 5.25 tonnes of food was provided from hunting, fishing, and gathering by the research community. Altman also undertook a food consumption survey (see pp.181-94) that provided an important cross-check on output levels. As output data were collected for all producers, Altman was also able to investigate the productivity of different individuals and households. This raised a host of questions about the social relations of production (Altman 1987: 97-127): Was the household an economic unit? Why were some individuals more successful producers than others? Why did some households regularly produce a 'surplus' while others were always in 'deficit'? What was the correlation between household production levels and household consumption? Were inter-household variations in productivity ameliorated by distribution and redistribution (see pp.203-8).

Hayami *et al.* (1978) conducted a benchmark survey of all households in Barrio Tubuan, Municipality of Pila, on the southern coast of Laguna de Bay, Philippines, in November 1974. Subsequently, the researchers chose eleven co-operative households from the ninety-five in the village. Included in the sample were the households of four large farmers (cultivating more than two hectares), three small farmers (cultivating less than two hectares), and four landless workers, two of whom subleased small parcels of paddy field (0.25 hectares each) from other tenant farmers during the course of the year-long survey. The researchers state that selection of households was not random, but was based on their judgement of the ability and willingness of households to participate in the project. Hayami *et al.* (1978: 5) present a table that contrasts the characteristics of their sample households with all households in the village, quantifying such variables as average family size, average per capita income, average farm size, average rice yield (during wet and dry seasons); and contrasting sample and village households within their categories of large farmer, small farmer, and landless worker.

In this output survey, co-operators kept daily records on economic activities in record books provided. The record period was from 1 June 1975 to 31 May 1976. April and May 1975 were used as test periods. The record book included a questionnaire on daily household income and expenses and on products sold, paid to labourers, given as gifts, consumed, fed to animals and stored in a replacement fund. These records were checked twice a week and new record books were issued weekly. The researchers set up a balance sheet for rice that quantified total receipts and total disposition and provided a rice balance based on record keeping that could be contrasted with an outputs survey. Hayami *et al.* also had comprehensive information on the size of landholdings, on land use, and on paddy yield per hectare, so they were able to monitor output data carefully. All told, they estimated (1978: 56-9) that their sample households produced between 10,271 and 10,446 kilograms of rice in the twelve months from June 1975; the statistical discrepancy between expected output (from the rice balance account) and rice output (from their outputs survey) was only 175 kilograms over the year.

Lest it appear that measuring outputs is too straightforward an exercise, let us present three very different situations where measurement has been problematic.

In studying fishing, statistics on the weight of fish brought in by each boat or net each day would be useful. But in many labour-intensive fishing communities the fish are not weighed. This means that, if direct observations are wanted, the investigator must either divert people to a weighing station or carry a weighing machine up and down the beach. This procedure is clearly impossible in most circumstances and indirect methods of obtaining approximate totals are needed. Firth suggests that the investigator

> can note, by sampling, the number of baskets of fish in a
> catch; he can find out in various ways the average weight of a
> basket. Again, from time to time, when fish are sold retail, or
> by number, he can count the fish in a basket; and on his own
> scales at home he can weigh individual series of fish of that
> type, thus getting a cross-check. Some idea of the physical
> volume of production can be obtained by such round-about
> means.
>
> (Firth 1946: 315)

It is especially important to recall that information collected on cash incomes from products sold can provide a means to estimate output so long as the price paid for items is known. The real challenge though is to measure output that is not sold but is either locally consumed or locally exchanged (for labour, land, technology).

The problems of collecting data on livestock production are particularly acute. The mobility of herds and people, unpleasant and often dangerous field conditions, and, in some cases, unfriendly and uncooperative informants have meant that very few statistical data have been collected. But, as McCabe's study (1987) of the Ngisonyoka Turkana of Kenya shows, the problems are not insurmountable if carefully selected samples are sufficiently small.

148

He chose four residential units (*awi*) with different household and livestock composition and paid periodic research visits to these groups collecting daily data on milk yields from the camels, cows, sheep, and goats they kept. Each household was also questioned about sales and purchases of animals since the last visit, the number of times animals were bled for extra food, and also about meat consumption. By interpreting these data within the context of climatic and other broader factors, important conclusions were drawn concerning the strategies different *awi* adopt to cope with periods of prolonged stress.

The third example comes from Hide's study of pig production and use in Sinasina, Papua New Guinea. Hide (1981: 642) notes that while the 'bag, scale and hasty record' is an important means to get direct weights of pigs (he recorded two hundred or so), it does have some obvious disadvantages. Hide lists these as the violent and noisy resistance to bagging by large pigs, the disturbance of such resistance for other pigs that become difficult if not impossible to catch, and the labour involved in counting and weighing a large pig population by this method. As Hide notes, after several months of attempting to weigh pigs directly, this method can be 'unnecessarily risky for both man and beast, as may be appreciated by anyone who has tried to remove one pig from a yard full of hungry animals in the rain at dusk' (1981: 642). Hide decided to seek an indirect method for estimating pig weight, and sought advice from the Tropical Pig Breeding and Research Centre in Goroka about the possibility of converting linear measures to weight. The centre suggested the use of heart girth and provided some data from villages near Goroka. Hide found measuring heart girth was relatively simple and quick and that it provided an indirect and approximate means of estimating the live weight of pigs. The main disadvantages were the quality of the conversion data and the crude 'eyeballing' of an average line around the heart girth. This example though illustrates how appropriate and useful methods can be devised in the field after attempts at an alternative method have proved unsatisfactory.

It is very important to observe the manner in which indigenous categories of measurement are used, especially when one is at least partially reliant on informants' reports. For example, among hunting people, fine distinctions are frequently made between species and within the same species on the basis of sex and stage of development. Such information can be of great assistance when estimating the weight of an animal. Freeman (1970: 254) found that the Iban measure rice by the basketful. An average basket or *baka* holds about one *pasu* or bushel (a measure of capacity for grain crops that is equivalent to eight gallons or 36.4 litres). About twenty *pasu* make one *dunjong* and four *dunjong* make one *lumpong* – a measure containing approximately eighty bushels. An understanding of local categories can be especially important when crop yield is expressed in these terms. In Bastar district of central India the most important standard is the *khundi*, a measure of capacity for quantifying both grain and land area. It is reckoned that one *khundi* of rice seed is required to sow one acre (0.40 ha) and that the return ranges between 10:1 to 40:1 depending on the quality of the soil. As one *khundi* holds approximately 30 kg, this implies yields of between 300 kg to 1,200 kg per acre (740 kg/ha to 2,965 kg/ha). Information of this kind should be treated with due caution and cross-checked where possible. Indigenous standards are notoriously variable; indeed, they often tell us more about social relations than quantities (see p. 15).

Valuing output

If the annual output of a household is six cows, one tonne of rice, and one hundred gallons of milk, what is the total output? What is the relative importance of the different lines of production? Questions of this kind can only be answered by valuing, that is, by reducing the different quantities to a common measure and adding them up.

One of the central defining characteristics of the world economy is that almost everything is valued in money terms; things that are not valued are, by definition, worthless. Every minute of every day tonnes of rice, bushels of wheat, ounces of gold, and hours of labour time are being reduced to equivalent money units (see pp.208-12). This process now occurs everywhere. Even non-marketable things obtain implicit valuations: clan lands in Papua New Guinea have acquired implicit values in those areas where coffee trees have been planted; the rising price of gold has transformed old mining dumps into valuable property.

Valuations of this type are made by the 'invisible hand' of the world market for the purposes of making profits; but when

Table 7.1 Valuation of Momega production, 1979–80

Activity	Labour time (hrs/day)	Kilocalories (,000s)	Protein (Kg)	Money (A$s)
Primary	2.6 (72%)	11,800 (46%)	944 (81%)	36,100 (64%)
Secondary	0.8 (22%)	n.a.	n.a.	5,850 (10%)
Tertiary	0.2 (6%)	13,900 (54%)	221 (19%)	14,980 (26%)
Total	3.6 (100%)	25,700 (100%)	1,165 (100%)	56,930 (100%)

Source: Altman (1982b)

ethnographers value products that are not marketed, ethical and epistemological questions are raised. Is this a Eurocentric process that hinders rather than helps the analysis of non-market activities? Is it a male-centric process that undervalues the domestic labour of raising children and housekeeping? Questions of this type cannot be answered in the abstract; the particular research problem in hand will determine the strategy to be adopted. In any case, prices are only one of many possible ways of valuing outputs. Other standards include consumption units, such as protein weight and number of kilocalories, and production standards such as hours of labour time or tonnes of rice.

The standard of valuation chosen will affect the interpretation to be given to the data. This is illustrated in Table 7.1 which shows estimates of the relative importance of primary, secondary, and tertiary economic activity for the Momega band (see pp.76-80).

The methods for valuing these activities using labour time, kilocalories, and protein are discussed elsewhere (see pp. 103-14 and pp. 181-94). The main problem in this case involved allocating monetary values to products that have no price as they are not sold. Altman (1982b; 1987: 47-57) used a combination of market and market replacement prices to calculate the monetary value of output. Market prices applied to products (like artefacts) that were sold for cash; market replacement values were applied to output that was locally produced and consumed. The returns from hunting, fishing, and gathering were classified by broad category (mammal, bird, fish, reptile, and so on). As indigenous flora and fauna could not be purchased, a number of market commodities had to be used as proxies for these items. For example, chicken was used as a proxy for birds and reptiles, beef for kangaroo and buffalo meat. The imputed value of locally consumed items was derived by multiplying the quantity of output (measured in kilos) by the estimated market replacement valuation.

Table 7.1 values the output from activities described in Table 4.3 (p. 77). It shows that hunting, fishing, and gathering are the most important economic activities when time, protein, and money are used as standards, but that welfare is most important when kilocalories are used as the basis of valuation. In other words, flour, sugar and other purchases with cash received from welfare and craft production provide more kilocalories than bush foods. What conclusion is to be drawn? To what extent is the Momega group reliant on welfare?

This question is complicated by the fact that the money figures are determined by the prices chosen as the standard. Prices vary from time to time and place to place and arbitrary assumptions about the appropriate prices to be used have to be made. Altman used Northern Territory producer prices in his calculations of the imputed value of produce that was locally consumed and not sold. However, as Fisk (1985: 22-3) showed in a re-analysis of Altman's (1982b) data, if Sydney consumer prices are used, then the relative importance of primary production drops to 48 per cent while that of tertiary activity rises to 38 per cent.

The implication of this, it seems to us, is not that one strategy is 'correct' and the others 'wrong', but that one must investigate a subject from all possible angles before reaching a conclusion. Ambiguity is a fact of life that must be confronted directly rather than avoided. In many situations, however, monetary valuation will not be as complicated as this. In the rice village studied by Hayami *et al.* (1978) a similar imputation exercise was undertaken to estimate the value of rice that was locally consumed and used as a medium of exchange (to pay for hired labour and land rent). As a proportion of rice output was sold the adoption of a market price was less problematic. The imputed value of rice was $US 0.14 per kg for paddy and $US 0.30 for milled rice. While Hayami *et al.* (1978: 5) initially collected data on output using a local measure (*cavan*) and local currency (*peso*) these were subsequently converted to metric weights and US dollars. The former conversion (one *cavan* of rough rice equals 45 kg) was a straightforward exercise, but the latter required an assumption that the exchange rate was fixed at seven *pesos* to the US dollar. This raises further issues about world prices and currencies (see pp.208-11).

Ultimately the link between valuation and interpretation is political. Marx's revolutionary critique of capitalism, for example, uses abstract labour time as the basis of its theory of value and interpretation. Neoclassical economists, on the other hand, use a utility theory of value as the basis for their decidedly non-revolutionary interpretations and policy prescriptions. An ethnographer does not have to work within the boundaries of either of these paradigms, but the necessary political implications of any valuation procedure is an issue that must be confronted.

Illegal products

A dilemma that a fieldworker may face is whether to collect data on illegal production. The methodology for collecting such information is no different than for other products. For example, if one were collecting quantitative information among alcohol traders in the Mexican state of Chiapas (Crump 1987) then rum would be quantified using a measure of capacity (metric, American liquid or British); if one were working in Ethiopia or Kenya among producers of the quasilegal drug Qat (Cassanelli 1986) then weight would be the likely measure. Similarly, these illegal or quasilegal commodities could be valued, although it is likely that the market price would be an unofficial 'street value'. Information can also be collected on small-scale artisan and commercial activity that is characteristic of the 'street corner economy' discussed in Pinnarò and Pugliese's (1985) article on the formal and informal economy of Naples.

Recording and reporting such activities raises ethical issues, as does a great deal of other confidential material collected during fieldwork. The difference, though, between recording confidential information on, say, disputes and on illegal activities is that the latter may result in criminal charges being laid and prosecutions brought. We do not need to go into the issues in great detail here, but we do suggest that the ASA's *Ethical Guidelines for Good Practice* (1987) is consulted if there are any doubts. It should be emphasized that social research data are not privileged under law and may be subject to legal subpoena. The onus is on the researcher to anticipate potential threats to confidentiality and anonymity and to consider whether it is necessary, or even a matter of propriety, to record certain information at all (ASA 1987: 5, 10). It goes without saying that these risks must be fully explained to informants.

The issue of illegal activity can be demonstrated by discussing how it related to a project Altman took part in during 1983 and 1984. The government-sponsored research sought to collect quantitative economic information about rural land-sharing communities (communes or alternative communities) in New South Wales. An issue that arose when designing questionnaires for the project (in consultation with the Australian Association for Sustainable Communities) was whether a question would be asked on the production of marijuana for sale. It was quickly determined that this was an inappropriate question and it was dropped. Indeed the only reference to drugs in the final report was linked to a common concern of the twenty communities studied about police harassment; community members were concerned that they were harassed unnecessarily and often violently for no cause other than a generally prevailing stereotype that rural land-sharers are all automatically producers and consumers of psychotropic drugs. It was found that in many religious communities there are rules which specifically ban the growth or consumption of all stimulants including alcohol (Sommerlad *et al.* 1985: 211-12). On the other hand, communities were not concerned about the reporting of commercial enterprises that were not strictly legal in that they contravened provisions of the Health Act and the Egg Marketing Board. This lack of concern was linked to the anonymity of communities maintained throughout the study and the trivial nature of these legal contraventions. The possibility was provided for land sharers to include illegal activities in the questions on cash income sources (under a miscellaneous category) but to the researchers' knowledge this was not done. Similarly, this study did not concern itself with issues such as whether people were exceeding their welfare entitlements (by participating, for example, in the 'black economy') or whether they were eligible to receive them.

Ultimately, whether to ask questions on illegal output is one of those existential dilemmas that must be left to individual researchers. In all research situations trade-offs are made, and in the case above it was decided that it was better to undertake the study and risk missing some 'potential' output rather than to alienate participants by asking ('culturally') inappropriate questions. Readers must decide for themselves whether this was justified or whether the research results were invalidated by self-censorship. Again we emphasize that with local co-operation the measurement of illegal output and its valuation will not cause undue methodological problems; it is the documentation and reporting that will raise ethical concerns.

PRODUCTIVITY

Productivity is the ratio of what is produced to what is required to produce it, and is usually expressed as an output-input ratio. If 100 tons of rice is produced using 100 hectares of land, then the productivity of land is one ton of rice per hectare; if 200 units of labour were used then labour productivity is half a ton of rice per unit of labour.

Comparative and historical measures of productivity provide indices of growth and measures of efficiency; they enable concise descriptions of complex processes to be made, and facilitate the posing of important questions. Data on the long term trends in national output per worker for the past century show that the USA's productivity has increased by a factor of three, the UK's by a factor of 1.6, and Japan's by 7.5 (Frankel 1982: 29). These data summarize important trends in the world economy and pose comparative questions concerning the causes of the relative wealth of some nations and the poverty of others.

Productivity measures are, therefore, among the most important statistical measures that a social scientist uses and many theoretical controversies in economic anthropology converge on them (Conklin 1961: 21). The problem is, however, that they are also among the most difficult to compile.

Productivity of land

Crop yields depend on literally hundreds of variables: climate, soil, pests, skill and intensity of labour, machines used, crop variety, fertilizer, and so on. Agricultural scientists try to control these variables by growing crops in carefully controlled environments. Experiments of this type are beyond the scope of anthropology and the question arises as to the worth of any anthropological investigation of land productivity.

Anthropological opinion of the matter differs. We agree with Conklin (1961: 28) who argues that although the difficulties involved in measuring productivity are great, adequate techniques of indirect as well as direct checking can be devised.

The methods used to collect data on yields might include the following:

a detailed measurements of selected plots;
b rough measurements of granaries of selected households;
c verbal testimonies.

If detailed measurements of selected plots are done, every endeavour should be made to describe as many of the complicating variables as possible: What is the history of the use of the plot? Soil type? Slope? Aspect? Who farmed it? Was it weeded? Trial plots can be selected on a contrasting basis: a plot on good quality soil should be paired with one on bad soil; a rich farmer's plot with a poor farmer's; a skilled farmer's plot with an unskilled farmer's plot; a plot fertilized by manure and one by chemicals; and so on. The assistance of knowledgeable informants can be invaluable here because they will be able to identify the meaningful contrasts much better than the ethnographer. It is important to plan the study very carefully to ensure that accurate measurements of the selected plots can be made within the limited research time available.

Where crops are stored in granaries, rough estimates of yields can be obtained by measuring outgoings and incomings of selected household bins at various key times throughout the year. This inventory approach has similarities to some techniques used in food consumption surveys (see pp.181-94). It assumes that the researcher has knowledge of the arable landholdings of each family and that reasonably accurate estimates of the withdrawals and additions made to the bin for purposes of consumption, sales, and other purposes can be made.

Verbal testimonies are sometimes useful guides to the productivity of different plots; but data of this type must be carefully cross-checked by collecting the statements of many people and situating the data in the light of comparative ethnographic and scientific evidence on yields..

Many unexpected problems can arise in work of this kind and it is important to report all these problems so that others can assess the value of the estimates and use them with due caution. Freeman's (1970: 250-8) account of his attempt to measure the yields of Iban dry rice farms is exemplary in this respect and it is instructive to examine his report briefly.

Freeman's intention was to establish test plots on as many farms as possible and to collect a detailed series of measurements. But the Iban claimed that the paddy spirits would be deeply offended by such treatment and, because of the fear of disastrously poor crops, Freeman was unable to get co-operation. He eventually persuaded one farmer to let him measure the yield of a 22 ft by 11 ft test patch, but only after many set-backs resulting from the opposition of other family members to this idea. The plot he selected was on land that was first felled in 1944, farmed again in 1945, left fallow from 1946 to 1948, and cultivated for the third time in 1949. On 25 April 1950 the land was ready to be reaped. He marked out the boundaries with wooden stakes and had it harvested under his supervision. The plot, he noted, was thoroughly weeded and contained top quality paddy. Freeman carried the paddy back to the village and once again took detailed observations while it was threshed and winnowed. Capacity measurements of the yield were taken both before and after winnowing and yields per acre calculated. As a cross check, it was planned to take measurements of the contents of paddy bins after the grain had been stored away. Once again, problems arose because many families refused him access to their bins for ritual reasons. Freeman managed to gain the permission of four families, however, and obtained rough estimates of yields which showed great household variability. The lowest yield came from a household which was unable to weed its fields properly because of a shortage of female labour. The yields as a whole were low because of an unusually poor season. In sum, his figures showed a range from 8-43 bushels per acre. He compared this with comparative data from other places in south-east Asia and drew the conclusion that 'the growing of hill *padi* by the method of shifting cultivation is characterized by wide variations in yield' (Freeman 1970: 258).

This conclusion, it could be argued, is obvious and does not justify the effort required to establish it. But this criticism ignores the fact that the range of the variation in yield is never obvious and must be determined empirically. In any case, an anthropologist's main concern should be with explaining diversity rather than with the computation of averages because this is where they have most to contribute. Freeman's data show that a social variable – the absence of female labour – was crucial; factors such as these are ignored in the experiments made by agronomists.

Productivity of labour

If the object of study is an agrarian economy, and data on land, labour time, and yields have been collected carefully, then measures of labour productivity are implicit in the information already collected. As a cross-check, detailed observations on labour time should be made when measuring yields.

This was the procedure adopted by Pospisil (1963). He selected three plots of 900 square metres each and made detailed observations of the yields and labour time required to produce the output. The Kapauku economy he studied used three methods of production and he selected trial plots accordingly. On the first plot, farmed by what he called an 'extensive shifting cultivation' method, 127 hours of female labour and 136 hours of male labour were needed to produce 730 kg of sweet potato. As productivity measures are usually expressed in per unit output terms, these data imply that the productivity of land was 0.81 kg/sq m (730/900), while the productivity of labour was 5.75 kg/hr for females and 5.37 for males. (This case is discussed in greater detail on pp.160-8).

Where returns are of a heterogeneous nature these must be converted to a common value (see pp. 150–3) before labour productivity can be calculated. For example, Altman (1987: 108-12) estimated labour productivity for twenty-six adult Gunwinggu engaging in hunting, fishing, and gathering activities that yielded an extremely diverse range of flora and faunal species. Data collected on the imputed value of game hunted, flora collected, and fish caught by individuals were aggregated on a monthly basis and divided by the time spent in these activities by each individual. The standard used in this exercise was market replacement value, but weight (gross or net) or kilocalories could have been used. On a community wide basis, the average imputed return to labour was $2.40 per hour. This figure masked enormous variability in labour productivity between males and females, between different age sets, and over the seasonal cycle. Women's hourly returns varied from $0.20 to $1.50 and averaged $0.60; men's hourly returns varied from $0.40 to $9.20 and averaged $3.90. In imputed dollar terms men's returns were over six times higher than women's. But in terms of kilocalories produced per hour this divergence was even greater; over a four month period stratified over the year, Altman (1987: 92) calculated that men's returns were nine times greater than women's. It is no surprise that many of the valuation issues raised in measuring output (see pp.150-3) resurface when labour productivity is examined.

In industrial economies, measuring labour productivity involves the direct measurement of output per unit labour input. In most large industrial enterprises accurate measures of labour productivity are kept by management and access to these are needed if measures are wanted. It is now widely accepted that the social organization of work is a key determinant of labour productivity in industrial enterprises. This raises the general question of industrial relations, an area where anthropologists are beginning to work (Kriegler 1980), and one where they have an important contribution to make. Unions and management, shop-floor workers and managers have their own cultural beliefs and values and these can have a profound affect on labour productivity. Some of these values in an industrial culture are shared, while many others are in opposition; the ways these affect labour productivity can only be ascertained by direct observation.

It is significant that one of the people who played a key role in changing the face of industrial relations in England was an American consultant with training in anthropology. In 1960 a so-called 'productivity agreement' was signed between management and workers at the Esso refinery at Fawley (Flanders 1964); this was the first instance of what came to be one of 'the major phenomena in British industrial relations in the 1960s' (McKersie and Hunter 1973: 1). The Fawley Agreement, which was without precedent in the history of collective bargaining in Britain, embodied a 'productivity package deal' whereby the company agreed to pay large increases – of the order of 40 per cent – in return for the union's consent to changes in those working practices which were hampering a more efficient utilization of labour. These included relaxation of job demarcations and the withdrawal of craftsmen's mates and their redeployment on other work. The American consultant, who remains anonymous in Flanders's case study of the agreement, found British trade union practices were quite alien to him and became an interested observer. He became involved in regular daily discussions with the shop stewards and management in order to learn; his recommendations for change emerged only after many months of investigations.

This case illustrates the value of studying 'other' cultures, and the need for time, patience, and conversation when trying to learn about different economies using the ethnographic method.

RELATIVE INTENSITY

Intensity can be measured by input/output ratios; it is, therefore, the inverse of productivity which is measured by the ratio of output to input. Measures of relative intensity are comparative; they must be distinguished from measures of 'intensification' which are historical (see pp.168-71).

Measures of relative intensity can be obtained by performing some elementary arithmetic operations on the input-output ratios. Such calculations enable one method of production to be described as 'labour intensive' relative to another one described as 'machine intensive'. The calculation of intensity ratios involves the manipulation of data already collected; this raises the issue of the role of secondary data analysis during fieldwork.

Data analysis, it could be argued, is out of place in this chapter because it comes at the end of fieldwork, not during it. This argument is disputable. As Malinowski (1935: 317) has pointed out, the observer should not function as a mere automaton; while making observations, the 'fieldworker must constantly construct: he must place isolated data in relation to one another and study the manner in which they integrate'. This reflection not only facilitates the development of new hypotheses and new lines of inquiry, it also highlights gaps in the data already collected. Many months of research time can be wasted, and volumes of statistical data can be rendered useless, if measurements of a key variable are overlooked.

Another reason for discussing data analysis here is that it enables us to draw some scattered threads from the previous chapters together and to recapitulate some important methodological points. Finally, it enables us to clarify the meaning of the concept of 'intensity' which is much used, but also much abused, in anthropological circles. This is particularly so when it is analysed in conjunction with the notion of 'productivity'. The relationship is a straightforward unproblematic one, but conceptual confusion may arise because of the empirical complexity of certain production processes.

We intend to proceed by examining the detailed statistical data collected by Pospisil in his book *Kapauku Papuan Economy* (1963). Our interest in his work is not so much in the particular facts of the Kapauku case but the general methodological points it enables us to illustrate. Furthermore, his work is an exemplar because he is explicit about his methods, is comprehensive in his coverage of the relevant facts, and presents his data in a way that can be reinterpreted by others. The arguments of his critics and reinterpreters (Sahlins 1972; Gregory 1982) would be on much less solid ground were it not for this commendable feature of his research.

Table 7.2 is a synoptic table of the Kapauku farming sub-system. This is part of a larger production system that includes fishing, hunting, and pig raising, but, for ease of exposition, we ignore these activities in the discussion which follows.

Sweet potatoes are produced on the mountain slopes using a long fallow method (A) and on the fertile valley floor using short fallow crop rotation and composting methods (B and C). Labour is divided vertically on gender lines and horizontally on the basis of technique. There are six labour processes common to all methods – clearing, fencing, planting, weeding, harvesting and burning – and three specialized processes: felling is unique to method A, ditching to methods B and C, and bedding to method C. The specialized processes require special tools – axes for A and wooden spades for B and C – and special skills for fertilizing the land. Methods A and C produce sweet potatoes and a minor intercrop of 'spinach' (*idaja*), while method B is used for producing many crops, of which sugar cane, taro and sweet potato are of greatest significance. The Kapauku also breed pigs and chickens, fish, hunt and trap game, and gather various insects,

Table 7.2 The Kapauku farming sub-system

Method	Land		Labour		Technology		Output
	topography	soil	male	female	tools	fertilizer	
'extensive shifting cultivation' (A)	mountain slopes	brown	felling, clearing, fencing	clearing, planting, weeding, harvesting	steel axe, machete, wooden sticks	burning	sweet potato with some intercropping
'intensive shifting cultivation' (B)	valley bottom	black	ditching, clearing, fencing	clearing, planting, weeding, harvesting	wooden spades, machete, wooden sticks	crop rotation, burning	multiple cropping of sugar cane, taro, sweet potato, and other crops
'intensive complex cultivation' (C)	valley bottom	black	bedding, ditching, clearing, fencing	clearing, planting, weeding, harvesting	wooden spades, machetes	composting, ditch soil	sweet potato with some intercropping

Source: Pospisil (1963: 82–203)

eggs, and plants. Part of the output of sweet potato is used to feed pigs.

At this stage a number of questions are posed which can be put to informants such as Why are three methods of producing sweet potatoes used? and What are the advantages and disadvantages of each method? It also suggests a number of lines of inquiry: Do different households adopt different strategies? If so, why? (The reader is left to judge whether these are good or bad questions and to think about other questions that a fieldworker armed with this much information could raise.)

The next stage is to assess the relative significance of different productive activities. Three measures are possible: area under cultivation, time allocation, or kilos of food produced. In this particular case, all three measures reveal that sweet potato production is by far the most important activity. Using land as a measure, 90 per cent of arable land is planted with sweet potato, 5 per cent with sugar cane, 2 per cent with taro, and the remainder with minor crops such as beans, ginger, maize, and manioc. It is obvious, then, that the analysis of sweet potato production should be the central focus of attention.

In different fieldwork circumstances there may be many important activities to investigate, not just one central issue. The Yamiyufa of the highlands of Papua New Guinea have a sweet potato and pig economy like the Kapauku. The time spent on subsistence activities in this location has declined from 82 per cent of daylight hours to 44 per cent over the period 1933 to 1978 for women and from 80 per cent to 18 per cent for men. Nowadays (1978) women spend 10 per cent of daylight hours on cash earning activities and 9 per cent on introduced activities such as civic work, gambling and the like; the figures for men are 18 per cent and 16 per cent respectively (Sexton 1986: 50-4). Figures such as these highlight the continued importance of sweet potato production but pose different questions to be investigated concerning gender and cash earning activities.

To return to Table 7.2, the coexistence of three methods of production poses comparative problems concerning intensity that require further statistical investigation. Pospisil's description of method A as 'extensive shifting cultivation', method B as 'intensive shifting cultivation', and method C as 'intensive complex cultivation' illustrates the problems that arise when farming

163

Table 7.3a Kapauku production statistics: gender

Method	Land (sq m)	Male labour (hrs)	Female labour (hrs)	Output (kg)
A	900	136	127	730
B	900	119	180	1,240
C	900	259	196	1,520

Source: Pospisil (1963: 422, 444)

systems of varying input intensity are described by words. While his terms describe certain aspects of the different processes, a statistical analysis of his data shows that they are inconsistently applied: method A is 'extensive' in the sense of the absolute amount of land , method B is 'intensive' in terms of relative female labour inputs and method C is 'intensive' in terms of relative, specialized, male labour input. If a consistent set of comparative terms based on quantitative investigation is used, then method A is land intensive, method B female labour intensive, and method C male labour intensive; if intensity is calculated using the distinction between general and special labour rather than male/female, then method A is still land intensive, but method B is general labour intensive while method C is special labour intensive. This reinterpretation of Pospisil's categories, it is important to reiterate, could not have been made were it not for the fact that he paid special attention to collecting his statistical data in a consistent comparative manner that allows re-analysis.

Pospisil collected labour time inputs and yields from three selected plots of 900 square metres. These data, aggregated along gender lines, are presented in Table 7.3a.

The input-output ratios for each method can be calculated by dividing the inputs for each row by the outputs for each row. For example, for method A, 900 square metres of land can be divided by 730 kg of output to give an input-output ratio of 1.23; for

Table 7.3b Input-output ratios

Method	Land	Male labour	Female labour
A	1.23	0.19	0.17
B	0.72	0.10	0.15
C	0.59	0.17	0.13

Table 7.3c Input-output ratios as column percentages

Method	Land	Male labour	Female labour
A	49	41	38
B	28	22	33
C	23	37	29
	100	100	100

method B this ratio is 900/1,240 which equals 0.72, and so on. These ratios are presented in Table 7.3b.

This table shows that to produce one kg of sweet potato using method A, 1.23 square metres of land, 0.19 hours of male labour, and 0.17 hours of female labour are needed. If method A is compared with method C it is evident that the latter uses less of all inputs but relatively more male labour. To provide a precise measurement of this relative input intensity some more adding and dividing needs to be done.

The first step is to render the three methods comparable by expressing the input-output ratios as column percentages that add up to 100 per cent. This is done in Table 7.3c.

This procedure eliminates the influence of the arbitrarily chosen standards of measurement. In other words, if land was measured in acres and output in pounds the numbers in Table 7.3b would be different but those in Table 7.3c would not change.

The next step is to express the data in Table 7.3c as row percentages to restore the table to a modified version of Table 7.3b. This is done in Table 7.3d.

With this table, inputs can be compared to outputs for each method, and the relative input proportions compared to each other. It is clear that method A, with input proportions of 38:32:30 is relatively land intensive because land inputs, at 38 per cent of all inputs, are the highest; method B, with input proportions of 34:26:40 is female labour intensive for similar reasons; while

Table 7.3d Input-output ratios as row percentages

Method	Land	Male labour	Female labour	Total
A	38	32	30	100
B	34	26	40	100
C	26	42	33	100

Table 7.3e Output-input ratios (productivity)

Method	Land	Male labour	Female labour
A	0.81	5.37	5.75
B	1.38	10.42	6.88
C	1.69	5.87	7.75

method C, 26:42:33, is male labour intensive.

The question now arises as to the relationship between productivity and intensity. Productivity is measured by the ratio of output to inputs. Using the data in Table 7.3a, the figures in Table 7.3e can be calculated.

The data here are interpreted as follows: one square metre of land yields 0.81 kg sweet potatoes, one hour of male labour yields 5.37 kg of sweet potatoes, and so on. The data in this table, it should be noted, are the inverse of those in Table 7.3b: method A, the most land intensive, has the lowest productivity of land, while method C, the least land intensive, has the highest productivity of land. This inverse relation only holds if the comparison is made on an input by input basis. When comparisons are made on a method by method basis no simple relation holds. For example, it cannot be said that method C is most productive because, even though it has the highest land and female labour productivity, method B has the highest male labour productivity. This is the source of much confusion about the relationship between intensity and productivity and it arises because people fail to realize that any method of production always involves a combination of inputs. It is clear that the more inputs there are into a production process, the more complicated is the empirical relationship between productivity and intensity.

The above calculations were premised on the validity of being able to add general and special labour. An argument against this procedure is that it fails to distinguish the intensity and skill of different labour processes. An alternative approach would be to distinguish between general and special labour rather than male and female labour. The advantage of this approach is that special labour provides a proxy measure of technological inputs which have been hitherto ignored. It is clear from Table 7.2 that the central distinguishing feature of Kapauku technology is knowledge of soil conservation techniques rather than the use of

Table 7.4 Kapauku production statistics: technology

Method	Land	General labour	Special labour (= technology)	Output
A	900	228	35	730
B	900	268	31	1240
C	900	284	171	1520

special tools and machines. Steel axes are the most important material input, but as steel axes last for many years the annual depreciation cost of an ax is negligible. Specialized labour processes, then, are obviously what technology consists of in this economy. If this approach is taken then a different starting point for the calculation of relative intensity is needed. This involves aggregating labour input figures on technical lines as in Table 7.4.

If these figures are manipulated in a similar way to those above, the input proportions of method A (expressed in percentage terms) are 41:37:22 for land, labour, and technology respectively; those for B are 37:42:21 and for C 22:24:54. Thus, from this perspective, A is land intensive, B labour intensive, and C technology intensive.

The disadvantage of this approach is that it subordinates the social relations of production to the technical relations. Clearly, both sets of data are important; they can answer different questions and when considered in relation to one another pose further questions about gender and technology.

These methods of manipulating data may appear complicated to the numero-phobic but they involve nothing more than simple addition and division. Our calculations do not *per se* explain anything; but, by facilitating precise description, such analysis brings to the forefront information that was only implicit in data already collected. The advantage of this is that it may suggest new lines of inquiry and/or suggest new hypotheses.

This is clear from the research of Fox (1977), whose pioneering work on input proportions in the Roti economy has provided the principal stimulus for the preceding discussion. Fox obtained animal census data for the seventeen states of Roti and this formed the basis of his analysis of relative intensity (see pp.135-7). His comparative analysis suggested a number of hypotheses concerning the dynamics of the different systems which he was then able to investigate using oral and historical evidence.

Fox's analysis distinguished three inputs and seventeen methods of production. If a geometric representation of the data is needed (Fox 1977: 47), then obviously only three inputs can be used. However, if only statistical representation is required then there is no limit to the number of variables that can be used. Clearly, the more statistical data on inputs one has, the more time-consuming the computations become. It may be counter-productive to spend valuable fieldwork time undertaking calculations that can be done more efficiently with a computer (or calculator) in a post-fieldwork situation. Again, the issue is one of allocating fieldwork time as efficiently as possible. The simple point we are making here is that some attempt at summarizing the significant qualitative and quantitative features of the production process should be made during fieldwork in order to generate new lines of inquiry and to avoid errors of omission and commission in the data collection process.

EFFICIENCY AND INTENSIFICATION

Efficiency is measured by the ratio of the amount of useful work performed to the total time or energy expended. Thus a steel axe is more efficient for felling trees than a stone axe if the same work can be performed in less time; and a new variety of rice yielding 4 kg per hour of labour input is more efficient than an old variety that yielded only one kg per hour of labour.

Intensification can be defined as the substitution of an inefficient input by a more efficient one. This is an historical process and the collection of data on it obviously poses problems for the direct observation method. However, where important changes have occurred within living memory of informants, valuable oral evidence can be collected and the adequacy of this can sometimes be tested using either the comparative or the experimental method. For example, Salisbury (1962: 108), who conducted fieldwork among the Siane in 1953, was also able to reconstruct the situation in 1933 from the recollections of his informants and his assessment of the impact of post-contact changes on production.

Efficiency affects input-input and output-input ratios and the analysis of these ratios provide useful measures of efficiency and intensification. Where two or more methods of production coexist

168

the analysis of these ratios can suggest many new questions and interesting lines of inquiry.

Consider the case of the Kapauku yet again. Table 7.3e shows that method A is the least efficient method of production in all respects; it has the lowest productivity of land, of female labour and of male labour. A fieldworker confronted with these data should give immediate attention to the question of why this method is still used to produce more than 80 per cent of the sweet potato crop. (See Pospisil (1963: 83) for an answer in terms of risk and ecology.)

But productivity (or output-input ratios) is only one measure of efficiency; input-input ratios are another. From Table 7.3a the ratio of male to female labour input can be calculated as 1.07 for method A (136/127), 0.66 for method B (119/180), and 1.32 for method C (259/196). Given that method B is used primarily for mixed crop production, methods A and C compete as sweet potato production methods. From a male perspective method A is the more efficient in its use of male labour. Another question is thereby posed: Does this gender perspective provide an answer to the question posed above concerning the coexistence of three methods of production? What do Kapauku men and women think of this proposition? Pospisil does not appear to have asked such questions; they probably would not have occurred to the male authors of this book either had it not been for the rise of feminist anthropology in recent years and the research of female anthropologists like Sexton (1986) who worked on a similar economy in Papua New Guinea.

These illustrative examples show, once again, how a few elementary manipulations of comparative data already collected can pose new questions and suggest new lines of enquiry. But comparative data are not always available. This applies to those cases where efficient inputs have completely replaced the inefficient ones; where, for example, only steel axes, tractors or shotguns are to be found. One strategy here is to reconstruct comparative data using the experimental method. This was the method adopted by Salisbury (1962) in his famous 'stone to steel' argument. Subsequent researchers have tried to refine the statistical side of his argument by conducting experiments of their own (Godelier and Garanger 1978). The aim of exercises of this type is to obtain scientific measurements of efficiency using controlled experimentation in an artificially contrived situation. Such methods have their drawbacks, but they do provide one means of cross-checking informants' statements such as 'using this new tool has reduced our labour time by half'.

As the time when 'stone to steel' type experiments were possible has now passed in the New Guinea Highlands no purpose is served by examining this particular method. However, in many parts of the world new technologies coexist with older ones and useful measures of efficiency can be made.

In the South American context, Hames (1979) has undertaken an interesting study comparing the relative efficiency of the shotgun and bow; more recently Yost and Kelley (1983) compare the shotgun, blowgun, and spear. Both these studies measured productivity with output/input ratios, which were expressed in terms of mean yield of game per hunt divided by mean hours per hunt. Hames (1979: 245) calculated that the Ye'kwana obtained a yield of 1.49 kg of game per hour using the shotgun. This contrasts with a yield of 0.45 kg per hour for the Yanomamo who use the bow and arrow and suggests that the shotgun is 3.3 times as efficient as the bow and arrow. Yost and Kelley (1983) worked with the Waorani of east Ecuador, a society first colonized in 1958. They analysed data they collected in 1974–5 and 1979 on 867 day-hunts when spear, blowgun and shotgun were used. They found that the yield (kg/hr) for the spear was 3.95, for the blowgun 1.62 and for the shotgun 2.54 (Yost and Kelley 1983: 212). This implies that the spear is 1.6 times as efficient as the shotgun and 2.4 times as efficient as the blowgun. However, the efficiency issue is far more complicated than this in the Waorani context because spears, shotguns, and blowpipes are specialized technologies used for different types of game. Overall, the Waorani have increased their protein intake by about 30 per cent by utilizing the shotgun as well as traditional technology; interestingly Yost and Kelley note that the shotgun has been adopted to complement the spear and blowgun and not to supplant it.

To return to the New Guinea example, in the case of stone and steel axes, relative efficiency ratios of between 1.5:1 and 3:1 were obtained. In other words, steel axes are between 1.5 to three times more efficient than stone axes. Data of this type can be used to reconstruct stone-using input-output relations. According to Pospisil's data, the steel-axe-using method A produced 730 kg of

Table 7.5 Kapauku production statistics: impact of steel axe

Method	Land	Male labour	Female labour	Output
A* (stone)	900	206	127	730
A (steel)	900	136	127	730

sweet potatoes using 900 square metres of land, 136 hours of male labour, and 127 hours of female labour. Included in the male labour hours are 35 hours of axe work felling trees. If we assume, following Salisbury (1962), that steel axes cut this work by two-thirds, then an extra 70 hours must be added to the male labour time of method A to reconstruct a stone-using version of method A. This reconstruction, method A*, is compared with method A in Table 7.5.

Using these reconstructed data a number of ratios can be calculated and compared with method A. The significant ratios are the male to female labour ratio and the ratio of output to male labour. The former ratio falls from 1.62 (206/127) to 1.07 (136/127) while the latter rises from 3.54 (730/206) to 5.36 (730/136). From the point of view of western capitalism the latter ratio, which measures male labour productivity, is central; but in economies such as the Kapauku such assumptions should not be made. If it is hypothesized that gender relations are central in these economies then indigenous thinking on this matter must be investigated closely. The difficulty here is transforming these observer categories into questions that are culturally meaningful.

It is clear that these calculations express in a statistical form relations between men and women that were not obvious from casual observation. Even if they did turn out to be obvious, calculations like this are still useful. The fieldworker must constantly check and cross-check and this is one means of doing this. Casual empirical observation is not always reliable and the 'obvious' has a habit of becoming so only after it has been discovered. Preconceptions and misconceptions prevent us from seeing the obvious; anthropological fieldwork, when it is done properly, can help break down these conceptual barriers.

DIVISION OF TOTAL OUTPUT

Total output is divided into those products that are necessary for reproduction, such as the rice stored as seed for next year's harvest and the sweet potatoes fed to pigs; those products that are set aside for human consumption, such as the grain to be used as food and the pigs killed for bacon; and those products which are exchanged for other products or given away to fulfil an obligation such as the share of total product payable to a landlord.

Total output can also be divided into those products which are necessary for the survival of the producers and those which represent a surplus. This 'necessary product/surplus product' distinction raises many controversial methodological and theoretical issues, some of which we have already examined: How is the division of total output into its parts to be measured? (see pp.144-55) Does one use labour time, product shares, or money prices? What products are included in the necessary product? Is it limited to the minimum necessary for biological production or does it include those products necessary for social and cultural reproduction? These questions have no simple answers because the personal judgements and interpretations necessarily involved raise political questions of some moment: Is the producer being exploited? If so, what policy conclusions follow? If not, what other interpretations are possible?

The fieldworker cannot avoid these controversial issues. However, if the questions are approached concretely without preconceived theoretical ideas, it may be possible for a fieldworker to change the direction of the debate. Detailed observations on the empirical relation between production and consumption for different households can often throw new light on the meaning of concepts such as 'surplus' and 'deficit'. In a rice-producing village, for example, it is important to note which households are forced to buy rice before the harvest and which households are self-sufficient. The investigation can be pursued further by noting when during the agricultural cycle rice purchases are made. (Methods for recording household expenditure are outlined later, see pp.175-81). Information of this kind will provide a rough ranking of surplus, deficit, and break-even households which can then be cross-checked with other data collected in property censuses (see pp.48-57) or in monitoring distribution and redistribution (see pp.203-8).

It is obvious from this brief discussion that the study of the division of output is simultaneously the study of circulation and consumption; the topic raises other issues that are discussed in the next two chapters.

Chapter Eight

CONSUMPTION

INTRODUCTION

Consumption refers to the final use of food, clothing, and shelter produced by people. Logically, consumption is the end of an economic process; but, because it creates the need for reproduction, it is also the beginning of a new one. It follows, then, that production must bear a definite relationship to consumption. This relationship holds for the economic activities of an individual, a household, a community, and a nation state, but the nature of the relationship will, of course, vary for each of these different levels. The methodological significance of this is that consumption data can be used both to complement and cross-check production data (see pp.199-203).

Consumption involves both destruction and preservation, but the distinction is not clear cut. Perishable food is destroyed relatively quickly when it is eaten or wasted, clothing wears out slowly with use, and brick houses may last hundreds of years. As every anthropologist knows, the destruction and preservation of products cannot be explained solely in terms of biological need; religious beliefs, social status, and politics are at the basis of much consumption behaviour. The study of consumption, then, raises many issues of traditional anthropological concern which can be grouped under the general heading of 'culture and ideology' (see pp.34-40).

In order to limit the scope of this chapter a rather tight economic line has been drawn. The arbitrary division between the economic and the non-economic made in this chapter is not meant to be prescriptive; fieldworkers will have to draw their own

174

lines in the light of the particular circumstances of their study. This chapter begins with a discussion of techniques that can be used for collecting general data on household expenditure. It then considers the particular methodological problems involved in the collection of statistical and cultural data on specific items. Food and drink are the primary focus, but alcohol and drugs, shelter, clothing, and other consumer durables are briefly considered.

HOUSEHOLD EXPENDITURE

It is important to make a distinction between household expenditure and household consumption. In some situations expenditure patterns are similar to consumption patterns; but in other situations, where a large proportion of output is locally consumed, there will be a divergence between consumption and expenditure. In general, the greater the degree of self-provisioning, the smaller the correlation between expenditure and consumption.

Expenditure patterns reflect the money wealth and cultural values of people. Data of this kind, therefore, reveal a great deal about economic inequality between households, about the cultural obligations to consume in various conspicuous and inconspicuous ways, and about the degree of incorporation into the world economy. Data collected on the range of items bought at different points in time can highlight socially significant facts concerning changes in consumer preferences.

There are a number of different techniques that can be used to monitor household expenditure. At one end of the methodological spectrum are household surveys based on direct observation, at the other end are the indirect methods used in large-scale surveys, and in the middle are the hybrid methods. Data collected by these methods are normally collected from the place of consumption (such as the household) and can be cross-checked with data collected from the place of expenditure (such as the shop). In the discussion which follows we consider each of these methods in turn and suggest how they might be combined.

Household surveys based on direct observation. Pioneering work in this area was conducted by Rosemary Firth in *Housekeeping among Malay Peasants* (1966). While her husband was investigating the production and distribution of wealth, she attempted to find out

175

how this wealth was used (see p. 51–3). Besides making visits to markets and shops, as well as to weddings and other social occasions where unusual expenditure was taking place, Firth also made daily visits to houses every evening for consecutive periods ranging from one month to twenty-one weeks. She took notes on every cent expended each day; on the food eaten, received, and stored in the house; and in many instances on the manner of cooking it (Firth 1966: 4).

Similar methods were used by Altman to collect expenditure data at the small Aboriginal community of Momega. All the expenditures of community residents were recorded. Data were collected mainly when a fortnightly mobile store visited the community. On these visits, cash income was received and simultaneously spent. Momega people also spent some money at a nearby township and by arranging mail orders of larger items (like shotguns) from Darwin, an urban centre some 550 kilometres away. Altman collected detailed data on township transactions by interviewing people and noting items bought. As he was frequently the broker for mail order purchases from Darwin, Altman was able to maintain accurate records of these transactions. Altman (1987: 59-69) was therefore able to observe almost all expenditure by Momega residents; not only could a list of items bought be recorded, but also the names and household affiliations of purchasers.

This information allowed Altman to analyse expenditure by broad category, by variations over the seasonal cycle, and by variations between households. Interestingly, some households continually spent more than their cash income; these deficits were covered by households with 'surplus' cash and sanctioned by obligations to share (see pp.203-8). The expenditure categories used by Altman (1987: 63) were quite simple because the range of goods procured was limited. A broad division was made between consumer and producer goods. Consumer goods were sub-divided into foodstuffs, alcohol, tobacco products, personal items, household items, and items used for ceremonial exchange. Producer goods were subdivided into fishing equipment, hunting equipment, and other commodities used for housebuilding and the manufacture of arts and crafts.

It is especially important that expenditures on locally significant cultural events are recorded in as much detail as possible. Epstein

(1967: 178) suggests that data on weddings, ceremonies and feasts, mortuary rites, and so on, be collected separately from household budgets. In an earlier study, Epstein (1962: 102, 264) collected information on wedding expenses for selected households in the villages of Wangala and Dalena in south India. These data were used to contrast emerging economic inequality within and between villages. Rosemary Firth (1966: 157, 200) presents expenditure data for two feasts, one a Muslim circumcision, the other a wedding, that she observed in 1940 and 1963 respectively at Perupok village in north-east Malaysia. Her data not only allowed her to assess the overall economic significance of these feasts for the respective households, but also facilitated an analysis of change in household economic circumstances over time.

Large scale surveys involving indirect methods. An example of this approach is the recent household expenditure survey completed by the Australian Bureau of Statistics (ABS 1987). The ABS survey covered a random sample of 7,500 households distributed throughout urban and rural Australia. Data were collected using expenditure and income questionnaires, administered by an interviewer, and a personal expenditure diary kept by each spender in a household for a period of up to four weeks. The diaries were in the form of coded lists that included thirteen major expenditure categories, 100 sub-categories, and 440 sub-sub-categories. The thirteen broad categories were:

Current housing costs (e.g. rent, mortgage (interest only), insurance)
Fuel and power (e.g. electricity, gas, other fuel)
Food (including non-alcoholic beverages, meals out)
Alcohol
Tobacco
Clothing and footwear
Household furnishings, equipment (e.g. utensils, tools, appliances)
Household services, operations (e.g. non-durables, telephone, child care)
Medical care, health expenses (e.g. pharmaceutical products, charges)
Transport (e.g. vehicle purchase, running, fuel, public transport fees)

Recreation (e.g. radio, television, books, holidays, gambling)
Personal care (e.g. toiletries, cosmetics, hairdressing, beauty services)
Miscellaneous goods and services (e.g. jewellery and education fees)

A number of methodological difficulties were addressed by the ABS (1987: 7-8) prior to conducting the survey. It is useful to consider three of these problems because they illustrate some of the classification problems an ethnographer may encounter.

The first concerns the category 'housing'. This creates problems where the house is owner-occupied but mortgaged. In the ABS survey, interest payments on mortgages were regarded as current housing costs, but repayments of mortgage principal were classified as household asset formation or investment. Four broad categories (income tax, repayments of mortgage principal, other capital housing costs, and superannuation and life insurance) were called 'selected other payments' and were not counted as expenditure.

The second involves the distinction between 'payments' and 'acquisitions'. The payments approach to expenditure records the payments made during the survey period for goods and services whether or not acquired or consumed during that period. The acquisitions approach, on the other hand, emphasizes the cost of items during the survey period whether or not fully paid for or consumed. For most expenditure the two approaches yield identical results; the main difference occurs with durable consumer goods that are purchased on credit. For example, a vehicle that would ordinarily last for a number of years may be financed through periodic repayment of a loan; with the acquisitions approach the full purchase price of the vehicle is recorded as expenditure at the time of purchase.

The third problem concerns the definition of 'recreation'. The expenditure on gambling activities is recorded in the ABS survey as recreation; but in many societies gambling is regarded as a means to accumulate cash and to gain social status. Similar ambiguities arise with expenditure on items like televisions and radios. Should they be classified as household or recreation equipment? Or are they purchased for the purposes of prestige, for use, or for both? For example, Gell (1986) reports the case of

Sri Lankan fishermen who have spent cash on water tanks, televisions, and garages for cars, in a place where there is no reticulated water, electricity, or roads.

Hybrid methods. The methods used by Sommerlad *et al.* (1985) represent a methodological example of an intermediate point between the microsurveys using direct observation and large-scale surveys using indirect methods. This study, conducted in 1984, examined twenty New South Wales rural land sharing communities with an average size of eighteen persons (see pp. 154–5). Data were collected on the expenditure patterns of 140 households and 218 adults within these communities, and the data compared with the 1975–76 household expenditure survey conducted by the Australian Bureau of Statistics. A combination of direct observation and questionnaire techniques was used. Fieldworkers spent a week at each community assisting with the filling of questionnaires. There were three different types of questionnaire: the first was aimed at the community as a whole; the second at households; and the third was administered to individual adults. This style of research enabled cross-checking both within and between communities, and between questionnaire responses and the recorded observations of fieldworkers.

The above examples illustrate the full range of household expenditure survey methodologies. The advantage of the detailed surveys is that they allow a degree of verification by direct observation and recording of expenditure transactions. If a survey is conducted over a prolonged period, then it will also allow analysis of seasonal changes in expenditure patterns. The intermediate case combines direct observation with questionnaires. The advantage of this method is that it allows relatively widespread coverage with a degree of direct observation. Large scale surveys are based almost entirely on questionnaires and there is little opportunity to verify reported expenditure patterns with actual expenditure.

Shopping surveys. Data collected by the above methods can be cross-checked by taking the seller's perspective. The obvious means to do this is to situate oneself at the counter of a retail outlet and record all transactions. This approach is relatively simple if all transactions are undertaken at the one outlet and if shopping occurs infrequently. For example, Altman (1987) was able to record all purchases by residents of an Aboriginal community because the bulk of transactions were concluded in an hour or two every fortnight. Data on expenditures could subsequently be checked against the records of the regional retailer. Such a 'closed' economic situation is rare today.

When it is not feasible to monitor all expenditure, it will be necessary to undertake surveys on randomly selected days (see p. 109). It must be recognized, though, that surveys conducted at shops are extremely labour-intensive. However, data collected by direct observation can provide important information about the social relations of shopping. Who shops with whom? Who controls cash resources? Who shops for the household? How do buyers interact with sellers? How does the seller allocate scarce commodities? Are queues formed?

An alternative method for collecting information on community expenditure is to gain access to the books of retailers. Obviously this is only possible where accurate shop records are maintained. A problem with this approach is that expenditure categories may be predetermined by book-keeping styles. A high degree of co-operation from local traders will be required if access to financial records is to be gained. It is not unusual for such co-operation to be withheld on the grounds that information on business turnover is confidential. A means to gain access to such information may be to convince shopkeepers of the usefulness of such data, particularly for the assessment of the nutritional status of the community. An alternative strategy may be to request data at an aggregate level that will not reflect mark-up policies and other commercial practices. It is likely that co-operation will not be forthcoming in situations of unfair or illegal business practice.

Gregory's attempts to gain access to the books of merchants in central India were largely unsuccessful. Most of them are kept in secret codes known only to the families of the merchants. He was able to view these books, but only one merchant was prepared to spend some time translating the information. Data on this merchant's sales of glass bangles for just two weeks took three hours of tedious work to transcribe; this access was given on the condition that the data not be published. However, the data did support hypotheses made about the importance of credit. Many glass bangle sellers have gone bankrupt because of bad debts. This particular merchant stopped giving credit, but his weekly sales dropped dramatically as a result. The data, which spanned the week before and the week after this decision, provided a quantitative verification of this change.

This case illustrates, among other things, the difficulties likely to be encountered when working with shopkeepers; it is also another example of the problems inherent in differentiating household acquisition from household payment.

FOOD AND DRINK

Expenditure surveys provide data on purchased food and drink. As locally produced foods and drinks are often important components of consumption in many economies, other methods must be used to collect comprehensive information on these products. For example Dufour (1983) conducted research at the village of Yapú in the Colombian Vaupés among Tatuyo people who do not purchase food. Pospisil (1963: 261) notes that for the Kapauku Papuans food constitutes the most important article of consumption and that, with the exception of salt and pork, all food is locally produced. Clearly in such situations it is appropriate to concentrate on the measurement of food consumption because expenditure surveys, which apply only to the cash nexus, are meaningless. In this section we outline some of the techniques which can be used to both complement and cross-check expenditure survey data.

Food consumption surveys

Food consumption surveys can be used to answer a host of economic questions: Is the household meeting its basic consumption needs? To what extent does seasonality influence foodstuff consumption? What percentage of consumption is domestically produced? What are the determinants of variations in household consumption patterns? Is there any relationship between the control of economic resources and diet? Do cultural beliefs provide a barrier to food consumption? How do people adapt to the availability of a range of new foods? Are the nutritional implications of consuming new foods understood? Do new cash earning opportunities result in radical changes in consumption patterns?

Nutritional anthropology has become a highly specialized sub-discipline of anthropology (Jerome *et al.* 1980; Messer 1984) and many sophisticated techniques have been developed to undertake dietary analysis. A general guide to these is provided in Weiner and Lourie's *Practical Human Biology* (1981); an illustrative example of the application of these techniques can be found in the work of Norgan *et al.* (1974) in Papua New Guinea or Edmundson (1976) in Java. In the discussion that follows we emphasize the utility of some of these techniques for economic analysis.

It is important that ethnographers specify their economic aims in collecting data on food consumption. No attempt should be made to assess the nutritional status of a research population because dietary data must be be complemented by detailed clinical examinations and anthropometric measurements before they can be interpreted in this way. Such techniques are clearly beyond the scope of most ethnographic studies. For example, Altman (1987: 31) prefaced his research of consumption patterns among Aborigines in north Australia by stating that his prime concern was to make an economic rather than nutritional or health status statement. Today, these people receive all the welfare entitlements of Australian citizens and continue to participate in subsistence activities. The two specific questions Altman asked were: What proportion of the people's food comes from local production? and, What proportion is purchased? These questions were addressed by measuring community-wide food consumption using some of the techniques discussed below.

Survey techniques and problems

There are marked differences between the methods used in small scale surveys undertaken by anthropologists and large scale national nutritional surveys. The full range of survey methods available to measure food consumption has been listed by Wheeler (1981) in decreasing order of precision as follows:

The duplicate analysis method where all foods and drinks are weighed and measured, and identical weighed samples are taken at the same time for chemical analysis. This technique is usually undertaken under laboratory conditions; for fieldworkers it involves sending samples of foods for chemical analysis (see Norgan *et al.* 1974).

The weighing method where all foods are weighed before serving, and discarded food is subtracted after the meal. Nutrient intakes are then calculated from food composition tables. Using such tables introduces what is termed 'food table error' which means that the nutritional composition of foods actually consumed may vary from the standards. This error is liable to be magnified if foods consumed (e.g. kangaroo meat) are not listed in the tables and close substitutes (e.g. beef) are used.

Diary methods require the subject to keep a diary of all foods consumed (usually for a 24 hour period) in 'typical household measures' (like cupfuls, spoonfuls, bowlfuls). This approach introduces subject error, which may result in over- or under-reporting; and calibration error resulting from the conversion of household measures to estimated food weights.

Dietary interview requires the subject to recall food items and/or quantities consumed to an interviewer. A questionnaire, visual aids, and standard measures may be used. This method introduces greater subject and calibration error than the diary method.

The community food use survey provides a brief account of the foods used in a community and seasonal variations in supply. This approach can be conducted with a small number of key informants to provide qualitative, rather than quantitative, data.

This range of techniques can be divided into two broad categories, direct and indirect methods, with the first two belonging to the former and the last three to the latter. While it is clear from Wheeler's ranking that survey methods based on direct observation are preferable (from the point of view of statistical accuracy), in a field situation a variety of techniques may be used.

Ethnographers have tended to use a combination of the weighing method and dietary interviews, but have also had to develop special techniques to deal with the particularities of local economies. The following illustrative examples are drawn from Papua New Guinea and Mexico.

Sillitoe (1983: 230-2) worked with a sample of twelve households in his study of food consumption among the Wola of highlands Papua New Guinea. He weighed the garden foods brought back by women at the end of the day for household consumption. This food accounted for between 80 and 90 per cent of all food consumed. When Sillitoe was unable to weigh foods, he questioned members of each homestead in the survey to establish what other foods they had eaten. The weight of these foods was estimated from informants' statements about the amounts they had eaten, size of tubers, and so on.

Sillitoe (ibid: 267) used a questionnaire to collect daily information on the consumption of respondents. This was structured as follows:

Name:
Family group:
Sex:
Date:
For each crop (twenty-seven floral and faunal species):
   number
   weight
   remarks
Names of people consuming:
Numbers (and owners) of pigs consuming:
Garden harvested from:
Other foods consumed by this group during the day:
Remarks:

Prior to formulating this questionnaire, Sillitoe (1983: 230) staged a preliminary survey of twelve days' duration. The food consumption survey proper extended over a period of three months, with the most comprehensive coverage being eighty-two days for a number of individuals. Overall, 143 persons were included in his survey which generated food consumption data for 5,304 person days.

A different approach was taken by DeWalt *et al.* (1980: 205-21) in their study of nutritional variation among households at Il Puerto de las Piedras, a village of 1,300 people in the north-west part of Mexico. Their main concern was to analyse differentials in household access to food and the extent to which this differentiation was a result of economic, social, or cultural variables. Because income data were difficult to obtain in this poor community, the researchers developed a 'material style of life' (MSL) scale based on inventories of commodities and household goods owned by village families. A sample of sixty-two households was divided into quartiles on the basis of the MSL scale; the authors found a clear relationship between socio-economic status

184

and food intake. The statistical analysis was reinforced by a more detailed survey which examined a 'rich', a 'medium', and a 'poor' household over three-day periods. DeWalt *et al.* (1980: 218) draw three interesting conclusions from their study. First, economic resource control was an important predictor of dietary variation: richer households showed greater complexity in their diets and obtained protein from a greater variety of sources. Second, they found that traditional beliefs and food attitudes did not provide barriers to adequate nutrition: people's ratings of desirable foods, defined by such terms as 'tastiness' and 'healthiness', strongly favoured nutritious foods. Third, they demonstrated that within an economically marginal community there was a degree of microdifferentiation that was frequently overlooked. The researchers do not specify how their sample of sixty-two households was chosen or the populations of these households; it would have been interesting to know to what extent economic differentiation was linked to household demographic structure (see pp.48-57). In a recent study in Taiwan, Greenhalgh (1985) examined whether inequality was demographically induced; DeWalt *et al.* could have asked a similar question with their data on food consumption.

The undertaking of food consumption surveys may require the use of some specialized equipment. The basic 'tool-kit' will no doubt vary depending on the research location, but two spring-balance scales (one for heavy weights and one for finer measures), a measuring tape, and a camera are essential. If one is to work in a society where liquid foods, such as palm juice (Fox 1977) or milk and blood (McCabe 1987), are consumed as staples, then measurement cylinders or graduated beakers are important. A random numbers table is useful if sampling is to be undertaken, and simple hand-held counters can also be an invaluable aid. If one is to use a 24-hour recall method, then visual prompts, like photographs of different food items, and food lists may be useful; standardized vessels (Ramnath *et al.* 1985) will be needed for measuring consumption of grains like rice.

There are a number of methodological problems that must be addressed before undertaking a food consumption survey and the following discussion considers some of these; Wheeler (1981) and the National Research Council (1986) should be consulted for further details.

185

Allocation of research time. Food consumption surveys are labour intensive and they raise the now familiar question about the principles to be used for the allocation of research time. As a rule of thumb, Wheeler (1981) estimates that in a weighed food intake survey one observer can work with a maximum of three subjects. On the other hand, surveys based on dietary interview take about half an hour per subject per 24-hour recall (Australian Commonwealth Department of Health 1986). Even using this less precise method, one fieldworker could only work with about ten subjects. A possible approach for food consumption surveys is to use a random spot check technique (see p. 105). We are not aware of any study that has used this technique.

Problems of measurement and valuation. Anthropologists are rarely able to justify chemical analyses of foods, unless they are working as part of a multi-disciplinary team. As a result they will normally be obliged to use weighing and valuation methods in conjunction with food composition tables which introduce error in the vicinity of plus or minus 15 per cent (Wheeler 1981: 348). It is generally impossible to measure accurately the intakes of individuals, so a commensal unit will need to be defined and taken as the basic unit. This assumes that food is distributed according to physiological need. However, in many cultures adult males may receive a disproportionate share of certain foods (McArthur 1977; National Research Council 1986). There is no solution to this measurement problem, but the anthropologist can provide qualifications by observing the behavioural dimensions of food distribution (both between and within households) and food consumption. If average requirement benchmarks are to be used, then they must be interpreted with great caution. The conversion of weights into nutritional values such as calories, protein, fat, carbohydrates, fibre, calcium, iron, and the like (Sillitoe 1983: 241) raises problems of valuation. This issue has been discussed above using Altman's data as an example (see pp.150-3).

Duration of survey. The duration of food consumption surveys is an important consideration, particularly in research communities that grow seasonal crops or whose productive activities are greatly influenced by seasonality. Norgan *et al.* (1974) attempted to overcome this problem in their New Guinea surveys by spreading their observations over the year, but concentrating on individual households for periods of five to seven days. Their assumption (as in large-scale surveys) was that the distribution of observations over the year would eliminate the effects of seasonality. However, such an approach also precludes the possibility of testing for dietary variability between households. It is also important to avoid overgeneralizing from a 12- to 24-month study period. If possible, historical and comparative information should be collected on variables such as climatic conditions, production levels, employment opportunities, the prices paid for crops, the local rate of inflation, and the local availability of foods and other goods, for these will all influence foodstuff consumption.

Ethics. There is a trade-off between the scientific requirement that individual intakes are monitored and the social and cultural codes of acceptable behaviour within the society being studied. Paradoxically, fieldworkers undertaking long-term field research can be more constrained than outsiders in this regard because of their greater understanding of local languages and cultural norms. In many societies enquiring about food implies one wants a share and observing people preparing or eating food is tantamount to intrusion into the most private of domains. The ASA's *Ethical Guidelines for Good Practice* warns against undue intrusion and notes that like all social researchers, anthropologists have no special entitlements to study all phenomena (ASA 1987: 3).

Lest we make the task of conducting food consumption surveys appear too complicated, let us provide an anecdote from Edmundson (1976: 15) who reports that calculating food intakes of individuals in a Javanese village was somewhat easier than expected because of two factors. First, the villagers did not eat breakfast. Second, Javanese villagers normally took their meals as individuals and not as a family unit. This, plus the fact that the standard menu consisted of only a few items, made it a simple matter to weigh the food of the individual. The main 'problem' reported by Edmundson was the graciousness of the Javanese family; they were always anxious to share their food with him.

Restrictions, preferences and prescriptions

Data collected from food expenditure and food consumption surveys must be situated in their cultural context if they are to be of value. This is because food and drink are classified by different people in different ways. Distinctions are made between edible and non-edible foods on the grounds of religion, social tradition, and individual preference; edible foods are in turn subject to various restrictions depending on time, status, age, and sex, among other things. What is defined as edible varies markedly between cultures (Conklin 1957; Koestlin 1981; Pollock 1985). This point was made forcefully by Sahlins (1976: 170-9) in his discussion of western culture's rejection of horse and dog meat as a food. The use of ethno-categories of what constitutes food is extremely important for determining cultural definitions of edibility.

These non-economic factors affect the volume and structure of production, occupational specialization, and the mode of distribution and exchange of products. India is the classic example of a country where diverse dietary laws and complex rules concerning the giving and receiving of food have significant economic consequences of this kind. Different cultures have different modes of consumption and the following discussion contains some suggestions for how these might be described and analysed.

The participating observer will frequently be confronted with a complicated range of dietary laws and food customs when studying among unfamiliar people. When one first enters the field, these practices can be quite confusing, and it may take some time before sense can be made of the system. The following questions may be helpful in preparing an initial cultural classification of food:

What foods are rejected as inedible?
What accepted foods are subjected to restrictions:
What are the bases of these restrictions?
What is the role of the following in determining restrictions:
    Time (seasonal cycles, religious calendars, etc.)
    Status (of producer, of consumer; political, cultural, economic)
    Age and sex (of producers, of consumers)
    Kinship relations?

Consider the consumption practices of the Gunwinggu of north Australia (Altman 1987). They reject some foods like crow and dingo, but eat an extremely wide range of indigenous and exotic flora and fauna. However, many of these edible foods are frequently restricted (*djamun*). Sometimes this is based on a particular season: the river sawfish, for example, is not eaten during the wet. Other foods are subject to restrictions based on the phases in the ritual life cycle of males or the sexual cycle of females. For example, male ritual novices cannot eat kangaroo meat during ceremonies and women cannot eat reptiles during menstruation. The Gunwinggu also have complex consumer/producer taboos (*galngboi*) whereby the product of ritual novices' labour is consumable only by fully initiated men. They also have food prescriptions: lactating or pregnant women are encouraged to eat small fish and to avoid big ones; people with maladies are encouraged to eat certain species of food, and so on.

Having developed a cultural classification of foods an attempt should be made to assess their social and economic effects in the light of sanctions and social contexts. This is an issue that has received a great deal of attention in anthropology recently (see pp.38-40) and the scope of the subject is vast, as Messer's (1984) review of anthropological perspectives on diet indicates. A checklist of questions that the fieldworker concerned with the economy might ask include:

What is the religious significance of different foods?
What are the impacts of such prescriptions?
Are foods redistributed from the rich to the poor?
Does feasting result in the widespread sharing of seasonal
    surpluses?
Is there a correlation between nutritional and cultural values of
    food?
Are new foods used to break the monotony of the diet?
What is the link between restrictions and relations of production?
Do restrictions amplify or sanction gender inequalities?
Do sections of society have restricted access to foods they produce?
Is food used as a symbol of social/political/economic
    differentiation?
Are food transactions manipulated to improve relative status?
Is food used as a signifier of ethnic identity?
What are the social implications of food shortages?
What can be learnt during periods of seasonal shortage or famine?
What are the reasons for food avoidance?
Are avoidances linked to negative physiological effects?
Are avoidances due to culturally specific properties of foods?

Observations and case study material can be summarized using the tabular method discussed above (see pp.69-80). Table 8.1, a truncated version of Firth's table of Tikopian taboos (1939: 202), illustrates how the synoptic method might be applied in this case.

Tables of this type pose a number of further questions concerning the politics of sanctions, especially when a *tapu* results in economic hardship. Case study material is essential to answer such questions.

In Tikopia, for example, breaches of *tapu* are not always followed by evil consequences as the following shows:

> Pa Fenuatara set up a *sekilo* in Nuku. When the time came for it to be 'untied' he invited his father the chief to come and perform the kava. Not many coco-nuts had been saved through the *tapu*. Folk had gone and taken them regardless of the coco-nut frond standing there. The reason was that it was a time of distinct scarcity of food. Because of this Pa Fenuatara made no objection to their action when he found it out, and indeed removed the *tapu* earlier than otherwise in consequence.
>
> (Firth 1939: 210-11)

Furthermore, the breach of a *tapu* is not the only method of securing an alleviation from it:

> Sometimes a person closely related to the chief, or of rank in another clan, may make a direct appeal to him to limit its range or lessen its intensity. For instance, after the death of

Table 8.1 Economic effects of some Tikopian taboos

Type	Context	Sanction	Economic effects
Funeral prohibition on plucking coconuts	Specified areas set up by chief	Fiat of chief, fear of chief and of supernatural punishment	Accumulation of reserves to small extent
Restriction of access to taro land or individual cultivations	Imposed by individuals in their own interests or immediate interests of group	Respect for individual wish and sometimes fear of chief and/or supernatural punishment	Retention of individual advantage; limitation on general freedom of utilization

the grandson of the Ariki Tafua a general *tapu* was imposed upon sea fishing in his district. After a while it was limited to the shore waters only. I was told that the son of the Ariki Kafika requested that the waters off the reef should not be prohibited in order that the fish which collected in safety on the reef might be taken as they return to sea.

(Firth 1939: 211-12)

This example shows that the Tikopians modify religious *tapu* when its economic consequences are too severe.

When collecting case study material on the operation of a taboo it is essential that indigenous interpretations of the action are recorded. These can be analysed at a later date for their economic significance. The manner in which the cultural status of food can influence the process of distribution (see pp.203-8) is illustrated by the following example from northern Australia:

At Gukapangga two types of flying fox were shot in large numbers. One type called *murru* was black and Dua [moiety] and was an important Gunabibi totem. The other called *nagayelak* was brown and Yirritja [moiety] and was from Ubar, a ceremony that is not performed these days. There were three young men in camp who were *klawutu* [ritual novices] and could not eat *murru* but could eat *nagayelak.* Hence most of the brown flying foxes were directed to these young men and the black ones were eaten by other camp residents.

(Altman 1987: 180)

It is extremely difficult to quantify the economic effects of taboos, but it may be possible to do so in certain circumstances. Altman was able to measure the impact of producer/consumer taboos imposed on young men's output in Gunwinggu society. He found that about 17 per cent of their annual foodstuff production was restricted, with the monthly average ranging from zero to nearly 39 per cent. These restrictions excluded the hunters and women from consumption, but allowed fully initiated males and all children to partake. But these statistics relate to one restriction among many. In the absence of detailed dietary observations of individual intakes, Altman found it impossible to state categorically to what extent restrictions were observed; direct observation and verbal testimony suggested that the powerful sanctions incorporated both in public myths and in restricted ceremonies resulted in a close observance of taboos.

The impact of external forces such as the state and the world market raises other issues to be explored. In the Gunwinggu case, the existence of complex restrictions on indigenous foods contrasts with the general absence of restrictions on modern foods. New foods were readily adopted by them in the 1950s and 1960s in government settlements and missions when communal kitchens were established. The fact that these foods were not part of the indigenous classification system and, therefore, not subject to indigenous forms of social control that were imposed by elder males was probably an important reason they were so readily adopted. Another reason was that Aboriginal elders' authority was totally undermined by the white administrators who controlled the distribution of food in the communal kitchens (Altman 1987: 187-9).

Alcohol and drugs

This subject requires similar methods to those described in the previous section: namely, careful observations of the social context of drug and alcohol taking should be undertaken and its economic impact assessed using classificatory and, where possible, statistical techniques. Heath (1987a, 1987b) in two recent reviews has summarized the anthropological contributions to alcohol studies; he notes that poor data collection techniques were responsible for the uneven quality of earlier anthropological studies. Other economic questions that may arise (and some recent illustrative works) include:

1   What proportion of household income is spent on alcohol (see pp.175-81)?
2   Is alcohol produced or bought?
3   How does alcohol consumption affect productive activities (Grossman 1984a)?
4   Does alcohol have an economic impact via incorporation into ceremonial contexts (Warry 1987; Sexton 1986)?
5   Is alcohol used to create employment opportunities (Mars 1987)?
6   Is drinking a means to build social credit? Can it be

regarded as consumptive investment rather than hedonistic expenditure (Collmann 1988)?

7 How is alcohol consumed? Is it done in a generalized manner or in binges (Warry 1987)?

8 Does alcohol (Crump 1987) and drug (Cassanelli 1986) production constitute an important component of output in an economy?

9 Are different alcoholic drinks used to signal different social occasions (Thornton 1987; Ngokwey 1987)?

10 Does alcohol and drug consumption provide any indicators of inequality?

When studying an emotive subject such as the economic impact of drugs and alcohol it is important to avoid Eurocentric assumptions and personal prejudice. For example, in certain social contexts wines and beers are regarded as general tonics and good food. Richards (1939), Goody (1982), and Ngokwey (1987) all emphasize the beneficial nutritional impact of beer and palm wine on the Bemba, LoDagaa and Lele societies of Africa. For the LoDagaa, beer is food; the LoDagaa often apply the same term to beer as they do to the basic cereal elements of the meal, porridge. This is because beer and porridge are made from the same basic ingredient, sorghum (Goody 1982: 72).

The manner in which drugs affect labour productivity must be carefully observed too. Nash, in *We Eat the Mines and the Mines Eat Us* (1979), discusses the use of coca, a drug that is derived from cocaine and used extensively by miners in the Bolivian tin mines. She quotes a tin miner who said 'It gives us courage, it serves us as energy, and it serves us as food. We can work sixteen hours below the ground with coca' (ibid: 199). She notes further that:

> Management is well aware of the importance of coca in that it makes the inhuman conditions of the mine tolerable. As a result they keep the pulpería well supplied with good coca from the Yungas. 'If we ran out of coca,' one administrative clerk told me, 'we would really have a revolution on our hands!'
>
> (Nash 1979: 200)

This case is particularly interesting because it illustrates that coca increases labour productivity in the shorter run. However, in the longer run it has deleterious effects because the imbibing of coca allows workers to increase their exposure to silicone in the mines (ibid: 201). People are invalided out of the work force early and many die prematurely from silicosis. Such a situation raises general issues concerning work-place industrial relations (see pp.98-101).

Alcohol consumption may play a pivotal role in ceremonial exchange (see pp.215-25). Warry (1987) in his study of Chauve politics in the Papua New Guinea Highlands collected quantitative information on beer expenditures, consumption, and exchange. He demonstrates how beer has been incorporated into the range of valuables exchanged at marriage in the 1970s. In ten reported cases, when data were collected by interview, between 30 and 240 cartons of beer were exchanged. Warry directly observed a ceremony which provided important substantiating data. In this marriage ceremony the father of the groom spent about $PNG1,000 to provide 100 cartons of beer. Warry (1987: 135) notes that clans greatly enhance their reputation if day long drinking occurs at ceremonies; the most successful wedding feasts entail virtual sobriety for the host clan and widespread drunkenness for the visiting clan.

It is important to note that quantitative data on alcohol consumption and drug use can be collected by analysing household expenditure patterns (see pp.175-81) and household consumption patterns (see pp.182-2). Grossman (1982) provides an example of data collection on beer expenditure over a year (1977) at Kapanara village in the Kainantu District of the Papua New Guinea Highlands. In alcohol studies it is particularly important to identify the sample carefully and to quantify individual variations in consumption. The measurement of alcohol and drug consumption may be particularly problematic in situations where it is either illegal or a socially sensitive issue. Time allocation data may assist by providing information on time spent distilling palm wine or beer (see pp.103-14); and output data, like litres of palm wine or beer produced and not sold (see pp.144-55), can provide useful cross checks on consumption data.

SHELTER, CLOTHING AND OTHER DURABLES

Expenditure pattern analysis (see pp.175-81), property census data (see pp.48-57), and general observation will determine the relative significance of these relatively durable forms of consumption. The discussion which follows is concerned mainly with housing, but it is obvious that the general methodological issues raised here can be applied to cloth and clothing (Schneider 1987) and other consumer durables.

Many of the variables discussed in housing consumption can in fact be linked to housing production. We discuss them here partly because the consumption of housing (depreciation) is closely linked to the nature of its production (materials, complex or simple, permanent or seasonal) and partly because we did not address housing in our discussion of technological inputs or output (see pp.144-55).

Humphrey (1988) in reviewing Paul Oliver's book *Dwellings: The House across the World* (1987), notes that housing has been generally ignored by anthropologists. A fascinating aspect of Oliver's comprehensive work is the sheer diversity of housing types in different societies. He illustrates the interrelated roles that belief systems, status, territoriality, wealth, technology, and climate play in determining the form housing takes.

The study of a community often begins with mapping the layout of housing (see pp.48-57 and pp.62-9), but it may be equally important to examine the nature of houses in some detail, especially if there are obvious differences in their quality and size. A check-list of questions that could be addressed includes:

What materials are used in house construction?
Is the housing suitable for climatic conditions?
What is the size of each house?
How many rooms are there? What are their functions?
How many people occupy each house? (see pp.48-57)
What family group type occupies each house? (see pp.48-57)
Who owns each house? The community, family, or the state?
What is the estimated value of the house?
What furnishing and facilities does each house have?
Was there labour co-operation in housing construction?
What is the size of the housing lot?
Is there evidence of any garden crops?
What is the spatial relation of houses to each other?
Where are fields, water, and pastures located in relation to housing?

Are there links between housing types and economic stratification?
Is there any evidence of homelessness?
Are dwellings decorated?
What values and symbols are associated with dwellings?
Who pays for and cares for public buildings, ceremonial houses, etc?

Estimating the annual cost of housing is fraught with difficulty. Strictly speaking, the annual consumption of housing equals its rate of depreciation. However, houses often increase in value while they are being 'consumed'; in these cases appreciation rather depreciation occurs. In most locations, though, this appreciation is not realized because houses and land are rarely sold. Housing costs estimates will therefore have to be made in the light of particular circumstances. One strategy may be to quantify the cost of bought housing construction materials (see pp.175-81) or the labour time spent in construction (see pp.103-14).

Among some groups, like mobile Australian Aborigines who still construct housing from year to year, or season to season, the production and consumption of housing is of limited economic significance; houses are constructed in a few hours, abandoned after a few months, and then reconstructed the following year.

In other situations, housing is not just shelter, but can also be regarded as an input in production. This is particularly the case with informal activities (see pp.153-5) and cottage industries. For example, in Ennew's (1980) study of crofters on the Western Isles off Scotland, there is a putting-out system and many households participate in the weaving of Harris tweed at home. Houses must be regarded as a production input in such situations (see pp.137-40).

Many consumer durables have multiple uses. For example, modern four-wheel-drive vehicles are the most highly valued durable item in remote Australian Aboriginal communities. On the one hand, vehicles can markedly increase productivity in hunting and must be regarded as technological inputs; on the other hand, they are used for a range of other social and cultural activities (like visiting kin and attending religious ceremonies) that limit the time available for hunting activities (Altman 1987). Pelto (1973) discusses a similar mixed impact associated with the snowmobile revolution in Finland. The methodological challenge in such situations is to decide what component of consumption is materially productive and what part is significant for social or cultural reproduction.

CONCLUSION

Anthropologists do not need to be reminded that food, clothing, and shelter are symbols that convey messages about power, status, and authority, that they are modes of communication like language, kinesics, and proxemics. Economists, on the other hand, have to be reminded of the importance of symbolism. Douglas and Isherwood attempted to do this in *The World of Goods* (1978). This polemical book was addressed to economists who, for the most part, adopt a rather dogmatic utilitarian approach to consumption. Their book has had almost no impact within the economics profession.

What seems to be at stake here is a choice between an approach that emphasizes personal use (economics) and an approach that focuses on interpersonal relations (anthropology). But this is not the only issue. For anthropology 'value' has a symbolic meaning and refers to 'prestige', 'status', and the like; for economics, 'value' usually means 'price'. The two disciplines have a communication problem, the root cause of which is that anthropology is primarily concerned with primary data analysis, while economics usually involves tertiary data analysis (see pp.4-7). At the primary data level, drawing the artificial boundaries between economy and culture, economy and religion, economy and language, economy and ecology, and so on, is an extremely difficult task. Indeed, one of the great advantages of the ethnographic approach is that the complex relationship between these factors can be examined to a much greater extent than is possible at a more abstract level of analysis.

Methods for the analysis of symbols are beyond the scope of this book; however, some indication of how these issues might be integrated into an economic analysis is given in the next chapter.

Chapter Nine

CIRCULATION

INTRODUCTION

Circulation mediates production and consumption; it includes the distribution of the means of production (land, labour, technology), the exchange and distribution of output, and the redistribution of stocks between members of a given population. Flows of output are often mediated by currencies; these are distinguished by their high velocity of circulation and their relative independence from the production process. Circulation is also the sphere from which many tertiary economic activities such as money lending, transport, and other services originate.

This chapter discusses a number of techniques for analysing these different aspects of circulation. The emphasis is on the economy as a totality: not only do we examine the methodological implications of the fact that circulation mediates production and consumption, we also stress the need to see the economy as a total social phenomenon where religion, politics, and the like find simultaneous expression (Mauss 1925: 1).

Analysis of circulation in any economy is an extremely complex task. This is because data must be collected from three different perspectives: the giver's, the receiver's, and the observer's. If these three perspectives are not distinguished, fieldwork data will be of limited value and the analysis confused. The ethnographer who can master the general ethno-accounting principles outlined here will, we believe, find it relatively easy to organize data on any exchange system, whether it be the mechanics of *kula* (Campbell 1983) or the workings of the 'invisible hand' of world markets.

RECONCILING PRODUCTION AND CONSUMPTION

The previous chapters have been concerned with techniques for collecting data on production, with particular emphasis being given to primary production. The fact that the majority of the world's population is engaged in agricultural activity of one form or another has provided the justification for this bias. However, it is also true that many primary producers diversify by engaging in different forms of secondary production and tertiary activity. In the village of Torand (see pp. 69–76) rice farming was the central focus of the villagers' lives; but they also hunted, gathered, fished, traded, worked as wage labourers, drove rickshaws and trucks, lent and borrowed money, and gambled. At Momega outstation (see pp. 76–80), hunting, fishing, and gathering were the main economic activities; but the people there also produced artefacts for sale, worked as wage labourers, received welfare, and gambled. By concentrating on the dominant economic activity – whether primary, secondary, or tertiary – the fieldworker has no option but to spend proportionally less time investigating subsidiary, but nevertheless important, activities. However, by reconciling data collected on production with those on consumption, gaps in the data base will be highlighted and new research questions posed.

The key to reconciling production with consumption is the following simple equation:

$$\text{income} = \text{expenditure} + \text{net savings} + \text{net transfers.}$$

'Income' refers to the revenue derived from primary, secondary or tertiary economic activity; 'expenditure' refers to the outlays for food, clothing and shelter; 'net savings' equal savings minus dissavings; and 'net transfers' equal net outflows from the study area. The equation can be applied to data collected for individuals, households, villages, communities and even nations. Its use presupposes that the relevant economic units have been defined (see pp.45-57) and that cash and non-cash data on production and consumption for a given time period have been collected using consistent criteria.

At Momega outstation, cash income totalled $20,830 in 1979–80. Of this, $5,850 was received from the sale of art and craft and $14,980 in the form of welfare payments from the government. Cash expenditure of $16,285, savings of $1,355, and net cash transfers to other communities of $1,210 were recorded for the ten-month study period. These items totalled $18,850, leaving an unaccounted proportion of income that amounted to $1,980. Altman collected information on the incomes and expenditures of individuals and households; disaggregation revealed that the statistical discrepancy was the sum of a number of small errors and omissions.

Another of Altman's aims was to examine the claim that outstation communities in Arnhem Land such as Momega were entirely dependent on social security transfers from the welfare state. He kept detailed daily records of the bush foods that were hunted and gathered; values were imputed to these products by calculating how much producers would have to spend in order to procure the equivalent foods He found that primary subsistence production accounted for 64 per cent of total cash and imputed income; art and craft 10 per cent; and pensions 26 per cent. A time allocation study revealed that 72 per cent of productive labour time was spent on subsistence activities; this important cross-check (see pp.103-14), together with others (see pp.181-94), enabled him to disprove the claim that the economy was entirely dependent on social security (Altman 1987: 54).

The particular circumstances of Altman's fieldwork made it possible to collect comprehensive cash data on income and expenditure. For example, supplies were delivered fortnightly by a mobile store and Altman recorded all the transactions that took place on these occasions. However, situations like this are rare; most researchers will be forced to adopt less precise techniques for reconciling production with consumption.

In Torand village the existence of numerous markets and shops made it impossible for Gregory (n.d.) to collect comprehensive cash flow data when he was there in 1982-3. However, reasonably accurate measures of the production/consumption balance for each household were derived from data on the distribution of population, rice-land holdings and cattle between households. Table 9.1 shows the relevant details for four of the thirty-one households in the village.

Gregory calculated that a rice-land to population ratio in excess of one implied that rice production exceeded rice consumption. This was checked by direct observation and inquiry. It was found that Gopi's household always produced a surplus of rice, that

Table 9.1 Wealth of selected households in Torand village

Head	Population	Cattle (nos)	Land/population (ha per capita)
Gopi	12	16	1.67
Sukhchand	14	13	0.46
Panka	12	6	0.25
Chamru	10	nil	0.10

Source: Gregory (n.d.)

Sukhchand's household sometimes broke even, but more often than not ran out of rice three months before harvest, that Panka's household never broke even and had to buy rice for up to nine months of the year, while Chamru's was virtually landless and had to buy rice every week. Direct observation and questioning revealed how the deficit households survived. Chamru, for example, a member of the herder caste, earned most of his income from following his caste specialization. Panka's household presented an initial problem because it was difficult to reconcile Panka's wealth in terms of cattle and relatively affluent lifestyle with the poverty of his landholdings. Being a member of the gardening caste meant that his wife earned some income from daily market sales of vegetables. His son also earned some extra money working as an occasional day labourer for the public works department. However, the little money this brought in could not have sustained his lifestyle. The puzzle was solved one day when Gregory observed a member of the Gond tribe pay Panka ten rupees (equivalent to slightly more than a day's wages) for palm juice collected from a tree on Panka's land. A quick check on the distribution of palm trees revealed that most happened to lie on Panka's land; it became obvious that Panka was receiving a monopoly rent. An additional culturally significant fact is that Panka's caste rules do not permit the consumption of fermented palm juice; gardeners in this area smoke marijuana, which is readily available from government controlled stores.

Rice surplus households of Gopi's type pose different methodological problems. This is because there is no discrepancy to be explained, which makes it easy to overlook important additional sources of income. Cross-checks can pick up some of these omissions. An interview with Chamru, for example, revealed that he had borrowed money from Gopi. Interviews with other households revealed that Gopi had lent them money too. This gave Gopi's household access to additional land because money lending in this village involves the pawning of land for cash rather than the payment of interest on money borrowed (Gregory 1988). It must not be assumed that relatively well-off households are always money lenders though. An abundance of assets can sometimes mean an abundance of both debt and credit, as Hobson's (1978) study of a south Indian joint family illustrates.

The following check-list of some of the different types of economic activity may be useful when reconciling data on production and consumption:

Primary economic activity
  Hunting
  Fishing
  Foraging
  Herding
  Farming
  Mining
Secondary economic activity
  Manufacturing (artisan)
  Manufacturing (industrial)
  Building and construction
Tertiary economic activity
  Transport (road, water, air, maintenance and repair)
  Communication
  Commerce (wholesale, retail, storage)
  Finance (banking and money lending, insurance, investment)
  Education
  Health
  Government services
  Professional services (legal, accounting, hairdressing, contracting)
  Religious services
  Personal services (gambling, hotels, domestic service, hospitality)

This list can be further subdivided into so-called 'formal' and 'informal' categories: road transport includes motor taxis and rickshaws; health includes doctors and shamanic healers; hospitality includes entertainers and prostitutes, and so on (see pp.153-5). This formal/informal distinction was developed by an ethnographer (Hart 1973) who argued, *pace* orthodox economic theory, that people in the informal sectors were positively employed, 'even if often for erratic and low returns' (Hart 1987: 845). Hart's essay, which has now become part of the development economist's orthodoxy, has led to much debate over the validity of the formal/informal distinction but very little direct observation of the 'erratic and low returns' of the slum dwellers in cities. Hart's contribution was to draw attention to an important subject of study, not to develop abstract distinctions. Books such as Guinness's (1986) on an Indonesian urban slum should be consulted by those with a specialist ethnographic interest in this subject.

SOCIAL RELATIONS OF DISTRIBUTION AND EXCHANGE

What is the principle whereby the thing received has to be repaid? This question, a modified version of Mauss's (1925: 1), can be a useful starting point for research in this area. Mauss's claim is that the answer should be found in the total social phenomenon where 'all kinds of institutions find simultaneous expression: religious, legal, moral, and economic'. It may be necessary to divide up a society into discrete parts for analytical purposes. Our concept of the 'economy' is one such example, but this theoretical device is a tool for understanding social complexity not for eliminating it.

The existence of a plethora of theory on exchange is both an aid and an obstacle for the contemporary fieldworker. Consider the distinction between gifts and commodities (Gregory 1982). This is a simplified abstraction from ethnographic data; its primary use lies at the secondary data level of analysis. While abstractions of this kind may help the ethnographer in the formulation of a research programme, they should not be used as instruments of field research because they are always subject to revision in the light of new empirical evidence. The ethnographer's concern should be with ambiguity and complexity when it comes to the analysis of di tribution and exchange; attempts should be made to develop new exchange taxonomies by analysing transactions in the light of social relations of which they are part.

Exchange can be defined in general terms as the simultaneous action that occurs when transactor A gives transactor B object x and B gives A object y (where A and B are individuals or groups and x and y are things). Logically speaking, circulation is where more than two transactors exchange a number of products. It also includes the distribution of the means of production between households (see pp. 48-57).

In a simple exchange there are three categories of exchange relations to investigate: the relationship between the transactors (A and B), the relation of the transactors to the objects exchanged (A to x, B to y), and the relations between the objects exchanged (x to y). The following range of questions could be asked in such a situation:

Relations between transactors
    1 What is the place of origin of the transactors?
    2 What is the economic status of the transactors?
    3 What is the social status of the transactors?
    4 Are transactors linked by kinship or marriage?
    5 Are they friends, enemies, or strangers?
    6 What is the history of their relationship?
Relations between transactors and objects
    7 Did the giver produce the object exchanged?
    8 If not, then how was it acquired from the producer?
    9 What rights of disposal does the giver have?
    10 Is the giver acting on behalf of others?
    11 For what purpose does the receiver intend to use the object?
    12 What rights and obligations does the receiver have over objects?
Relations between the objects
    13 What is the physical nature of the objects transacted?
    14 Are they symbols? If so, of what?
    15 What quantities are transacted?
    16 Are the objects equivalent in any sense?
    17 What is the basis of any equivalence: identity? synonymy? equality? (see pp. 16–17)
    18 Are the magnitudes of these objects measured by an ordinal or cardinal scale? (see p. 16)

This list can be extended by posing questions concerning the function of the transaction, its history, and the future obligations it creates. The aim should be to construct a synoptic table of the categories of transactors involved, the types of objects, and the forms of exchange. Malinowski's (1922: 177-94) discussion of seven forms of exchange and eight types of relationship between transactors found in the Trobriands remains a model of the method to be followed, although it has proved to be incorrect in some matters of detail (Leach and Leach 1983).

His list of the forms of exchange included:

1 Pure gifts
2 Customary payments, re-paid irregularly, and without strict equivalence
3 Payment for services rendered
4 Gifts returned in economically equivalent form (see pp. 16–17)
5 Exchange of material goods against privileges, titles and non-material possessions
6 Ceremonial barter and deferred payment
7 Trade, pure and simple

His list of the forms of personal relationship included:

a Matrilineal kinship
b Marriage ties
c Relationships-in-law
d Clanship
e The relationship of personal friendship
f Fellow-citizenship in a village community
g Relationship between chiefs and commoners
h Relationship between any two tribesmen

Lists like this can then be used to form new matrices linking forms of exchange with types of relationship. In this case, for example, '1' occurs with 'b'; '2' occurs mainly with 'c', but also with 'g', and so on (Malinowski 1922: 191).

Matrices are useful means of summarizing complex data on transactions involving many people and objects. They allow many complex linkages to be grasped at a glance, and are also extremely useful for highlighting gaps in one's data. Suppose, for example, that food transaction data of the following form were collected in an Indian village:

Brahmins (B) will only eat food cooked by members of their caste. Carpenters (C) and Gardeners (G) said they would only

eat from the Brahmins; Blacksmiths (S) maintained that they
would eat from Rajputs (R) and Farmers (F) as well, but not
from Carpenters; Farmers said that they would eat from
Rajputs and Blacksmiths, but not from Carpenters.

(adapted from Mayer 1960: 39)

These data have many gaps which are immediately apparent when
these relations are expressed in matrix form:

		Receivers					
		B	R	C	G	S	F
	B	o	?	o	o	o	?
	R	x	o	x	x	o	o
Givers	C	x	?	o	o	x	x
	G	x	?	x	o	?	?
	S	x	?	x	x	o	o
	F	x	?	x	x	o	o

Acceptance of food is represented by 'o' and rejection by 'x'; the
question marks represent the gaps. Thus, the Rajputs must be
interviewed to determine their commensal rules; the Farmers must
be asked whether they would accept food from Gardeners and
Brahmins; and the Blacksmiths must be asked whether they accept
food from Gardeners.

Once these data are gathered, the matrix can be used to analyse
the hierarchy of caste ranking as Marriott (1968) and Dumont
(1966) have done. An example of the usefulness of matrices for
analysing kinship terms and prices can be found in Gregory
(1982).

Much can be learnt about the social relations of exchange and
distribution by paying careful attention to the details of particular
cases, especially those involving disputes. Consider the following
case from the Papua New Guinea Highlands:

One Friday night Amara was in her house talking with three
fellow villagers. Amara's husband and another man and
woman came into the house. All had been drinking. Amara's
husband asked for her money to buy more beer. She refused,
saying they needed the money to look after their children. If
she gave him the money for beer they would have none left.
Amara's husband hit her and she fought back, losing her grip
on the infant she was holding. The child was caught by one of
the men who had been in the house chatting with her. As

Amara and her husband fought, the inebriated woman accompanying the husband joined the fight against Amara and the contents of the house were strewn on the floor.

Amara filed a complaint in the Village Court against her husband and her other assailant. A judge summed up the case after the three parties testified. He said that Amara was justified in keeping the money because it would have been wasted on beer. Amara's husband and the female assailant were each ordered to pay three kina court fines.

(Sexton 1986: 68)

An analysis of cases of this type will provide insights into gender relations, the impact of cash cropping, the role of the state, and the effectiveness of brute force in bringing about desired ends. Cases like the following one from northern Australia provide interesting information about the social obligations to share:

there was a Lorrkun ceremony at Marrgulidban and en route two Momega men, Mar and Jar, shot thirty-four ducks and a wallaby. They openly presented half the ducks to their father-in-law Dja, and consumed or gave away the rest of the ducks. The wallaby was hidden to be cooked later, but a child discovered the wallaby under some blankets in the back of the Toyota in which they were travelling. Dja heard of this and immediately demanded that the young men cook the wallaby. The hunters complied with his wishes somewhat shame-facedly.

(Altman 1987: 147-8)

Malinowski also stressed the importance of paying close attention to the language of exchange (and production). Much can be understood about the process of price determination by recording details of particular transactions. This technique was pioneered by Firth (1946: 202) and utilized by Alexander in her *Trade, Traders and Trading in Rural Java* (1987). She taped bargaining sessions and her analysis of these dialogues not only enabled her to understand how prices are agreed upon, but also provided many insights into other aspects of Javanese culture.

Finally, it is important to remember that much can be learnt about exchange by simply watching. As Alexander notes; 'The most important source of information ... was the hours I spent watching the business activities of thirty women traders' (Alexander 1987: 8). The importance of this form of observation cannot be over-emphasized. It is necessary to spend many long hours, even months, just watching transactions in the early stages of fieldwork (Smith 1985: 300). When Gregory began fieldwork on the rural markets of Bastar he made the mistake of thinking this was unnecessary because the people in the markets seemed to be buying and selling objects in a very familiar way. After a couple of abortive attempts to conduct a survey he decided to adopt the watching technique. He spent two months travelling with a relatively wealthy silver merchant on his daily rounds to the weekly markets in various towns. The merchant had a fixed daily and weekly routine: on Monday he left at 8 a.m. to travel the 20 kilometres to Sampur by jeep with twenty other merchants of his caste; on Tuesday he left at 7 a.m. to travel the 50 kilometres to Makdi; and so on. By adopting this routine Gregory became a familiar face; he slowly began to develop a 'feel' for silver merchants' marketing behaviour and the social relations of the seven daily markets attended. Over time he gradually began to widen the circle of merchants he observed, starting first with other silver merchants and then moving on to the poorer glass bangle merchants. This qualitative overview of the market provided the basis of later informed questioning and quantitative data collection.

WORLD PRICES AND MONEY

The growth and expansion of the market economy has created a high degree of interdependence in the world economy. The economic livelihood of previously isolated people is now influenced by political and ecological events in distant regions. The economic vehicles for the transmission of these effects are prices: frosts in Brazil send coffee prices soaring and the coffee producing areas of highlands Papua New Guinea become flush with money; a fall in the world price of tin upsets the delicate balance between wages, prices, and profits and sets off a wave of protest and political action or of repression among the Bolivian tin miners (Nash 1979: 210).

The aim of studying world prices is not so much to understand how the world economy works as to assess the impact of changing prices on the lives of farming and labouring households. World prices are part of the economic environment and their influence must be studied in a way analogous to that in which the effects of the sun and the rain are assessed. This presupposes some knowledge of world economic history, but it is important to remember that the impact of the world market is everywhere different.

An immediate orientation can be obtained by taking a broad historical overview. Books such as Wolf's *Europe and the People without History* (1982) and Wallerstein's *The Modern World System* (1974) are useful starting points because they give a synoptic view of the evolution of the present world economy over the past four centuries. Of more immediate interest to fieldworkers, though, are the trends of the past four decades.

The standard source of international statistics on many aspects of contemporary international and domestic finance is the International Monetary Fund's *International Financial Statistics*. This is a monthly report and is published in conjunction with a year-book containing annual data for thirty years beginning in 1953 (IMF 1985). The reports contain information on, among other things, world commodity prices; for each member country there are data on exchange rates, prices, production, balance of payments, population and literally hundreds of other economic variables. Almost any data on world markets that an anthropologist is likely to need will be found here.

Like all official data, the IMF figures must be treated with due caution, but it is impossible to take a critical approach to the data unless one has some notion of what the terms 'money' and 'price' mean. The IMF statistics are premised on the validity of the US dollar as an adequate standard of price. While this was a reasonable assumption to make in the 1950s and 1960s, the declining relative value of the dollar in the 1970s and 1980s has rendered this assumption suspect. The interpretative problems this gives rise to are best illustrated with a simple example.

Suppose the researcher is doing fieldwork in a Japanese village where surplus wealth is accumulated in the form of gold, wheat is grown for export, and rice for domestic consumption. Such a fieldworker will need to know something about trends in world prices for rice, wheat, gold, and the yen in order to ask informed questions during fieldwork.

An historical approach to the problem will yield the following statistical series from the IMF's 1985 statistical yearbook:

Table 9.2 World prices of selected commodities

Year	Rice*	Wheat*	Gold*	Yen*
1960	179	1.73	35	.0028
1965	183	1.88	35	.0028
1970	190	1.66	35	.0028
1975	419	5.23	161	.0033
1980	496	5.43	608	.0049
1985	382	2.68	317	.0048

Source: International Monetary Fund (1985)

* US dollars per tonne of rice
* US dollars per bushel of wheat
* US dollars per fine ounce of gold
* US dollar per one Japanese yen

Consider the world price of rice. This is expressed in US dollars per tonne. It is obvious that this rate remained relatively stable until 1970 when rapid inflation set in; prices more than doubled in the five years to 1975, increased by a third in the next five years, and dropped back by somewhat in the five years to 1985.

Different measures of the world price of rice can be obtained by using other standards such as wheat, gold or yen. These standards can be calculated by dividing the dollar price of rice by the dollar prices of wheat, gold, and yen respectively. In 1960, for example, the wheat price of gold was 103 bushels of wheat per tonne of rice which is calculated by dividing the price of rice by the price of wheat ($179/1.73 = 103$). The gold price of rice for 1960 is 5.11 fine ounces of gold per tonne of rice ($179/35$), while the yen price is

Table 9.3 World price of rice using different standards

	Wheat standard*	Gold standard*	Yen standard*
1960	103	5.11	63,900
1965	97	5.23	65,300
1970	114	5.43	67,800
1975	79	2.60	126,900
1980	91	0.82	101,200
1985	142	1.20	79,600

* price of rice/price of wheat = bushels of wheat/tonne of rice
* price of rice/price of gold = fine ounces of gold/tonne of rice
* price of rice/price of yen = yen/tonne of rice

63,900 (179/.0028). Calculations of this type for the other years will produce three new series for the world price of rice as shown in Table 9.3.

It is clear from Table 9.3 that the standard of world price affects the interpretation that can be given to the trend in the world price of rice: when wheat is used as standard, the world price of rice fluctuates widely; when gold is used as standard the price declines sharply; and when the yen is used prices rise to 1975 and decline thereafter.

These various measures of the world price of rice are a further illustration of the problems inherent in any valuation exercise (see pp.150-3). The conclusion to be drawn is not that valuation is a useless exercise, but that any problem must be approached from as many different angles as possible before a final interpretation is reached. In this particular case, the fluctuations in the wheat price of rice are a reflection of changing world conditions in the production of wheat and rice; the gold and dollar prices of rice reflect the global instability caused by the persistent US balance of payment deficit and, in the Reagan years, of the ballooning budget deficit; while a comparison of the yen price of rice with the dollar price reflects the relative decline of labour productivity in the USA.

Issues such as this are too often seen as being beyond the scope of anthropology. Every anthropologist is familiar with Malinowski's *Argonauts of the Western Pacific* (1922) but how many have read his *Freedom and Civilization* (1947) which contains his reflections on a world at war and prospects for post-war settlement? World issues affect anthropology and anthropologists whether we like it or not. As Marcus and Fischer (1986) demonstrate, developments in the world political economy not only affect the mode of livelihood of both observer and observed, they also affect the way anthropologists think and write. The current trends in western thought, which focus on micropatterns of disorder rather than macropatterns of order, they argue, 'may have much to do with the unfavorable shift in the relative position of American power and influence in the world, and the widespread perception of the dissolution of the ruling post-war model of the liberal welfare state at home' (Marcus and Fischer 1986: 9).

CEREMONIAL EXCHANGE

Ceremonial exchanges can be defined as those exchange transactions such as *kula, moka, potlatch,* and the giving that occurs at Christmas time, weddings, and other ritualized occasions. These events obviously have an economic dimension; but this is inextricably combined with religion, myth, politics, and the like. As any attempt to draw an arbitrary line isolating the economic from the non-economic will seriously limit the value of data collected on these occasions, the researcher should strive to analyse the event as a Maussian total social phenomenon.

The collection of data on ceremonial exchange activities raises many complex accounting, conceptual, and interpretative issues. In the following discussion we address some of these through the use of an imaginary example. Our aims in this exercise are threefold. First, it provides a comprehensive example of how economic data should be cross-checked from a number of different perspectives. Second, it attempts to illustrate interpretative problems inherent in primary data analysis. Finally, by using an imaginary example we hope to be able to convey something of the human dimension of fieldwork that is very difficult to illustrate in a methods book of this type.

The myth of the Marché

Imagine yourself suddenly set down surrounded by all your gear, alone on a Mediterranean beach, while the helicopter that has brought you to this island disappears into the clouds. You have discovered an island society that has survived to the present day in its pristine form. Imagine further that you are a beginner, without previous experience, with only a manual of research methods on economic anthropology to guide you. This exactly describes the experiences of our ethnographer on first entering the Isle of Bourse. He was intoxicated with delight at his discovery and set about his fieldwork like a man possessed. He worked sixteen hours a day, never stopping to read a novel, worried that other anthropologists might find the place before he had finished his fieldwork.

Our ethnographer has now been in the field eleven months. He has discovered that the island is divided into three groups: *les*

212

propriétaires des terres, la classe productive, and *la class stérile* whose functions are to manage, to produce wheat, and to manufacture iron products respectively. He arrived at the beginning of the agricultural year in October (according to the local calendar); harvest has just been completed, and the year is about to end with the annual *marché*, which is held each year on the autumnal equinox. We take the following extracts from his diary:

22 September Annual market (*marché*) day. Much general merriment and drinking. No women were to be seen, as usual. Most exciting day of fieldwork so far, but conditions of work the worst ever. My normally co-operative informants were most unhelpful and downright rude to me. I was totally overwhelmed by the events of the day and was unable to record anything accurately. Furthermore, just as I was beginning to feel that I was getting to know the language they began to use words I had never heard before. Fortunately I was able to record the oratory used in the elaborate exchange ritual called *Marché* (as distinct from *marché*) but a magus who was in attendance tried to smash my equipment when I tried to record his chants. *Marché* with a small 'm' refers, it seems, to the thousands of small transactions that precede the big 'M'. My attempts to record the small transactions were a total failure because the transactors would turn their backs on me when I tried to question them. However, I did notice that secrecy seemed to be a feature of all the transactions. Some people seemed to be using a sign language to speak to each other, while others used what looked like a special script. My failure to record details of just one of these transactions was somewhat offset by the realization that unless I recorded all of them, which was clearly impossible, the data would have been useless anyway. The secrecy and multiplicity of the *marché* transactions contrasted sharply with the public nature of the six ritualized *Marché* transactions. The transactions were conducted with just two bags of silver and mediated on every occasion by a ritualized chant. The proceedings were opened when Emile, leader of the *productives*, danced up to Jean-Paul, leader of the *propriétaires*, and aggressively threw two bags of silver at Jean-Paul's feet. Jean-Paul picked up one bag and threw it back at Emile's feet and then picked up the other and threw it at Marcel, the leader of the *stériles*. Marcel picked up his bag and threw it at

Emile who promptly picked it up and threw it back. Marcel once more threw it back to Emile who picked up the two bags he arrived with and walked away. The ceremony was over. This ceremony reminded me of a speeded up version of *kula*. It does not have the symmetry of *kula* though. The two bags do not move in opposition to each other; furthermore, one bag of silver has a velocity of two moves per *Marché*, the other a velocity of six. Of course I must not jump to interpretative conclusions too soon. What is the function of *Marché*? What is its structure? What is the principle whereby the gift received has to be repaid? What force is there in the thing given which compels the recipient to make a return? These are the questions I must pursue over the next few weeks. But I am anxious that I will never find out. When I attempted to pursue the meaning of *Marché* transactions with Emile, Marcel, and Jean-Paul immediately after the event they were extremely rude to me. Frustrated and depressed I decided to give up observing and participate in the drinking.

23 September Bad hangover. Stayed in my cabin transcribing tapes. Preliminary translation of *Marché* oratory as follows:

First transaction
    Giver: '*Loyer.* 2,000 *livres.* 480,000 *deniers.* 12 *deniers* in a *sol.* 12 moons in a year. Hey! Hey! Hey!'
    Receiver: '*Loyer.* 80 *arpents.* One *domaine.* The Isle of Bourse. Hey! Hey! Hey!'
Second transaction
    Giver: '*Achat.* 1,000 *livres.* 240,000 *deniers.* 12 *deniers* in a *sol.* 12 moons in a year. Hey! Hey! Hey!'
    Receiver: '*Vente.* Wheat. 50 *setiers.* Hey! Hey! Hey!'
Third transaction
    Giver: '*Achat.* 1,000 *livres.* 240,000 *deniers*', and so on.
    Receiver: '*Vente.* Iron. 50 *milliers*', and so on.
Fourth transaction
    Giver: '*Achat.* 1,000 *livres*', and so on.
    Receiver: '*Vente.* Wheat. 50 *setiers*', and so on.
Fifth transaction
    Giver: '*Achat.* 1,000 *livres*', and so on.
    Receiver: '*Vente.* Iron. 50 *milliers*' and so on.

Sixth transaction
  Giver: '*Achat.* 1,000 *livres*', and so on.
  Receiver: '*Vente.* Wheat. 50 *setiers*', and so on.

I am feeling bewildered. What is the meaning of all these words?

24 September Tried to see Jean-Paul but he was being examined by the doctor who was in the village for his annual visit. Went to Emile's place instead. He was delighted to see me and invited me in for *café*. We talked about the *Marché*. He teased me about my drunken behaviour on the day and said that I was a real *productive* now. We spent the entire day going over the details of the six transactions. He could not have been more helpful. He explained the meanings of all the terms and I took copious notes.

25 September Spent the day indoors trying to put the information Emile gave me into some order. Produced the following synoptic table of terms.

The language of exchange
loyer = rent
marché = numerous small private transactions
Marché = the six public transactions
bourse = bags containing the silver
achat = purchase
vente = sale
livre = face value of gold and silver coins (£)
sol = gold coin (s)
denier = silver coin (d)
setier = measure of capacity
domaine = measures of area; district
arpent = measure of area; sub-district
millier = measure of weight
prix = price

Standards of value and price
1 *livre* = 20 *sols*
1 *sol* = 12 *deniers*
price of wheat = *livres*/*setier* = £20
price of iron = *livres*/*millier* = £20

Standards of weights and measures
1 *domaine* = 80 *arpents*
1 *muid* = 12 *setiers*
1 *millier* = 10 *cwt*

Some startling associations occurred to me. I figured that 1 livre = 20 sols = 240 denier. Using the first letters as symbols gives £1 = 20s =240d which was very familiar indeed! Furthermore, *sol*, the gold coin, also means 'soil', and is a cognate of *soleil*, which means 'sun'. The symbolic equations *sol: denier* :: sun:moon :: 1:12 suggested themselves because there are approximately 12 lunar cycles in each calendar year. The oratory of exchange suggests that this interpretation is valid. Emile dismissed the idea as nonsense. I must check this idea with Marcel and Jean-Paul.

26-8 September Left at 4 a.m. for Marcel's village and arrived at 12 noon. He, too, was delighted to see me. We talked about the *Marché* and he, too, teased me about my drunken behaviour. You are a real *stérile* now he said. I gave him my interpretation of the *Marché* using my new-found knowledge of its language. He understood what I had to say but was not impressed; he then proceeded to give his explanation of it in his terms. I was astounded. I did not understand a word he was saying. We spent the next few days trying to translate his *langue marché stérile* into *langue marché productive* which I now realized was the dialect I was speaking. Some of the words like 'purchase' and 'sale' were easy to translate, but the terms for the standards of weight and measurement really stumped me. It was only after many hours of calculation and discussion – in retrospect, the patience of Marcel was unbelievable because I must have seemed like such a complete fool to him – that I realized the standards of weights and measures used in Marcel's village sub-district were different from those used in Emile's sub-district. I learnt that not only are there different standards for each of the 80 *arpents* in the *domaine*, but that they vary from year to year to ensure that prices always remained fixed at £20 for both wheat and iron. The *marché* transactions, the thousands of minor transactions that proceed the *Marché*, affect annual adjustments in these standards of weight and measure to ensure that prices never change. Because of the secrecy surrounding *marché* transactions, the manner in which this is brought about must for ever remain a mystery. According to my calculations there must be a minimum of 19,200 transactions.

29 September Arrived home from Marcel's at midday. I began to dwell on what I now knew. My heart sank. Should I collect data on all different standards? After hours of deliberation, and much anxiety, I decided against. It would take me at least a year and I simply have not got the time. I decided to create my own standard of weights and measures based on the system used in Emile's sub-district.

Ethnographer's standard for weights and measures
1 unit of wheat = 1 W = 1 *setier*
1 unit of iron = 1 I = 1 *millier*
1 bag of coins = 1 B = £1,000 = 20,000s = 240,000d
1 unit of land = 1 D = 1 *domaine*

This cleared away a host of false problems. I was now in a position to prepare the synoptic table of transactions.

Synoptic table of Marché transactions

Reference	Giver	Receiver	Description	Quantity	Value
1g	farmers	landlords	loyer	2B	£2,000
1r	landlords	farmers	domaine	1D	£2,000
2g	landlords	farmers	achat	1B	£1,000
2r	farmers	landlords	vente	50W	£1,000
3g	landlords	artisans	achat	1B	£1,000
3r	artisans	landlords	vente	50I	£1,000
4g	artisans	farmers	achat	1B	£1,000
4r	farmers	artisans	vente	50W	£1,000
5g	farmers	artisans	achat	1B	£1,000
5r	artisans	farmers	vente	50I	£1,000
6g	artisans	farmers	achat	1B	£1,000
6r	farmers	artisans	vente	50W	£1,000

The structure of the *Marché* was now obvious. The fundamental opposition *loyer/domaine* is the basis upon which an elaborate series of *achat/vente* oppositions are arrayed to form an encompassed totality. But what is the function of *Marché*? Are my inference about the landlord's role correct?

10 October Finally caught up with Jean-Paul, the landlord. He was not glad to see me. My relations with him are now at their lowest point ever. My drunken behaviour at the *Marché* was the end so far as he was concerned. He let it be known in no uncertain terms that I had become a *stérile* in his eyes. 'Why do you associate with those low class people? How many times have I told you not to have anything to do with them? Look at the food they eat. Look at the way they dress. They are not real people'. He did consent, however, to give a perfunctory account of the *Marché* from his perspective. It was in an aristocratic language which I did not understand. This did not confuse me. To the contrary, it was exactly what I had predicted. It left me feeling supremely confident that my inference about his structural role in the ceremonial exchange was correct.

12 October I met the doctor for the first time today as he was leaving the village for his next port of call. We chatted for a while about his work which involves circulating around the isle on an annual basis administering health care to the class of *propriétaires*. His route is set and he returns to Jean-Paul's village every year just before the time of *Marché*. He had being observing it for over twenty years now. He told me how it repeated itself exactly year in and year out, and that, yes, he had a diagnosis of its function. According to him the *Marché* is the central organ of the Isle of Bourse's economy and the bags of silver are the blood that is pumped through the organ to keep the economy alive. I thought his use of medical metaphors quaint and quite inappropriate. But then he took out a piece of paper and quickly sketched a zig-zag model of the *Marché*. I was thunderstruck and now knew exactly how Deacon must have felt when one of his informants sketched a diagrammatic model of the complicated Ambrym kinship system. He then proceeded to give me his exegesis of the *Marché*. I was dizzy with excitement. Not only did his analysis explain the functioning of the system, it also explained the origin of the terms *productive* and *stérile*. Up until now no one had the foggiest notion of why these classifications were used. When I pointed out to people that *stérile* meant 'sterile' they raised their eyebrows,

218

confessed that the connection had never occurred to them before, and thought no more about it (although I did notice that Marcel's consciousness seemed to have been raised by the revelation). For me, the contradiction between the obvious productiveness of the artisan class and its 'sterile' label was a source of some anxiety. I felt that unless I could explain the use of this term I would never understand the society. The good doctor solved this dilemma for me: 'The soil alone is productive', he said, 'because only mother earth has a womb; only she can create. The landowners are the brains; the iron workers unproductive like an appendix.' With this startling revelation, he bade me *au revoir*. After he left I spent the rest of the day thinking about his metaphor and the zig-zag diagram. I surrendered myself completely to the logic of metaphor. In a short time the penny dropped and the whole shebang fell into place. I formulated the following synoptic table of the doctor's symbolic equations:

Isle of Bourse = mother earth
silver coins = blood
les propriétaires = brain
la classe productive = womb
wheat = ?
la classe stérile = appendix
iron = ?

Damn it. Gaps in the data. Why did I not think to draw up this table while he was talking? No matter. It still gives me a new perspective on the *Marché* transactions.

The circulation of money in the Marché (the giver's perspective)

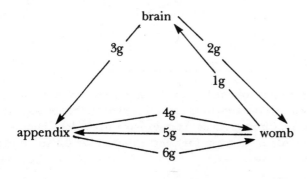

Starting with the womb, the blood flows to the brain (transaction 1g) where half of it is sent back to the womb (2g), and the other half flows to the appendix (3g). From the appendix, the blood pumps back and forth between the appendix and the womb (4g and 5g) and eventually returns to the womb (6g). This flow revitalizes the body for another year, during which time the blood sits in the womb ready for the circulation process to be repeated. The *Marché* is obviously a periodic market: a menstruating market where the blood flows annually. The metaphorical flow of blood, I inferred, literally facilitates the redistribution of newly produced stocks of wheat and iron in preparation for next year's production. This redistribution does not happen on the day of the *Marché*. Iron workers redistribute their products at various times throughout the year; farmers deliver before, during, and after the *Marché*. All we see during the ritual is the public declaration of the contracts.

Data on redistribution of stocks was, I now realized, implicit in my synoptic table. By taking the perspective of the receiver (r) rather than the giver (g) the following graphic representation of the redistribution of stocks is obtained:

The redistribution of stocks in the Marché (*the receiver's perspective*)

Class	Stocks held prior to the *Marché*	Stocks held after the *Marché*
Landlords	nil	50W + 50I
		(2r) (3r)
Farmers	150W	50I
		(5r)
Artisans	100I	100W
		(4r & 6r)

Thus the payment of rent gives the landowners the ability to purchase wheat (2r) and iron (3r). The money the artisans get from the sale of iron enables them to buy wheat (4r). When the farmers buy iron from them (5r), the artisans have the money to buy more wheat (6r).

24 October I have spent the past ten days working day and night trying to reconcile the doctor's analysis of the *Marché* with the data I have gathered to date. I have decided that his analysis is in error. He has confused metaphors with reality when in fact they are always models of reality. This leads him to the demonstrably false claim that the *stérile* class is unproductive and that the surplus product of the society is only £2,000 when it is in fact £5,000. I came to this conclusion when I prepared household budgets for each of the three classes. There can be no doubt: the doctor's model contains a brilliant error. It is 'erroneous' in that it is a logically coherent conceptual framework based on false assumptions; but it is 'brilliant' in that it clarifies relations and leads to the truth. From my observations of the production and consumption process I knew that the wheat purchases by artisans in transaction (6) are used as raw materials in the manufacture of sculptures and that there were some intra-class non-market transfers: 100 units of wheat (imputed value £2,000) that the farmers retain for domestic consumption and the 100 units of iron (imputed value £2,000) that the artisans use to make their own tools. It was only through my discussions with the transactors that I ascertained which transactions are for final consumption and which are for future production. I generated a simplified, but more accurate synoptic table of transactions:

Total market and non-market transactions

Cash (market) transactions

1. Payment of rent by farmers to landowners £2,000
2. Food purchases by landowners from farmers £1,000
3. Sculptures purchased by landowners from artisans £1,000
4. Food purchases by artisans from farmers £1,000
5. Tool purchases by farmers from artisans £1,000
6. Raw materials purchases by artisans from farmers £1,000

Imputed (non-market) transactions

7. Wheat used as food by farmers, imputed value £2,000
8. Wheat used as seed by farmers, imputed value £2,000
9. Iron used as tools by artisans, imputed value £2,000

Using these production, consumption, and circulation data I made the following calculations:

Household budgets (ethnographer's perspective)

	Income (£)	Expenditure (£)
Landlord		
rent (1)	2,000	
food (2)		1,000
sculpture (3)		1,000
sub-total	2,000	2,000
Farmers		
sales (2+4+6)	3,000	
tools (5)		1,000
rent (1)		2,000
food [wages] (7)	2,000	2,000
seed (8)	2,000	2,000
sub-total	7,000	7,000
Artisans		
sales (3+5)	2,000	
raw materials (6)		1,000
food [wages] (4)		1,000
iron (9)	2,000	2,000
sub-total	4,000	4,000

I calculated the surplus of the society, the value added by the real producers, to be £5,000 by realizing that the farmers and artisans are self-employed workers and that transactions (4) and (7) are the wages they pay themselves. The society's surplus can be calculated as follows:

Surplus (value added)

Farmers	
rent (1)	£2,000
wages (7)	£2,000
Artisans	
wages (4)	£1,000
Total	£5,000

It is clear that the real productive classes are the farmers and the artisans, whereas the landlords are the unproductive class. The doctor not only cares for the health of the landlord class, but has also provided an indigenous explanation of the *Marché* that expresses the ideology of the élite.

*****

We interrupt our imaginary ethnographer's field diary at this point. Readers may be interested to learn that he interviewed the magus and collected the following comprehensive set of symbolic equations:

Magus's symbolic equations

sun = gold
moon = silver
mars = iron
Venus = copper
Jupiter = tin
Saturn = lead
Mercury = mercury
Isle of Bourse = androgyne
soil = womb
wheat = seed of womb
iron products = semen
artisans = sons of sun
farmers = daughters of the moon
landowners = appendix
Marché = sacred union

From some young women he collected the following truncated version of a myth which is transmitted from mother to daughter:

In the beginning the Sun created the race of landlords, the Men [sic] of Gold. In those days men lived like gods in unalloyed happiness. They did not toil with their hands, for earth brought forth her fruits without their aid. They did not know the sorrows of old age, and death was to them like passing away in a calm sleep. After they had gone hence, their spirits were appointed to dwell above the earth, guarding and helping the living. Sol next created the farmers, the Men of Silver, but they could not be compared in virtue and happiness with the Men of Gold. For many years they remained mere children, and as soon as they came to the full strength and stature of manhood they refused to do homage to the gods and fell to slaying one another. After death they became the good spirits who live within the earth. The artisans, the Men of Iron, followed, springing from ash-trees and having hearts which were hard and jealous, so that with them 'lust and strife' began to gnaw the world. All the works of their hands were in bronze. Through their own invention they fell; they passed away to the dark realm of Mars in the bowels of the earth unhonoured and unremembered.

On returning home our ethnographer wrote up his material using a radically new ethno-accounting perspective. He developed a theory of the Market based on the principle that for every purchase there must be a corresponding sale. Using this principle he proposed that the sterile class was productive and argued that emic perspectives are ideological constructions of élites. The book was received with critical acclaim, but it did not please everybody. Feminists attacked it for failing to give primacy to gender relations, marxists attacked it for not giving primacy to class relations, world system theorists attacked it for ignoring the role of the world economy, Freudians attacked it for ignoring sexual symbolism, and kinship specialists attacked it for completely failing to examine intra-class kinship relations. Everybody found the data fantastic and obliquely accused him of inventing many of them. However, before our ethnographer had time to reply to these criticisms it was discovered that scholars such as Quesnay (1756), Fox (1916), and Eliade (1956) had also visited the Isle of Bourse and made similar observations. Their work was well-known in other disciplines but, because of the barriers to the free trade of information within universities, it had taken many years to reach the anthropology discipline.

Meanwhile, on the Isle of Bourse, the inherent instability and disequilibrium in the island's economy intensified and class warfare broke out. The social structure of the island was turned upside down and the *stérile* class became dominant. They immediately set about instituting a host of economic and linguistic reforms. Uniform standards of weight and measure were established and prices were allowed to vary in markets which were now held daily. The new leaders referred to themselves as the 'industrial' class and the body metaphor of the island's economy was replaced with a mechanical one. The industrial class saw themselves as the 'engine' of economic growth. The word *bourse* acquired a new meaning. The bags containing the silver coins transacted at the annual *Marché* were destroyed in the revolution. The silver coins were demonetized and symbolic paper money began to circulate in its place. A new *Marché* building was constructed and the name *bourse* given to it. This new institution enabled the velocity of circulation of money to increase at an exponential rate, but then, one day, the bubble burst.

BIBLIOGRAPHY

Alexander, J. (1987) *Trade, Traders and Trading in Rural Java*, Singapore: Oxford University Press.

Alexander, P. (1982) *Sri Lankan Fishermen: Rural Capitalism and Peasant Society*, Monograph on South Asia No. 7, Canberra: Australian National University.

Altman, J.C. (1982a) 'Maningrida outstations: a preliminary economic overview', in E.A. Young and E.K. Fisk (eds) *Small Rural Communities*, Canberra: Development Studies Centre, Australian National University.

Altman, J.C. (1982b) 'Hunter-gatherers and the state: the economic anthropology of the Gunwinggu of north Australia', unpublished PhD thesis, Australian National University, Canberra.

Altman, J.C. (1983) *Aborigines and Mining Royalties in the Northern Territory*, Canberra: Australian Institute of Aboriginal Studies.

Altman, J.C. (1987) *Hunter-Gatherers Today: An Aboriginal Economy in North Australia*, Canberra: Australian Institute of Aboriginal Studies.

Altman, J.C. (1988) *Aborigines, Tourism, and Development: The Northern Territory Experience*, Darwin: Australian National University North Australia Research Unit.

Altman, J.C. and Dillon, M.C. (1988) 'Aboriginal land rights, land councils and the development of the Northern Territory', in D. Wade-Marshall and P. Loveday (eds) *North Australia: Problems and Prospects. vol. 1: Contemporary Issues in Development*, Darwin: Australian National University North Australia Research Unit.

Appadurai, A. (ed.) (1986) *The Social Life of Things: Commodities in Cultural Perspective*, Cambridge: Cambridge University Press.

ASA (1987) *Ethical Guidelines for Good Practice*, London: ASA.

Asad, T. (ed.) (1973) *Anthropology and the Colonial Encounter*, New York: Humanities Press.

Australian Bureau of Statistics (1987) *1984 Household Expenditure Survey, Australia: Household Characteristics*, ABS Cat. No. 65310, Canberra: Australian Bureau of Statistics.

226

Australian Commonwealth Department of Health (1986) *National Dietary Survey of Adults: 1983*, Canberra: Australian Government Publishing Service.

Balfet, H. (1965) 'Ethnographic observations in North Africa and archaeological interpretation: the pottery of the Maghreb', in F.R. Matson (ed.) *Ceramics and Man*, London: Methuen.

Baran, P. (1957) *The Political Economy of Growth*, New York: Monthly Review Press.

Baran, P. and Sweezy, P. (1966) *Monopoly Capital*, Harmondsworth, Middx: Penguin.

Baric, L. (1964) 'Some aspects of credit, saving and investment in a "non-monetary" economy (Rossel Island)' in R. Firth and B.S. Yamey (eds) *Capital, Saving and Credit in Peasant Societies*, Chicago: Aldine.

Barnard, A. and Good, A. (1984) *Research Practices in the Study of Kinship (ASA Research Methods in Social Anthropology 2)*, London: Academic Press.

Baudrillard, J. (1981) *For a Critique of the Political Economy of the Sign*, St Louis: Telos.

Becker, G.S. (1974) 'A theory of marriage', in T.W. Schultz (ed.) *Economics of the Family*, Chicago: University of Chicago Press.

Berger, T.R. (1985) *Village Journey: Report of the Alaska Native Review Commission*, New York: Hill & Wang.

Berlin, B., Breedlove, D.E. and Raven, P.H. (1973) 'General principles of classification and nomenclature in folk biology', *American Anthropologist* 75: 214-42.

Bernard, H.R., Killworth, P., Kronenfeld, D. and Sailer, L. (1984) 'The problem of informant accuracy: the validity of retrospective data', *Annual Review of Anthropology* 13: 495-517.

Bliss, C.J. and Stern, N.H. (1982) *Palanpur: the Economy of an Indian Village*, Oxford: Clarendon Press.

Bloch, M. (1954) *The Historian's Craft*, Manchester: Manchester University Press.

Bohannan, P. and Bohannan, L. (1968) *Tiv Economy*, Evanston, Ill: Northwestern University Press.

Borgerhoff Mulder, M. and Caro, T.M. (1985) 'The use of quantitative observational techniques in anthropology', *Current Anthropology* 26 (3): 323-35.

Borrie, W.D., Firth, R. and Spillius, J. (1957) 'The population of Tikopia, 1929 and 1952', *Population Studies* 10: 229-52.

Bourdieu, P. (1984) Distinction: A Social Critique of the Judgement of Taste, London: Routledge.

Bronson, B. (1972) 'Farm labour and the evolution of food production', in B. Spooner (ed.) *Population Growth: Anthropological Implications*, Cambridge, Mass.: MIT Press.

Campbell, S.F. (1983) 'Kula in Vakuta: the mechanics of Keda', in J.W. Leach and E. Leach (eds) *The Kula: New Perspectives in Massim Exchange*, Cambridge: Cambridge University Press.

Cane, S. and Stanley, O. (1985) *Land Use and Resources in Desert Homelands*, Darwin: Australian National University North Australia Research Unit.

Carlstein, T. (1982) *Time Resources, Society and Ecology*, London: Allen & Unwin.

Carrier, J. (1981) 'Ownership of productive resources on Ponam Island, Manus Province', *Journal de la Société des Océanistes* 37: 205-17.

Carroll, V. (ed.) (1975) *Pacific Atoll Populations*, Honolulu: University Press of Hawaii.

Cassanelli, L.V. (1986) 'Qat: changes in the production and consumption of a quasilegal commodity in northeast Africa', in A. Appadurai (ed.) *The Social Life of Things: Commodities in Cultural Perspective*, Cambridge: Cambridge University Press.

Chayanov, A.V. (1925) *The Theory of Peasant Economy*, edited by D. Horner, B. Kerblay and R.E.F. Smith, Homewood, Ill.: Irwin (1966).

Christy Jr., F.T. and Scott, A. (1965) *The Common Wealth in Ocean Fisheries*, Washington, DC: Resources for the Future Foundation.

Clammer, J. (ed.) (1978) *The New Economic Anthropology*, London: Macmillan.

Clammer, J. (ed.) (1987) *Beyond the New Economic Anthropology*, London: Macmillan.

Collmann, J. (1988) *Fringe Dwellers and Welfare: The Aboriginal Response to Bureaucracy*, St. Lucia, Queensland: University of Queensland Press.

Conant, F.P. (1984) 'Remote sensing, discovery and generalizations in human ecology', in E.F. Moran (ed.) *The Ecosystem Concept in Anthropology*, Boulder, CO: Westview Press.

Conklin, H.C. (1957) *Hanunóo Agriculture: A Report on an Integral System of Shifting Cultivation in the Philippines*, Rome: FAO.

Conklin, H.C. (1961) 'The study of shifting cultivation', *Current Anthropology* 2 (1): 27-61.

Conklin, H.C. (1980) *Ethnographic Atlas of Ifugao: A Study of Environment, Culture, and Society in Northern Luzon*, New Haven, CT: Yale University Press.

Cordell, J. (1974) 'The lunar-tide fishing cycle in northeastern Brazil', *Ethnology* 13: 379-92.

Crump, T. (1987) 'The alternative economy of alcohol in the Chiapas highlands', in M. Douglas (ed.) *Constructive Drinking: Perspectives on Drink from Anthropology*, Cambridge: Cambridge University Press.

Cutileiro, J. (1971) *A Portuguese Rural Society*, Oxford: Clarendon Press.

Dalton, G. (1978) 'Introduction', in G. Dalton (ed.) *Research in Economic Anthropology: An Annual Compilation of Research*, Greenwich, CT: JAI Press.

Dalton, G. and Köcke, J. (1983) 'The work of the Polanyi group: past, present, and future', in S. Ortiz (ed.) *Economic Anthropology: Topics and Theories*, Lanham, MD: University Press of America and Society for Economic Anthropology.

Davis, J. (1973) *Land and Family in Pisticci*, London: Athlone.

Debreu, G. (1959) *Theory of Value: An Axiomatic Analysis of Economic Equilibrium*, New Haven and London: Yale University Press (1971).

Dennis, N., Henriques, F., and Slaughter, C. (1969) *Coal is Our Life: An Analysis of a Yorkshire Mining Community*, London: Tavistock.

Devereux, G. (1967) *From Anxiety to Method in the Behavioral Sciences*, The Hague: Mouton and Company.

DeWalt, K.W., Kelly, P.B. and Pelto, G.H. (1980) 'Nutritional correlates of economic microdifferentiation in a Highland Mexican community', in N.W. Jerome, R.F. Kandel and G.H. Pelto (eds) *Nutritional Anthropology: Contemporary Approaches to Diet and Culture*, New York: Redgrave Publishing Company.

Douglas, M. (ed.) (1984) *Food in the Social Order: Studies of Food and Festivities in Three American Communities*, New York: Basic Books.

Douglas, M. (ed.) (1987) *Constructive Drinking: Perspectives on Drink from Anthropology*, Cambridge: Cambridge University Press.

Douglas, M. and Isherwood, B. (1978) *The World of Goods: Towards an Anthropology of Consumption*, Harmondsworth, Middx: Penguin (1980).

Dufour, D.L. (1983) 'Nutrition in the Northwest Amazon: household dietary intake and time energy expenditure', in R.B. Hames and W.T. Vickers (eds) *Adaptive Responses of Native Amazonians*, New York: Academic Press.

Dumont, L. (1966) *Homo Hierarchicus: The Caste System and its Implications*, Chicago: University of Chicago Press (1980).

Durrenberger, E.P. (ed.) (1984) *Chayanov, Peasants, and Economic Anthropology*, New York: Academic Press.

Edmundson, W.C. (1976) *Land, Food, and Work in Java*, Monograph 4, Armidale: Department of Geography, University of New England.

Eliade, M. (1956) *The Forge and the Crucible*, Chicago: University of Chicago Press (1978).

Ellen, R.F. (ed.) (1984) *Ethnographic Research: A Guide to General Conduct (ASA Research Methods in Social Anthropology 1)*, London: Academic Press.

Engels, F. (1884) *The Origins of the Family, Private Property and the State*, reprinted in *The Selected Works of Karl Marx and Frederich Engels*, Moscow: Progress Publishers (1970).

Ennew, J. (1980) *The Western Isles Today*, Cambridge: Cambridge University Press.

Ennew, J. (1986) *The Sexual Exploitation of Children*, Cambridge: Polity Press.

Epstein, T.S. (1962) *Economic Development and Social Change in South India*, Manchester: Manchester University Press.

Epstein, T.S. (1967) 'The data of economics in anthropological analysis', in A.L. Epstein (ed.) *The Craft of Social Anthropology*, London: Tavistock.

Erasmus, C.J. (1955) 'Work patterns in a Mayo village', *American Anthropologist* 57: 322-33.

Erasmus, C.J. (1980) 'Comment on Minge-Klevana "Labor time and industrialization" (1980)', *Current Anthropology* 21(3), 289-91.

Evans-Pritchard, E.E. (1962) *Essays in Social Anthropology*, London: Faber.

Evans-Pritchard, E.E. (1976) *Witchcraft, Oracles, and Magic among the Azande*, abridged with an introduction by Eva Gillies, Oxford: Clarendon Press.

FAO/WHO (1973) *Energy and Protein Requirements: Report on a Joint FAO/WHO Ad Hoc Expert Committee*, Technical Series No. 522, Geneva: World Health Organization.

Farmer, B.H. (1977) *Green Revolution? Technology and Change in Rice-growing Areas of Tamil Nadu and Sri Lanka*, Boulder, CO: Westview Press.

Firth, R. (1939) *Primitive Polynesian Economy*, London: Routledge & Kegan Paul (1974).

Firth, R. (1946) *Malay Fishermen: Their Peasant Economy*, London: Kegan Paul, Trench, Trubner & Co.

Firth, R. (1957) 'Malinowski as scientist and as man', in R. Firth (ed.) *Man and Culture: An Evaluation of the Work of Bronislaw Malinowski*, London: Routledge & Kegan Paul.

Firth, R. (1959) *Social Change in Tikopia: Re-Study of a Polynesian Community after a Generation*, London: Allen & Unwin.

Firth, R. and Yamey, B.S. (eds) (1964) *Capital, Saving and Credit in Peasant Societies*, London: Allen & Unwin.

Firth, Rosemary (1966) *Housekeeping among Malay Peasants*, London School of Economics Monograph on Social Anthropology 7 (2nd edition), London: Athlone.

Fischer, E. and Shah, H. (1970) *Rural Craftsmen and their Work: Equipment and Technique in the Mer Village of Ratadi in Saurashtra, India*, Ahmedabad: National Institute of Design.

Fisk, E.K. (1985) *The Aboriginal Economy in Town and Country*, Sydney: Allen & Unwin and Australian Institute of Aboriginal Studies.

Flanders, A. (1964) *The Fawley Productivity Agreements*, London: Faber.

Forge, J.A.W. (1972) 'Normative factors in the settlement size of Neolithic cultivators (New Guinea)', in P.J. Ucko, R. Tringham, and G.W. Dimbleby (eds) *Man, Settlement and Urbanism*, London: Duckworth.

Fox, J.J. (1977) *Harvest of the Palm: Ecological Change in Eastern Indonesia*, Cambridge, Mass.: Harvard University Press.

Fox, J.J. (1987) 'The ecology of sustainable green revolution: past developments and current problems in Java', unpublished paper presented at the Workshop on the Green Revolution in South and Southeast Asia, Australian National University, Canberra, 10-12 April 1987.

Fox, W.S. (1916) *The Mythology of All Races, vol. I: Greek and Roman*, New York: Cooper Square Publishers (1964).

Frank, A.G. (1967) *Capitalism and Underdevelopment in Latin America*, New York: Monthly Review Press.

Frank, A.G. (1974) 'Dependence is dead, long live dependence and the class struggle', *Latin American Perspectives* 1 (1): 87-106.

Frankel, M. (1982) 'Productivity, economic', in *The New Encyclopaedia Britannica*, Chicago: Encyclopaedia Britannica, Inc.

Freed, R.S. and Freed, S.A. (1964) 'Calendars, ceremonies and festivals in a north Indian village: necessary calendric information for fieldwork', *Southwestern Journal of Anthropology* 20: 67-90.

Freeman, D. (1970) *Report on the Iban*, London: Athlone.

Freeman, J.M. (1979) *Untouchable: An Indian Life History*, London: Allen & Unwin.

Friedman, A.L. (1987) 'Taylorism', in J. Eatwell, M. Milgate and P. Newman (eds) *The New Palgrave: A Dictionary of Economics*, London: Macmillan.

Friedman, M. (1935) 'The methodology of positive economics', in W. Breit and H.M. Hochman (eds) *Readings in Microeconomics*, New York: Holt, Rinehart & Winston (1971).

Friedman, M. (1962) *Price Theory: A Provisional Text*, Chicago: Aldine.

Friedman, M. and Schwartz, A.J. (1963) *A Monetary History of the United States 1867-1960*, Princeton NJ: Princeton University Press for the National Bureau of Economic Research.

Fussell, G.E. (1982) 'Agriculture, the history of', in *The New Encyclopaedia Britannica*, Chicago: Encyclopaedia Britannica, Inc.

Galbraith, J.K. (1967) *The New Industrial State*, Boston, Mass.: Houghton Mifflin.

Geertz, C. (1963) *Agricultural Involution*, Berkeley, CA: University of California Press.

Geertz, C. (1984a) 'Culture and social change', *Man* 19: 511-32.

Geertz, C. (1984b) 'Anti anti-relativism', *American Anthropologist* 86 (2): 263-78.

Gell, A. (1986) 'Newcomers to the world of goods: consumption among the Muria Gond', in A. Appadurai (ed.) *The Social Life of Things: Commodities in Cultural Perspective*, Cambridge: Cambridge University Press.

Godelier, M. (1977) *Perspectives in Marxist Anthropology*, Cambridge: Cambridge University Press.

Godelier, M. (1986) *The Making of Great Men: Male Domination and Power among the New Guinea Baruya*, Cambridge: Cambridge University Press.

Godelier, M. and Garanger, J. (1978) 'Stone tools and steel tools among the Baruya of New Guinea: some ethnographic facts and quantitative data', *Social Sciences Information* 4: 633-78.

Goody, J. (1982) *Cooking, Cuisine and Class: A Study in Comparative Sociology*, Cambridge: Cambridge University Press.

Goody, J.R. and Tambiah, S.J. (1973) *Bridewealth and Dowry*, Cambridge: Cambridge University Press.

Gramsci, A. (1971) *Selections from the Prison Notebooks of Antonio Gramsci*, edited and translated by Q. Hoare and G.N. Smith, New York: International Publishers (1985).

Greenhalgh, S. (1985) 'Is inequality demographically induced? The family cycle and the distribution of income in Taiwan', *American*

Anthropologist 87: 571-94.

Gregory, C.A. (1982) *Gifts and Commodities*, London: Academic Press.

Gregory, C.A. (1987a) 'Economic anthropology', in J. Eatwell, M. Milgate and P. Newman (eds) *The New Palgrave: A Dictionary of Economics*, London: Macmillan.

Gregory, C.A. (1987b) 'Gifts', in J. Eatwell, M. Milgate and P. Newman (eds) *The New Palgrave: A Dictionary of Economics*, London: Macmillan.

Gregory, C.A. (1988) 'Village money, the World Bank and landlessness in central India', *Journal of Contemporary Asia* 18: 47-58.

Gregory, C.A. (1989) 'How the USA made the Third World pay for the Vietnam war', in P. Limqueco (ed.) *Partisan Scholarship: Essays in Honour of Renato Constantino*, Manila: Journal of Contemporary Asia Press.

Gregory, C.A. (n.d.) 'Markets and merchants in Bastar', unpublished manuscript.

Griffen, K. and Gurley, J. (1985) 'Radical analysis of imperialism, the third world and the transition to socialism: a survey article', *Journal of Economic Literature* 23: 1089-143.

Gross, D.R. (1984) 'Time allocation: a tool for the study of cultural behaviour', *Annual Review of Anthropology* 13: 519-58.

Grossman, L.S. (1982) 'Beer drinking and subsistence production in a highland village', in M. Marshall (ed.) *Through a Glass Darkly: Beer and Modernization in Papua New Guinea*, Boroko, Papua New Guinea: Institute of Applied Social and Economic Research.

Grossman, L.S. (1984a) *Peasants, Subsistence Ecology, and Development in the Highlands of Papua New Guinea*, Princeton, NJ: Princeton University Press.

Grossman, L.S. (1984b) 'Collecting time-use data in Third World rural communities', *Professional Geographer* 36 (4): 444-54.

Guha, R. (1982) 'Preface', in R. Guha (ed.) *Subaltern Studies I: Writings on South Asian History and Society*, Delhi: Oxford University Press.

Guha, R. (1983) *Elementary Aspects of Peasant Insurgency in Colonial India*, Delhi: Oxford University Press.

Guinness, P. (1986) *Harmony and Hierarchy in a Javanese Kampung*, Singapore: Oxford University Press.

Halpern, J.M. and Brode, J. (1967) 'Peasant society: economic change and revolutionary transformation', in B.J. Siegel and A.R. Beals (eds) *Biennial Review of Anthropology*, Stanford, CA: Stanford University Press.

Hames, R.B. (1979) 'A comparison of the efficiencies of the shotgun and the bow in neotropical forest hunting', *Human Ecology* 7 (3): 219-52.

Hames, R.B. (1983) 'The settlement pattern of a Yanomamö population bloc: a behavioral ecological interpretation', in R.B. Hames and W.T. Vickers (eds) *Adaptive Responses of Native Amazonians*, New York: Academic Press.

Hames, R.B. and Vickers, W.T. (eds) (1983) *Adaptive Responses of Native Amazonians*, New York: Academic Press.

Harriss, J. (1982) *Capitalism and Peasant Farming: Agrarian Structure and Ideology in Northern Tamil Nadu*, Bombay: Oxford University Press.
Hart, K. (1973) 'Informal income opportunities and urban employment in Ghana', *Journal of Modern African Studies* 11: 61-89.
Hart, K. (1982) *The Political Economy of West African Agriculture*, Cambridge: Cambridge University Press.
Hart, K. (1987) 'Informal economy', in J. Eatwell, M. Milgate and P. Newman (eds) *The New Palgrave: A Dictionary of Economics*, London: Macmillan.
Hawkes, K., Kaplan, H., Hill, K. and Hurtado, M. (1987) 'A problem in scan sampling', *Journal of Anthropological Research* 43: 239-46.
Hayami, Y. (in association with M. Kikuchi, P.F. Moya, L.M. Bambo, and E.B. Marciano) (1978), *Anatomy of a Peasant Economy: A Rice Village in the Philippines*, Manila: The International Rice Research Institute.
Heath, D. (1987a) 'A decade of development in the anthropological study of alcohol use, 1970-1980', in M. Douglas (ed.) *Constructive Drinking: Perspectives on Drink from Anthropology*, Cambridge: Cambridge University Press.
Heath, D. (1987b) 'Anthropology and alcohol studies: current issues', *Annual Review of Anthropology* 16: 99-120.
Herskovits, M.J. (1938) *Acculturation: The Study of Culture Contact*, Gloucester: P. Smith (1958).
Herskovits, M.J. (1940) *The Economic Life of Primitive People*, New York: Knopf.
Hide, R.L. (1981) 'Aspects of pig production and use in colonial Sinasina, Papua New Guinea', unpublished PhD thesis, Columbia University, New York.
Hill, K. and Hawkes, K. (1983) 'Neotropical hunting among the Aché of eastern Paraguay', in R.B. Hames and W.T. Vickers (eds) *Adaptive Responses of Native Amazonians*, New York: Academic Press.
Hill, P. (1963) *The Migrant Cocoa-Farmers of Southern Ghana*, Cambridge: Cambridge University Press.
Hill, P. (1966) 'Notes on traditional market authority and market periodicity in West Africa', *Journal of African History* 7(2): 295-311.
Hill, P. (1972) *Rural Hausa: A Village and a Setting*, Cambridge: Cambridge University Press.
Hill, P. (1977) *Population, Prosperity and Poverty: Rural Kano 1900 and 1970*, Cambridge: Cambridge University Press.
Hill, P. (1982) *Dry Grain Farming Families: Hausaland (Nigeria) and Karnataka (India) Compared*, Cambridge: Cambridge University Press.
Hill, P. (1986) *Development Economics on Trial: The Anthropological Case for a Prosecution*, Cambridge: Cambridge University Press.
Hoben, A. (1982) 'Anthropologists and development', *Annual Review of Anthropology* 11: 349-75.
Hobson, J.A. (1894) *The Evolution of Modern Capitalism*, London: Walter Scott.
Hobson, S. (1978) *Family Web: A Story of India*, London: John Murray.
Hogbin, H.I. (1957) 'Anthropology as public service and Malinowski's

233

contribution to it', in R. Firth (ed.) *Man and Culture: An Evaluation of the Work of Bronislaw Malinowski*, London: Routledge and Kegan Paul.

Howell, N. (1986) 'Demographic anthropology', *Annual Review of Anthropology* 15: 219-46.

Huber, R. (1977) *From Pasta to Pavlova: A Comparative Study of Italian Settlers in Sydney and Griffith*, St. Lucia, Queensland: University of Queensland Press.

Hull, V. (1975) 'Fertility, socioeconomic status, and the position of women in a Javanese village', unpublished PhD thesis, Australian National University, Canberra.

Humphrey, C. (1983) *Karl Marx Collective: Economy, Society and Religion in a Siberian Collective Farm*, Cambridge: Cambridge University Press.

Humphrey, C. (1988) 'No place like home in anthropology: the neglect of architecture', *Anthropology Today* 4(1): 16-18.

International Monetary Fund (1985) *International Financial Statistics, Yearbook, 1985*, Washington, DC: IMF.

Jerome, N., Kandel, R.F. and Pelto, G.H. (eds) (1980) *Nutritional Anthropology: Contemporary Approaches to Diet and Culture*, New York: Redgrave Publishing.

Jevons, W. (1871) *The Theory of Political Economy*, Harmondsworth, Middx: Penguin (1970).

Johnson, A. (1975) 'Time allocation in a Machiguenga community', *Ethnology*, 14(3): 301-10.

Johnson, A. (1978a) *Research Methods in Social Anthropology*, London: Edward Arnold.

Johnson, A. (1978b) 'Comment on Nag, White and Peet "Economic value of children" (1978)', *Current Anthropology* 19(2); 302-3.

Johnson, A. (1980) 'Comment on Minge-Klevana "Labor time and industrialization" (1980)', *Current Anthropology* 21(3); 292.

Josephides, L. (1985) *The Production of Inequality: Gender and Exchange among the Kewa*, London: Tavistock.

Kahn, J.S. (1981) 'Marxist anthropology and segmentary societies: a review of the literature', in J.S. Kahn and J.R. Llobera (eds) *The Anthropology of Pre-capitalist Societies*, London: Macmillan.

Kahn, J.S. (1985) 'Peasant ideologies in the Third World', *Annual Review of Anthropology* 14: 49-75.

Kaplan, A. (1964) *The Conduct of Inquiry: Methodology for Behavioral Science*, San Francisco, CA: Chandler Publishing Company.

Kearney, M. (1986) 'From the invisible hand to visible feet: anthropological studies of migration and development', *Annual Review of Anthropology* 15: 331-61.

Kelly, R.C. (1977) *Etoro Social Structure: A Study in Structural Contradiction*, Ann Arbor, Mich.: University of Michigan Press.

Kerblay, B. (1966) 'A.V. Chayanov: life, careers, works', in A.V. Chayanov *The Theory of the Peasant Economy*, edited by D. Thorner, B. Kerblay and R.E.F. Smith, Homewood, Ill.: Irwin.

Keynes, J.M. (1936) *The General Theory of Employment Interest and Money*, London: Macmillan (1967).

Knight, F.H. (1941) 'Anthropology and economics', *Journal of Political Economy* 49: 247-68.

Koestlin, K. (1981) 'Taboo and preference: culture construct and reality', in A. Fenton and T.M. Owen (eds) *Food in Perspective*, Edinburgh: John Donald Publishers.

Kriegler, R.J. (1980) *Working for the Company: Work and Control in the Whyalla Shipyard*, Melbourne: Oxford University Press.

Krishnamoorthy, S. and Muthiah, A. (1985) 'Age', in D. Lucas with P. Kane (eds) *Asking Demographic Questions*, Canberra: National Centre for Development Studies, Australian National University.

Kuttner, R. (1985) 'The poverty of economics', *The Atlantic Monthly* February 1985: 74-84.

Lamb, H.H. (1982) 'Climate', in *The New Encyclopaedia Britannica*, Chicago: Encyclopaedia Britannica, Inc.

Layton, R. (1973) 'Social systems theory and a village community in France', in C. Renfrew (ed.) *The Exploration of Culture Change: Models in Prehistory*, London: Duckworth.

Leach, E.R. (1961) *Pul Eliya: A Village in Ceylon. A Study of Land Tenure and Kinship*, Cambridge: Cambridge University Press.

Leach, E.R. (1967) 'An anthropologist's reflections on a social survey', in D.G. Jorgmans and P.C. Gutkind (eds) *Anthropologists in the Field*, Assen: Van Gorcum.

Leach, J.W. and Leach, E. (eds) (1983) *The Kula: New Perspectives on Massim Exchange*, Cambridge: Cambridge University Press.

Lee, R.B. and De Vore, I. (eds) (1976) *Kalahari Hunter-Gatherers: Studies of the !Kung San and Their Neighbours*, Cambridge, Mass.: Harvard University Press.

Lenin, V.I. (1899) *The Development of Capitalism in Russia, vol. III; Collected Works*, London: Lawrence & Wishart (1956).

Lepervanche, M.M. de (1984) *Indians in a White Australia*, Sydney: Allen & Unwin.

Levi, M. (1981) *Economics Deciphered: A Survival Guide for Non-Economists*, London: Pan (1984).

Lévi-Strauss, C. (1949) *The Elementary Structures of Kinship*, London: Eyre & Spottiswoode (1969).

Liep, J. (1983) 'Ranked exchange in Yela (Rossel Island)', in J.W. Leach and E. Leach (eds) *The Kula: New Perspectives on Massim Exchange*, Cambridge: Cambridge University Press.

Lourie, J.A., Peterken, G.F. and Smith, C.G. (1981) 'Description of the physical environment', in J.S. Weiner and J.A. Lourie (eds) *Practical Human Biology*, London: Academic Press.

Lucas, D. with Kane, P. (eds) (1985) *Asking Demographic Questions*, Canberra: National Centre for Development Studies, Australian National University.

McArthur, M. (1977) 'Nutritional research in Melanesia: a second look at the Tsembaga', in T. Bayliss-Smith and R. Feachem (eds) *Subsistence and Survival: Rural Ecology in the Pacific*, London: Academic Press.

McArthur, N. (1961) *Introducing Population Statistics*, Melbourne: Oxford University Press.

McCabe, J.T. (1987) 'Inter-household variation in Ngisonyoka Turkana livestock production', *Research in Economic Anthropology* 8: 277-93.

McCarthy, F.D. and McArthur, M. (1960) 'The food quest and time factor in Aboriginal economic life', in C.P. Mountford (ed.) *Records of the American-Australian Scientific Expedition to Arnhem Land, vol 2: Anthropology and Nutrition*, Melbourne: Melbourne University Press.

McCarthy, W.J. (1982) 'Tools', in *The New Encyclopaedia Britannica*, Chicago: Encyclopaedia Britannica, Inc.

McClelland, D. (1961) *The Achieving Society*, Princeton, NJ: Von Nostrand.

MacFarlane, A. (1976) *Resources and Population: A Study of the Gurungs of Nepal*, Cambridge: Cambridge University Press.

McKersie, R.B. and Hunter, L.C. (1973) *Pay, Productivity and Collective Bargaining*, London: Macmillan.

Maddock, K. (1983) *Your Land is Our Land: Aboriginal Land Rights*, Ringwood, Victoria: Penguin.

Madeley, J. (1988) 'Restoring land to the people', *South* April 1988: 114.

Malinowski, B. (1916) 'Baloma; the spirits of the dead', in *Magic, Science and Religion and Other Essays by Bronislaw Malinowski*, with an introduction by Robert Redfield, London: Souvenir Press (1982).

Malinowski, B. (1922) *Argonauts of the Western Pacific*, New York: Dutton & Co. (1961).

Malinowski, B. (1935) *Coral Gardens and their Magic: A Study of the Methods of Tilling the Soil and of Agricultural Rites in the Trobriand Islands*, London: Allen & Unwin.

Malinowski, B. (1947) *Freedom and Civilization*, with a preface by Valetta Malinowska, London: Allen & Unwin.

Malinowski, B. and de la Fuente, J. (1957) *Malinowski in Mexico. The Economics of a Mexican Market System*, edited and with an introduction by S. Drucker-Brown, London: Routledge & Kegan Paul (1982).

Marcus, G.E. (1983) 'The fiduciary role in American family dynasties and their institutional legacy', in G.E. Marcus (ed.) *Elites: Ethnographic Issues*, Albuquerque, NM: University of New Mexico Press.

Marcus, G.E. (1985) 'Spending: the Hunts, silver and dynastic families in America', *Archives Européennes de Sociologie* 26 (2): 224-59.

Marcus, G.E. and Fischer, M.M.J. (1986) *Anthropology as Cultural Critique: An Experimental Moment in the Human Sciences*, Chicago: University of Chigaco Press.

Marriott, McK. (1968) 'Caste ranking and food transactions, a matrix analysis', in M. Singer and B.S. Cohn (eds) *Structure and Change in Indian Society*, Chicago: Aldine.

Mars, G. (1987) 'Longshore drinking, economic security and union politics in Newfoundland', in M. Douglas (ed.) *Constructive Drinking: Perspectives on Drink from Anthropology*, Cambridge: Cambridge University Press.

Marx, K. (1857) *A Contribution to the Critique of Political Economy*, edited with an introduction by Maurice Dobb, Moscow: Progress Publishers (1970).

Marx, K. (1867) *Capital, vol. 1: A Critical Analysis of Capitalist Production*, Moscow: Progress Publishers.

Marx, K. (1894) *Capital, vol. III: A Critique of Political Economy*, Moscow: Progress Publishers (1971).

Mason, I.L. (1982) 'Draft animals', in *The New Encyclopaedia Britannica*, Chicago: Encyclopaedia Britannica, Inc.

Mauss, M. (1904) *Seasonal Variations of the Eskimo: A Study in Social Morphology*, translated with a foreword by J.J. Fox, London: Routledge & Kegan Paul (1979).

Mauss, M. (1925) *The Gift: Forms and Function of Exchange in Archaic Societies*, London: Routledge & Kegan Paul (1974).

Mayer, A.C. (1960) *Caste and Kinship in Central India: A Village and its Region*, London: Routledge & Kegan Paul.

Meehan, B. (1982) *Shell Bed to Shell Midden*, Canberra: Australian Institute of Aboriginal Studies.

Meek, R.L. (1956) *Studies in the Labour Theory of Value*, London: Lawrence & Wishart (2nd edition 1973).

Meillassoux, C. (1981) *Maidens, Meal and Money: Capitalism and the Domestic Community*, Cambridge: Cambridge University Press.

Mencher, J.P. (1974) 'The caste system upside down, or the not-so-mysterious east', *Current Anthropology* 15 (4): 469-93.

Mencher, J.P. (ed.) (1983) *Social Anthropology of the Peasantry*, Bombay: Somaiya Publications.

Menger, K. (1871) *Principles of Economics*, Illinois: Glencoe (1950).

Messer, E. (1984) 'Anthropological perspectives on diet', *Annual Review of Anthropology* 13: 205-49.

Metcalfe, A.W. (1988) *For Freedom and Dignity: Historical Agency and Class Struggle in the History of the Coalfields of NSW*, Sydney: Allen & Unwin.

Miles, D. (1979) 'The finger knife and Ockham's razor: a problem in Asian cultural history and economic anthropology', *American Ethnologist* 6 (2): 223-43.

Mill, J.S. (1848) *Principles of Political Economy with Some of Their Applications to Social Philosophy*, London: Longman, Green & Co. (1923).

Miller, D. (1987) *Material Culture and Mass Consumption*, Oxford: Blackwell.

Minge-Klevana, W. (1980) 'Does labor time decrease with industrialization: a survey of time allocation studies', *Current Anthropology* 21 (3): 279-98.

Mitchell, C.W. (1973) *Terrain Evaluation: An Introductory Handbook to the History, Principles and Methods of Terrain Assessment*, London: Longman.

Mitchell, D.D. (1976) *Land and Agriculture in Nagovisi, Papua New Guinea*, Boroko, Papua New Guinea: Institute of Applied Social and

Economic Research.

Montgomery, E. and Johnson, A. (1977) 'Machiguenga energy expenditure', *Ecology of Food and Nutrition* 6: 97-105.

Morgan, L.H. (1877) *Ancient Society, or Researches into the Lines of Human Progress from Savagery through Barbarism to Civilization*, London: Macmillan.

Morgan, L.H. (1881) *Houses and House Life of the American Aborigines*, Washington DC: Government Printing Office.

Mueller-Willie, C. (1984) *Images of The World: An Atlas of Satellite Imagery and Maps*, Harlow, Essex: Collins Longman.

Mundy, M. (1979) 'Women's inheritance of land in highland Yemen', *Arabian Studies* 5: 161-7.

Myrdal, G. (1968) *Asian Drama: An Inquiry into the Poverty of Nations*, New York: Twentieth Century Fund.

Nadel, S.F. (1957) 'Malinowski on magic and religion', in R. Firth (ed.) *Man and Culture: An Evaluation of the Work of Bronislaw Malinowski*, London: Routledge & Kegan Paul.

Nag, M., White, B.N.F. and Peet, R.C. (1978) 'An anthropological approach to the study of the economic value of children in Java and Nepal', *Current Anthropology* 19 (2): 293-306.

Nash, J. (1979) *We Eat the Mines and the Mines Eat Us: Dependency and Exploitation in Bolivian Tin Mines*, New York: Columbia University Press.

Nash, J. (1981) 'Ethnographic aspects of the world capitalist system', *Annual Review of Anthropology* 10: 393-423.

National Research Council (1986) *Nutrient Adequacy: Assessment Using Food Consumption Surveys*, Washington DC: National Academy Press.

Newell, C. (1988) *Methods and Models in Demography*, London: Belhaven Press.

Ngokwey, N. (1987) 'Varieties of palm wine among the Lele of the Kasai', in M. Douglas (ed.) *Constructive Drinking: Perspectives on Drink from Anthropology*, Cambridge: Cambridge University Press.

Norgan, N.G., Ferro-Luzzi, A. and Durrin, J.V.G.A. (1974) 'The energy and nutrient intake and the energy expenditure of 204 New Guinean adults', *Philosophical Transactions of the Royal Society of London* 268: 309-48.

Notes and Queries on Anthropology (1951), sixth edition revised and written by a committee of the Royal Anthropological Institute of Great Britain and Ireland, London: Routledge & Kegan Paul.

Oliver, P. (1987) *Dwellings: The House across the World*, Oxford: Phaidon.

Ortiz, S. (ed.) (1983) *Economic Anthropology: Topics and Theories*, Lanham, MD: University Press of America and Society for Economic Anthropology.

Packard, V. (1959) *The Status Seekers: An Exploration of Class Behaviour in America*, Harmondsworth, Middx: Penguin (1971).

Padilla, A.M. (ed.) (1980) *Acculturation: Theory, Models and some New Findings*, Boulder CO: Westview.

Pahl, R.E. (1984) *Divisions of Labour*, Oxford: Blackwell.

Palmore, J.A. and Gardner, R.W. (1983) *Measuring Mortality, Fertility and*

Natural Increase: A Self-Teaching Guide to Elementary Measures, Honolulu: East West Center.

Parry, J.K. (1979) *Caste and Kinship in Kangra*, London: Routledge & Kegan Paul.

Pedersen, J. (1987) 'Plantation women and children: wage labour, adoption and fertility in the Seychelles', *Ethnology* 26 (1): 51-61.

Pelto, G.H., Pelto, P.J. and Lung'aho, M.S. (1981) '"Modern" and "traditional" food use in West Finland: an example of quantitative pattern analysis', *Nutrition Research* 1: 63-71.

Pelto, P.J. (1973) *The Snowmobile Revolution: Technology and Social Change in the Arctic*, Menlo Park, CA: Cummings.

Pelto, P.J. and Pelto, G.H. (1978) *Anthropological Research: The Structure of Inquiry* (second edition), Cambridge: Cambridge University Press.

Peterson, N. and Langton, M. (eds) (1983) *Aborigines, Land and Land Rights*, Canberra: Australian Institute of Aboriginal Studies.

Pinnarò, G. and Pugliese, E. (1985) 'Informalization and social resistance: the case of Naples', in N. Redclift and E. Mingione (eds) *Beyond Employment: Household, Gender and Subsistence*, Oxford: Blackwell.

Polanyi, K. (1944) *The Great Transformation*, New York: Holt, Rinehart & Winston.

Polanyi, K. (1957) 'The economy as instituted process', in K. Polanyi, C.M. Arensburg and H.W. Pearson (eds) *Trade and Market in the Early Empires: Economics in History and Theory*, New York: The Free Press.

Pollock, N.J. (1985) 'The concept of food in a Pacific society: a Fijian example', *Ecology of Food and Nutrition* 17: 195-203.

Pospisil, L. (1963) *Kapauku Papuan Economy*, Yale University Publications in Anthropology Number 67, New Haven CT: Human Relations Area Files Press (1972).

Postan, M.M. (1970) *Fact and Relevance: Essays on Historical Method*, Cambridge: Cambridge University Press.

Preston, P.W. (1982) *Theories of Development*, London: Routledge & Kegan Paul.

Purseglove, J.W. (1968) *Tropical Crops: Dicotyledons*, London: Longman.

Purseglove, J.W. (1972) *Tropical Crops: Monocotyledons*, London: Longman.

Quesnay, F. (1756) 'Farmers', in P.D. Groenewegen (ed.) *Reprints of Economic Classics, Series 2, No. 2*, Sydney: University of Sydney.

Quesnay, F. (1759) 'The "Tableau Economique"', in R. Meek (ed.) *The Economics of Physiocracy*, London: George Allen (1962).

Rabinow, P. (1977) *Reflections on Fieldwork in Morocco*, Berkeley and Los Angeles CA: University of California.

Ramnath, T., Rau, P., and Rao, N.P. (1985) 'A pitfall in the estimation of rice consumption through oral questionnaire method of diet survey', *Ecology of Food and Nutrition* 16: 351-62.

Rehfisch, F. (1987) 'Competitive beer drinking among the Mambila', in M. Douglas (ed.) *Constructive Drinking: Perspectives on Drink from Anthropology*, Cambridge: Cambridge University Press.

Ricardo, D. (1817) *On the Principles of Political Economy and Taxation*, vol. 1 of *The Works and Correspondence of David Ricardo*, edited by P. Sraffa with the collaboration of M.H. Dobb, Cambridge: Cambridge University Press (1951).

Richards, A. (1939) *Land, Labour and Diet in North Rhodesia: An Economic Study of the Bemba Tribe*, London: Oxford University Press.

Richards, A. (1957) 'The concept of culture in Malinowski's work', in R. Firth (ed.) *Man and Culture: An Evaluation of the Work of Bronislaw Malinowski*, London: Routledge & Kegan Paul.

Robbins, L. (1932) *An Essay on the Nature and Significance of Economic Science*, London: Macmillan (1952).

Robinson, K.M. (1986) *Stepchildren of Progress: The Political Economy of Development in an Indonesian Mining Town*, Albany, NY: State University of New York Press.

Rodman, M.C. (1987) *Masters of Tradition: Consequences of Customary Land Tenure in Longana, Vanuatu*, Vancouver BC: University of British Columbia Press.

Ronan, C.A. (1982) 'Calendar', in *The New Encyclopaedia Britannica*, Chicago: Encyclopaedia Britannica, Inc.

Rostow, W.W. (1960) *The Stages of Economic Growth*, Cambridge: Cambridge University Press.

Sahlins, M. (1972) *Stone Age Economics*, Chicago: Aldine Atherton.

Sahlins, M. (1976) *Culture and Practical Reason*, Chicago: University of Chicago Press.

Salisbury, R.F. (1962) *From Stone to Steel: Economic Consequences of a Technological Change in New Guinea*, Melbourne: Melbourne University Press.

Salisbury, R.F. (1970) *Vunamami: Economic Transformation in a Traditional Society*, Berkeley, CA: University of California Press.

Salisbury, R.F. (1986) *A Homeland for the Cree: Regional Development in James Bay 1971-1981*, Kingston and Montreal: McGill-Queens University Press.

Samuels, W.J. (1987) 'Institutional economics', in J. Eatwell, M. Milgate and P. Newman (eds) *The New Palgrave: A Dictionary of Economics*, London: Macmillan.

Scaglion, R. (1986) 'The importance of night time observations in time allocation studies', *American Ethnologist* 13 (3): 537-45.

Schneider, H.K. (1974) *Economic Man: The Anthropology of Economics*, New York: The Free Press.

Schneider, J. (1987) 'The anthropology of cloth', *Annual Review in Anthropology* 16: 409-48.

Schultz, T.W. (1964) *Transforming Traditional Agriculture*, New Haven, CT: Yale University Press.

Scott, J.C. (1985) *Weapons of the Weak: Everyday Forms of Peasant Resistance*, New Haven, CT: Yale University Press.

Seddon, D. (ed.) (1978) *Relations of Production: Marxist Approaches to Economic Anthropology*, London: Frank Cass.

Sexton, L. (1986) *Mothers of Money, Daughters of Coffee: The Wok Meri Movement*, Ann Arbor, Mich.: University of Michigan Research Press.

Sharma, U. (1980) *Women, Work, and Property in North-West India*, Tavistock: London.

Sillitoe, P. (1983) *Roots of the Earth: Crops in the Highlands of Papua New Guinea*, Sydney: New South Wales University Press.

Sismondi, M. de (1847) *Political Economy and the Philosophy of Government: Selected Essays*, London: Chapman.

Smith, A. (1776) *An Inquiry into the Nature and Causes of the Wealth of Nations*, London: Everyman (1970).

Smith, C.A. (1985) 'Methods for analyzing periodic market places as elements in regional trading systems', in B.L. Isaac (ed.) *Research in Economic Anthropology*, London: JAI Press.

Somerville, J. (1941) 'Umbrellaology, or, methodology is social science', *Philosophy of Science* 8 (4): 557–66

Sommerlad, E.A., Dawson, P.L. and Altman, J.C. (1985) *Rural Land Sharing Communities: An Alternative Economic Model?*, Canberra: Australian Government Publishing Service.

Sraffa, P. (1960) *Production of Commodities by Means of Commodities: Prelude to a Critique of Economic Theory*, Cambridge: Cambridge University Press.

Stewart, R.E. (1982) 'Agriculture, technology of', in *The New Encyclopaedia Britannica*, Chicago: Encyclopaedia Britannica, Inc.

Stockley, L. (1985) 'Changes in habitual food intake during weighed inventory surveys and duplication diet collections: a short review', *Ecology of Food and Nutrition* 17: 263-9.

Strathern, A. (1971) *The Rope of Moka: Big-Men and Ceremonial Exchange in Mount Hagen, New Guinea*, Cambridge: Cambridge University Press.

Strathern, M. (1972) *Women in Between: Female Roles in a Male World*, London: Seminar Press.

Strathern, M. (1975) *No Money on Our Skins: Hagen Migrants in Port Moresby*, Port Moresby and Canberra: New Guinea Research Unit of the Australian National University.

Szalai, A. (ed.) (1972) *The Use of Time: Daily Activities of Urban and Suburban Populations in Twelve Countries*, The Hague: Mouton.

Taussig, M. (1978) 'Peasant economics and the development of capitalist agriculture in the Cauca Valley, Colombia', *Latin American Perspectives* 18: 62-90.

Taylor, J.G. (1979) *From Modernization to Modes of Production: A Critique of the Sociologies of Development and Underdevelopment*, London: Macmillan.

Thornton, M.A. (1987) '*Sekt* versus *Schnapps* in an Austrian village', in M. Douglas (ed.) *Constructive Drinking: Perspectives on Drink from Anthropology*, Cambridge: Cambridge University Press.

van Gennep, A. (1911) *The Semi-Scholars*, translated from the French and edited with an introduction by Rodney Needham, London: Routledge & Kegan Paul (1967).

Veblen, T. (1899) *The Theory of the Leisure Class: An Economic Study of Institutions*, London: Unwin Books (1970).

241

Vogt, E.Z. (ed.) (1974) *Aerial Photography in Anthropological Field Research*, Cambridge, Mass.: Harvard University Press.

Wallerstein, I. (1974) *The Modern World System*, New York: Academic Press.

Walras, L. (1874) *Elements of Pure Economics*, translated by W. Jaffe, London: George Unwin (1954).

Warry, W. (1987) *Chuave Politics: Changing Patterns of Leadership in the Papua New Guinea Highlands*, Department of Political and Social Change Monograph 4, Canberra: Australian National University.

Weber, M. (1927) *General Economic History*, New Brunswick: Transaction Books (1981).

Weber, M. (1948) *From Max Weber: Essays in Sociology*, translated, edited and with an introduction by H.H. Gerth and C. Wright Mills, London: Routledge & Kegan Paul (1977).

Weiner, J.S. and Lourie, J.A. (eds) (1981) *Practical Human Biology*, London: Academic Press.

Werner, O. and Schoepfle, G.M. (1987) *Systematic Fieldwork*, London: Sage.

Wheeler, E. (1981) 'Food consumption survey', in J.S. Weiner and J.A. Lourie (eds) *Practical Human Biology*, London: Academic Press.

White, B.N.F. (1976) 'Production and reproduction in a Javanese village', PhD dissertation, Bogor, Indonesia: The Agricultural Development Council.

Whyte, W.F. (1955) *Street Corner Society*, Chicago: University of Chicago Press.

Willis, P. (1977) *Learning to Labour: How Working Class Kids Get Working Class Jobs*, Westmead, Farnborough: Saxon House.

Winterhalder, B. and Smith, E. (eds) (1981) *Hunter-Gatherer Foraging Strategies*, Chicago: Chicago University Press.

Wolf, E. (1982) *Europe and the People without History*, Berkeley, CA: University of California Press.

Womersley, J.S. (1976) *Plant Collecting for Anthropologists, Geographers and Ecologists in Papua New Guinea*, Lae, Papua New Guinea: Division of Botany, Office of Forests.

Yorke, M. (1982) 'The situation of the Gords of Asifabad and Laksetipet Taluks, Adilabad district', in C. von Furer-Haimendorf (ed.) *Tribes of India: The Struggle for Survival*, Berkeley, CA: University of California Press.

Yost, J.A. and Kelley, P.M. (1983) 'Shotguns, blowguns and spears: the analysis of technological efficiency', in R.B. Hames and W.T. Vickers (eds) *Adaptive Responses of Native Amazonians*, New York: Academic Press.

Young, M.W. (1971) *Fighting with Food: Leadership, Value and Social Control in A Massim Society*, Cambridge: Cambridge University Press.

Ziadeh, N.A. (1982) 'Muslim calendar', in *The New Encyclopaedia Britannica*, Chicago: Encyclopaedia Britannica, Inc.

NAME INDEX

SUBJECT INDEX